BATTLE FOR KOREA

BATTLE FOR KOREA

A History of the Korean Conflict

Robert J. Dvorchak

DA CAPO PRESS
A Member of the Perseus Books Group

Originally published by Combined Publishing in 2001

Copyright © 1993 by The Associated Press

Cataloging-in-Publication data is available from the Library of Congress

ISBN 0-306-81244-4

First Da Capo edition, 2003

Published by DA CAPO PRESS
A Member of the Perseus Books Group
www.dacapopress.com

Printed in China

Director of APN Special Projects: Norm Goldstein
Author: Robert J. Dvorchak
Editor: Nate Polowetzky
Photo Researcher: Julia Wilson
News Library Researchers: Ben Meyers, Jeff Tishman

Illustration on half-title page: Gen. Douglas Mac-Arthur (center) leads his staff ashore after the Inchon landing to inspect the front lines, September 1950.

Illustration on page 2: The smoke from burning buildings fills the air and rubble chokes the streets as tanks lead U.N. forces in the recapture of Seoul, September 1950.

Illustration on title-page: Like a pied piper, an un-identified soldier from the U.S. 3rd Division is cheered by South Korean youngsters as he walks the recaptured streets of Seoul.

Below: A U.S. destroyer stands guard as demolition teams ashore blow up usable supplies and installa-tions as U.N. forces pull out of Hungnam on Christmas Eve 1950.

Contents

Maps

Sidebars

1

Surprise Invasion and U.S. Intervention

It was 4 a.m. on June 25, 1950, a rainy Sunday morning at the beginning of the monsoon season when North Korea's artillery barrels flung shells and flame across a man-made dividing line called the 38th parallel. Skirmishes between the communist North and the non-communist South were not uncommon, but this was more than just another border raid. The big guns proclaimed a full-scale invasion by seven assault divisions of infantry supported by 150 Soviet-made T-34 tanks. The first

Above: President Syngman Rhee signs South Korea's Constitution, August 1949.

Korea

ROK soldiers with full battle gear march to the front somewhere in Korea, July 1950.

blow by 89,000 soldiers, one-third of them battle-hardened veterans of the Chinese civil war won by the communists, included six major thrusts plus two amphibious landings on the peninsula's west coast. The communists still had three divisions of 23,000 men in reserve.

Korea, the Land of the Morning Calm, was now the flashpoint where the cold war got hot.

Opposing the invaders were four understrength divisions of 38,000 men in South Korea, or the formal Republic of Korea (ROK). Four other divisions were spread out in the south. The entire army was little more than a police force. It had no tanks and/or artillery to stop an armored invasion. Indeed, many of the soldiers were away on weekend passes when

the attack came. The United States had 500 advisors in the country as part of its Korea Military Advisory Group(KMAG). American combat troops inserted at the end of World War II had been withdrawn a year earlier.

South Korea, the bottom half of a thumb of land jutting southward from the Asian mainland, wasn't even in America's sphere of influence. In a January 12 speech before the National Press Club, Secretary of State Dean Acheson said the American defensive perimeter ran along the Aleutian Islands to Japan, then to Okinawa and the Philippine Islands. These positions would be defended militarily, he said. Korea was not mentioned.

North Korea's strategy was a lightning thrust through the southern half of the mountainous peninsula before any opposition could be organized. The communists wanted to unite the country by force without the need for elections. In this battle plan, they had the unstoppable land weapon in the T-34 tank. These 32-ton, armor-plated, metal monsters were the workhorses that stopped the German blitzkrieg outside Moscow in World War II. Each tank had an 85-millimeter gun, and one of its few vulnerable points was the engine grating in the rear where the armor was thinnest. Three-fourths of Korea is unsuitable for tanks; much of it is as craggy as a crumpled piece of paper, and the lowlands are flooded as rice paddies that would swallow a tank. But with nothing to stop them, the tanks brazenly rolled in single file columns along the roads.

The immediate target was the South Korean capital of Seoul, the heart of government, transportation and communications, located 25 miles south of the 38th parallel. The charge, bolstered by 120 tanks and led

Ex-President Harry Truman, the wars behind him, relaxes on the eve of his 71st birthday in his office at the Federal Reserve Building in Kansas City. He is cataloging his personal papers for the Truman Library to be built in his hometown, Independence, Missouri, May 1955.

by the 105th Armored Brigade, came down the shortest route from the artificial border. The *3rd* and *4th Divisions* supplied the infantry. Two more divisions, the *2nd* and the *7th*, struck the South in the central mountains. And the attack down the east coast included the *5th Infantry Division*, a motorcycle regiment and an infantry unit, plus the remaining 30 tanks. Two amphibious assaults provided more teeth. There was no question an invasion in the rain that was as coordinated as this one had been planned for some time.

It was a stunning success by the *North Korean Peoples Army*. By June 27, Seoul was abandoned by the Republic of Korea army headquarters and the government fled south to Taejon. Seoul fell to the communists in just four days, and panic had clearly set in.

To slow the North Koreans, plans were made to blow up three railroad bridges and a highway bridge over the Han River. Despite assurances that more time was available, the final three-lane bridge was destroyed without warning at 2:15 a.m. on June 28. It was jammed with soldiers and refugees, and an estimated 500 to 800 people died in the catastrophe. The responsibility fell to the ROK army chief of staff, Gen. Chae Pyong Duk, also known as Fat Chae, a 300-pound ex-sumo wrestler who was killed in action a few weeks later. The demolition occurred just after Fat Chae crossed the span in his jeep. What's worse, three ROK divisions and the 500 Americans with the Korea Military Advisory Group were cut off on the north side of the river. The North Koreans were at least six to eight hours away when the order was given. The South Koreans had abandoned most of their equipment before crossing the river. KMAG escaped in small boats, and its acronym in the grim humor of its soldiers became known as Kiss My Ass Goodbye.

Of the 98,000 men in the South Korean army on June 25, only 54,000 could be accounted for a week later. A rout was on.

Washington was almost deserted that last weekend in June. President Harry Truman was in Independence, Missouri, with his family. Secretary of State Dean Acheson was at his Harewood Farm in Sandy Spring, Maryland, Secretary of Defense Louis Johnson and Gen. Omar Bradley, chairman of the Joint Chiefs of Staff, were resting after a tour of duty in Asia. The calm was shattered by an urgent message from U.S. Ambassador John J. Muccio in Seoul to the State Department—North Korea had invaded. "It would appear from the nature of attack and manner in which it was launched that it constitutes all out offensive against ROK," Muccio cabled Washington. In Tokyo, John Foster Dulles, a special advisor to Acheson, flashed his interpretation of the events: "Believe that if it appears the South Koreans cannot themselves contain or repulse the attack, United States forces should be used even though this risks Russian counter moves. To sit by while Korea is overrun by unprovoked armed attack would start (a) disastrous chain of events leading most probably to world war."

When the secure phone rang in Missouri, Truman answered it himself. "Mr. President," Acheson said, "I have serious news. The North Koreans are attacking across the 38th parallel." Truman instructed Acheson to notify the United Nations, the fledgling world organization that was created to deal with armed conflict after the carnage of World War II. Secretary-General Trygve Lie of Norway said of the North Korean invasion: "This is war against the United Nations." He called an emergency session of the Security Council that approved a U.S.-sponsored resolution blaming North Korea for a "breach of the peace" and calling for the "immediate cessation of hostilities" and withdrawal of North Korean forces to the 38th parallel.

After the U.N. vote, Acheson contacted Truman with more details.

"Mr. President, the news is bad. The attack is in force all along the parallel," Acheson said.

"Dean, we've got to stop the sons of bitches no matter what," said Truman, an ex-haberdasher and former artillery captain who had been in the White

Gen. MacArthur joins South Korea's President Syngman Rhee as he debarks from MacArthur's plane, the "Bataan," June 1950.

House at the conclusion of World War II.

Then Truman flew back to Washington for a meeting of his top advisors at Blair House. The official minutes from that June 25 meeting in Washington said: "General Bradley said that we must draw the line (against Communist expansion) somewhere...The Korean situation offered as good an occasion for action in drawing the line as anywhere else." But Acheson later wrote: "If the best minds in the world had set out to find us the worst possible location to fight a war, the unanimous choice would had to have been Korea."

On the day the war broke out, General of the Army Douglas MacArthur was at his headquarters in Tokyo—the Dai Ichi building, which in Japanese means "No.1." The 70-year-old, five-star general was the Far East commander of U.S. forces on occupation duty in Japan. He had accepted Japan's unconditional surrender at the end of World War II, and he had been in charge of Japan's reconstruction. MacArthur was hardly alarmed at North Korea's audacity. "This is

American troops borrow a camouflaged South Korean truck for a ride to the front.

The First Marine Air Wing prepares to sail for Korea. Five-hundred-pound bombs are loaded aboard the attack cargo ship *Achernar* at Long Beach, California, July 1950.

probably only a reconnaissance in force. If Washington will not hobble me, I can handle it with one arm tied behind my back," the general said.

The North Koreans ignored demands sent through political channels. So at a June 27 meeting, the Security Council took the unprecedented action of resolving that "the members of the United Nations furnish such assistance to the Republic of Korea as may be necessary to repel the armed attack and to restore international peace and security in the area." Never before had a world body condemned aggression and then raised a force to fight a belligerent. This quick and decisive action was only possible because the Soviet Union, which as a permanent member had veto power on Security Council resolutions, had been boycotting meetings for five months because Communist China had not been recognized. Ultimately, 22 nations joined the U.S.-led coalition to evict the North Koreans, including 16 countries who sent ground forces. Within days, all U.N. forces were placed under the command of Douglas MacArthur.

The day of the U.N. vote and the day of panic in Seoul, President Truman by executive order authorized U.S. air and naval forces to attack North Korean troops, armor and artillery at will. "I have ordered United States air and sea forces to give the Korean government troops cover and support," he said in an address to the nation. "The attack upon Korea makes it plain beyond all doubt that Communism has passed beyond the use of subversion to conquer independent nations and will now use armed invasion and war." Truman said intervention in Korea was the toughest decision he had made as President. Later, he wrote he was checking Soviet desires of world domination: "If the communists were permitted to force their way into the Republic of Korea without opposition from the free world, no small nation would have the courage to resist threats and aggression by stronger communist neighbors." American prestige was on the line. The North Atlantic Treaty Organization had just been formed, whereby an attack by one country was viewed as an attack on the new alliance, and Korea was seen as a proving ground for that theory. The day Truman announced intervention, the House of Representatives voted a one-year extension of the draft, 315-14; and the Senate approved it 70-0 the next day. Clearly, there was political and popular support for Truman's order, but he did not ask Congress to declare war as the Constitution provides.

Republican Sen. Robert Taft of Ohio did not oppose Truman's decision but protested his procedures for the record. "If the incident is permitted to go by without protest, at least from this body, we would have finally terminated for all time the right of Congress to declare war, which is granted by Congress alone

A letter from the top. This South Korean farmer reads an air-dropped leaflet designed to boost civilian morale. President Truman's picture is on the front, MacArthur's on the back. July 1950.

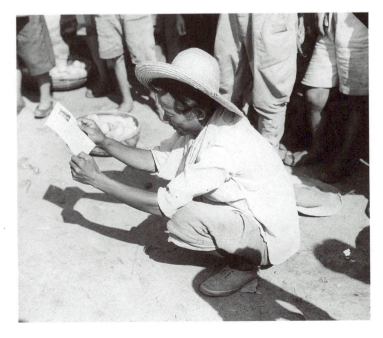

The terrain the foot soldier covered is viewed from on high by B-29 bombers.

Near the occupied town of Chonan, American soldiers coax their jeep across a blasted bridge, July 1950.

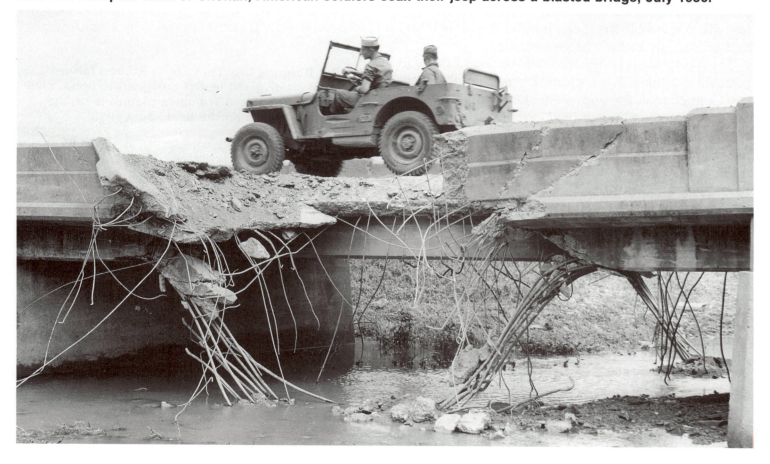

On their way to Korea, Marines of the 5th Regiment, 1st Division, load up on the Navy transport *Henrico* at San Diego. They are wearing their camouflaged backpacks. July 1950.

by the Constitution of the United States," Taft said. But Truman had set a precedent. No congressional approval was sought for later actions in Vietnam, Grenada, Panama or the Persian Gulf. The last formal declaration of war came in 1941.

The Korean War was also fought as a euphemism. Republican Sen. William F. Knowland of California had criticized Truman for prohibiting the Air Force to operate north of the 38th parallel, much like a policeman might chase a thug away from a crime scene." The action this government is taking is a police action against a violator of the law of nations and the charter of the United Nations," Knowland said in a floor speech.

Truman picked up on the phrase at a June 27 news conference, when he was repeatedly asked to characterize the U.S. response to getting involved in Korea's civil war.

Q. Mr. President, everybody is asking in this country, are we or are we not at war?

A. We are not at war....The members of the United Nations are going to the relief of the Korean Republic to suppress a bandit raid on the Republic of Korea.

Q. Mr. President, would it be correct under your explanation to call this a police action under the United Nations?

Two Russian-made North Korean tanks probably knocked out by U.S. air strikes are abandoned on a road somewhere in South Korea, July 1950.

A. Yes, that is exactly what it amounts to.

Although he didn't coin the phrase, Truman clung to it. Some Americans who fought, bled and died in the "police action" painted the sides of their tanks and landing craft with the words "Harry's Police."

The first contact between Americans and North Koreans was an air battle, and it came on the day Truman authorized the use of force. Three Yak piston-driven fighters fired on four U.S. jet fighters covering the Kimpo airfield. All three Yaks were shot down, and four more were eliminated that afternoon. One-sixth of the North Korean air force had been destroyed in a day. But on the ground, things were a disaster. MacArthur's advance commander, Brig. Gen. John Church, arrived in Korea the night before the Han River bridges were blown. On June 28, Church said planes and ships were inadequate to stop the North Koreans; only U.S. ground troops could do that job. MacArthur arrived in Suwon the next day for a first hand inspection, bringing along his familiar allotment of reporters and photographers. "The only way to judge a fight is to see the troops in action. Let's

go," said the general, clutching his familiar corncob pipe. His C-54 transport, named the "Bataan," had jet-fighter escort into the hostile environment. In those grim early hours, MacArthur began formulating a strategy that would strike a mighty blow at the North Koreans. But he had to stop them first to buy time, which in his mind could only be accomplished by U.S. ground forces. "The Korean army is entirely incapable of counter-action and there is grave danger of a further breakthrough....The only assurance for holding the present line and the ability to regain later the lost ground is through the introduction of U.S. ground combat forces into the Korean battle area," MacArthur cabled Washington.

The day after Seoul fell, MacArthur had Truman's approval to use whatever ground forces he had under his command and to put a naval blockade around North Korea. Less than five years after the mushroom clouds billowed over Japan at the end of World War II, the United States was in a full-blown shooting war, asking its sons and daughters to rescue a faraway land from conquest. It had not, however, equipped or prepared them for the task. This war would be fought like no other in U.S. history. Truman insisted on limiting the war to the Korean peninsula so as not to provoke the Soviet Union or Communist China into a wider war. No one wanted a nuclear holocaust. But MacArthur, among others, chafed at not being able to hit sanctuaries and supply points outside North Korea. The best way to fight a war, the generals felt, was an all-out effort fought to an unconditional conclusion using every weapon in the arsenal if need be.

Peacetime prosperity was on the minds of most Americans in 1950. The first color picture tube would fascinate the new TV generation, which tuned into such shows as "Ted Mack's Original Amateur Hour" and the "Cavalcade of Stars." The most popular song for the year was "Good Night, Irene" by the Weavers, and the sweet, smooth voice of Nat King Cole introduced "Mona Lisa." The Yankees were on their way to meeting and beating the Whiz Kids from Philadelphia in the World Series. And the French were pressing for U.S. dollars and advisors to help them in a place called Vietnam, a divided country whose southern half had just been recognized by the United States.

Few Americans had any idea where Korea was, let alone why it was suddenly necessary to send U.S. forces there to defend it. An old Korean proverb says that when the whales collide, the shrimp suffer. And Korea had suffered a lot in its history. It is surrounded by three of the world's great powers, bordered by China and Russia on the north and its less than 150 miles from its southern tip to Japan.

Given its position dropping down from the Asian mainland, Korea has historically been an invasion route for both China and Japan. Once known as the Hermit Kingdom, Korea looked upon China as its overlord, but its people developed their own language and alphabet. In 1910, the Japanese annexed Korea and made it a colony in its empire. Koreans chafed under the harsh rule of Japan, and some formed patriotic organizations in other lands to work for liberation. One was Syngman Rhee, the leader of a secret society who fled to the United States and studied at Harvard and Princeton. Rhee organized a government in exile, hoping to return to his homeland one day. Another organizer who took a different path was Kim Il Sung. He sought haven in the Soviet Union, graduating from a Russian university and serving as a Soviet officer in World War II. He also had dreams of making his country independent.

When Japan's defeat in World War II was imminent, the Americans proposed a plan that would divide Korea roughly in half. The dividing line was the 38th parallel, which in the United States runs just north of

San Francisco. There was no real intent to partition the country. It was an administrative demarcation between the Americans and the Soviets, allies against the Axis powers, to accept the surrender of their Japanese foes in the southern and northern halves. But the Soviets cut rail lines and set up roadblocks at the artificial and unnatural boundary, restricting the movement of people and goods and effectively creating two states that had no government and no money. Minerals and forests were concentrated in the communist northern half; the rice producing areas and most of the population were in the south.

The United Nations in 1947 scheduled elections in both halves to determine the government of a unified Korea, but the Soviets kept the world body out. An election resulted in the August 15, 1948, creation of the Republic of Korea, with 73-year-old Syngman Rhee as its autocratic but U.S.-supported president. The country, with 21 million people, was about the size of the state of Virginia. In the north, an area about the size of New York with 9 million people, the Russians installed Kim Il Sung as premier. Each side claimed to represent all of Korea, and each seemed dedicated to the destruction of the other. The Soviets had trained an efficient army and equipped it with tanks and artillery before pulling out in 1948. The United States organized South Korea's army but refused to give it tanks and cannons lest it entertain thoughts of striking the north. On June 25, 1950, North Korea played its military hand.

The American military in World War II was the mightiest in the world. It had defeated fascism in Europe and a militaristic empire in Japan. A sense of euphoria flourished because its land, sea and air forces were augmented by the ultimate weapon—the atomic bomb. (The U.S. monopoly was short-lived, however. The Soviet Union exploded it first atomic device in 1949.) But the 11 million Americans in uniform in 1945 returned to the civilian world rapidly. The bulk of the defense budget went to the Air Force, the branch of the armed forces capable of delivering the bomb. On the ground, the U.S. Army had become a hollow shell in just five years.

In 1950, the Army had 10 divisions and 11 separate regiments on active duty. There was one infantry division, two infantry regiments and a constabulary force equal to a division in Europe to discourage the Soviets from expanding their Iron Curtain over Eastern Europe. In addition to the divisions assigned to stateside duty, four infantry divisions were assigned to the U.S. Eighth Army on occupation duty in Japan.

The Eighth Army was under the command of Maj. Gen. Walton Walker, an experienced and aggressive

U.S. air power caught these North Korean tanks moving to the front. Rocket fire destroyed three, disabled three and sent the truck lying on its side down the embankment.

combat commander who earned the nickname "Bull-dog." He had commanded one of Gen. George Patton's corps in Europe; Patton had admiringly called Walker "a fighting son of a bitch." But of his four divisions in Japan, three of them—the 24th, the 7th and 1st Cavalry—were below their peacetime strength of 12,500 men, which was only 66 percent of their wartime strength of 18,900. Only the 25th Division exceeded its peacetime allotment with 13,000 men. Instead of the normal allotment of three battalions, most of the divisions had two. They were missing artillery and tank units. This was an army that did not expect to go to war. It was concerned with administration, not the grim and dirty task of fighting a determined foe. The duty was leisurely and relaxed, a Monday-to-Friday assignment. The business of war, such as fire support, weapons training, resupply and ammunition handling, all suffered. The ten-cent

drinks in Japanese bars and the geisha girls beckoned. There really was no room to train in the tight quarters of Japan, so fire and maneuver became textbook lessons. But the greatest single weakness was equipment and ammunition. In the whole of Japan, there were only 18 rounds of anti-tank artillery rounds, or high explosive, anti-tank (HEAT) shells. Everything from radios to batteries were leftovers.

"We were, in short, in a state of shameful unreadiness," said Lt. Gen. Matthew Ridgway, the Army's deputy chief of staff.

The alarms of war sounded at 10:30 a.m. on June 30 at Camp Wood on Kyushu, the southernmost island of Japan and home of the 24th Division, which would be the first to go to Korea simply because it was the closest. On this Friday night, a payday when many of the troops were out on the town, the phone rang in the home of Lt. Col. Charles B. (Brad) Smith,

Republic of Korea troops look on as a convoy of Americans pause on their way to the front. An overturned truck is in the background. July 1950.

commander of the 1st Battalion, 21st Regiment. Awakened by his wife, Smith was told by regimental commander Col. Richard Stephens: "The lid has blown off." Less than six hours later, Smith was on his way to Itazuke Air Base. Six C-54 transports were waiting to whisk him and about half his battalion to battle. A 1939 graduate of West Point, Smith had been at Schofield Barracks when the Japanese attacked Pearl Harbor on December 7, 1941. Now he was literally leading his country into war a second time. Maj. Gen. William Dean, the division commander, saw him off. "Good luck to you, and God bless you and your men," the general said. Dean and the rest of the division would journey later in whatever planes and ships could be scrounged up on short notice.

The first U.S. ground forces—designated Task Force Smith— were greeted by cheering Koreans outside of the port city of Pusan at Korea's southern tip. Serenaded by brass bands, the soldiers boarded trains for

a 12-hour ride to Taejon, where the reception was even more raucous. Bands played "Dixie" and "Columbia, the Gem of the Ocean," which they understood to be American favorites.

In Taejon, Gen. Church outlined Task Force Smith's mission—bolster the ROK army and meet the North Koreans as far north as possible. On a map, he pointed to a place called Suwon. "We have a little action up here. All we need is some men up there who won't run when they see tanks," Church told Smith on July 2. Later that day, Church confidently told reporters: "We will hurl back the North Koreans, and if the Russkies intervene, we will hurl them back too."

As more and more American troops funneled into Pusan by air and sea, Smith ventured 80 miles north by jeep up Route 1 to reconnoiter the terrain. It was the main highway between Seoul and Pusan, but in truth, it was a rutted, bumpy road that turned to goo during summer rains. Smith drove north to Osan, an assemblage of huts and shacks about 28 miles south of Seoul where a railroad line and a road met. In the opposite direction streamed vans, trucks, school buses, peasants pushing wheelbarrows and weaponless ROKs fleeing the steamroller of war. The roads were cluttered with the detritus of a beaten army—wrecked trucks and abandoned vehicles that had run out of gas. Smith picked out an advantageous spot on three hills north of Osan that overlooked the road and offered a view all the way to Suwon, eight miles to the north, where the North Koreans were coiling to strike. It was as good a spot as any for an ambush.

Although Smith had been told he could count on close air support, things had not gone well as his task force trucked to the north. Coordination between air forces and ground troops was sometimes disastrous in the early days of the war. On July 3, after a fog had lifted, friendly fighters mistakenly bombed a nine-car ROK ammunition train going north. Air attacks destroyed the Pyongtaek and Suwon train depots, shot up 30 ROK trucks and killed more than 200 ROK soldiers. A member of Task Force Smith, wounded by friendly air attacks, wondered: "What kind of screwy war is this?"

Shortly after midnight on July 5, the trucks carrying Task Force Smith departed Pyongtaek. It took three hours over puddled roads to reach the Osan ambush point. And at 3 a.m., U.S. soldiers drew a line in the reddish mud, a spot now marked by a monument built by the South Korean government. Task Force Smith had 540 Americans—406 infantrymen and 134 members of the 52nd Artillery Battalion, with an average age of 20—assigned to stop an entire marauding, armored army. Smith had six 105-millimeter howitzers, but only six rounds of armor-piercing (HEAT) shells. He had no tanks or land mines. He had no help on either flank and could not rely on any reinforcements. Because of the bad weather, he lacked air support. He had almost no contact with his South Korean allies—an example of the poor coalition and joint coordination in the war's early days. The U.S. Army had used superior firepower and lightning mobility in the broad land battles of World War II. Being outgunned and outnumbered was a totally foreign position. Still, morale was high. "We thought they'd back off as soon as they saw American uniforms," one

Two U.S. soldiers line up their bazooka and wait for North Korean tanks.

Side by side, an American GI and a South Korean soldier await their mutual enemy, July 1950.

Smith spotted a column of eight tanks clanking down the road—the tip of the spear leading the North Korean 4th Infantry Division. When the tanks reached a point a mile in front of the infantry, the artillery fired and provided man-made thunder for the rain. Gen. Barth instinctively looked at his watch. The U.S. Army's first shot of the Korean War came at 8:16 a.m. A 14-hour time difference meant it was still the Fourth of July back in the States, where volunteer firemen and communities everywhere were launching fireworks into the sky.

The opening bombardment had no effect on the tanks. Conventional artillery shells explode in thousands of hot, razor-like shards that can indiscriminately kill, main, amputate and castrate. But they can't penetrate thick steel, and North Korean tankers were safe behind their armored hulls. Then when the lead tank closed to within 700 yards, 75-millimeter recoilless rifles fired and scored direct hits. The tank didn't even slow down. With the tanks as close as 15 yards from the infantry, bazooka teams fired their 2.36-inch rockets, which were as ineffective as they were against

Heavy firepower moves to the front. Cpl. Coy Atkins (right) of Indiana carries a flame thrower and Pvt. Ray Blair of Maryland carries a bazooka. With the 1st Cavalry Division somewhere in South Korea, July 1950.

soldier said. Some riflemen had as little as two clips of ammunition for their M-1 Garand rifles. And Gen. George Barth, in command of the 24th Division artillery, said the GIs had an "overconfidence that bordered on arrogance." On the way north, Barth and Smith had berated ROK engineers for preparing to demolish bridges to stop North Korean tanks. "No thought of retreat or disaster entered our minds," Barth said.

In a steady morning rain that made July 5 unseasonably chilly, the Americans ate C-rations for breakfast. The North Koreans, who had captured the airstrip at Suwon the previous day and were rolling south, ate rice before revving up their tank engines at about 7 a.m. Most likely, they were unaware of the American trap. Flushed with success, they were 200 miles from Pusan, the only port and airstrip left that could accommodate modern military forces in numbers large enough to wage war. If Pusan fell, North Korea figured it could "cut the windpipe of the enemy."

Brad Smith had deployed his infantry on a mile-wide front. Five howitzers were a mile to his rear. The artillery piece with the six HEAT rounds was half a mile closer, set up as an antitank gun. At 7:30 a.m.,

GIs dig in a battery of 155mm howitzers to stem the advance of North Korean forces.

German tanks in the last war. Rockets hit tracks, turrets and rears of the machines, but the paint on the T-34s was barely scratched. "Colonel, we don't have anything that can stop them," one of the soldiers told Smith. Pre-battle anxieties now turned to downright uneasiness as the North Koreans rumbled past.

Finally, Lt. Col. Miller O. Perry, commander of the 52nd Artillery and also a West Pointer, ordered the HEAT rounds fired. The specially shaped charges bore into the metal of the two lead tanks as they came over a crest of a hill. Both were forced off the road. Two men came from their burning tank with their hands raised, but a third emerged with a burp gun and killed an American machine gunner. He was the first American killed in ground action, but his name has been lost to history. His comrades quickly gunned down the three North Koreans.

The tanks knocked out the northernmost howitzer,

and some artillerymen panicked and fled. But Perry rallied his men. He grabbed a bazooka and disabled a tank by hitting its treads, although he took a bullet in the right leg doing it. Another crew damaged a fourth Korean tank. But 29 T-34s had gotten through, shooting up American trucks and blowing up a stockpile of 300 artillery rounds.

The Americans, shaken that tanks were now behind them, held their positions to face a new menace—a six-mile long column of North Korean infantry and trucks, led by three more tanks. Smith's communication lines were cut by the first wave, so he was out of touch with his big guns for the second phase of the battle. Nobody expected the North Koreans to run now, and the Americans got their first taste of a deadly tactic their foe would use again and again and again during the war. The tanks pinned down the American front, then 5,000 men in two regiments deployed

The big guns roar and send their lethal message. The GIs turn away and protect their hearing.

At a railroad station somewhere in South Korea, the first American dead arrives from the front. A wounded soldier, hands raised, is on the stretcher in the background. Neither is identified. July 1950.

around either side in a maneuver called a double envelopment. The disciplined North Koreans did not have radios. They deployed at the sound of bugles, the low-technology communications that U.S. horse soldiers once followed to fight Indians. In Korea, bugles became a sound the Americans feared.

Task Force Smith, outnumbered 10-to-1, was now bracketed. These green U.S. soldiers were unprepared psychologically for an enemy that could overpower them and threaten their escape routes. They were almost encircled when Smith ordered a withdrawal at 2:30 p.m. "In an obviously hopeless situation, with many casualties, no communication, no transportation, ammo gone, and the enemy tanks now well behind us, I was faced with the decision: What the hell to do? The answer was simple: I chose to try to get out," Smith said later. A withdrawal under fire is a dicey maneuver, and most of the U.S. casualties that day came during the retreat. The withdrawal was supposed to be a leapfrog effort, with one company covering for another and then in turn pulling back. It was anything but orderly. Some soldiers discarded

their machine guns and rifles, slogging through the rice paddies around them. The dead and about 30 seriously wounded men on litters had to be left behind in the care of a medic who volunteered to stay with them. "That's the worst part of a deal like that, to leave wounded and dying men yelling for you to help them, and there was no way to help them," Smith said. Perry was still holding his position when Smith found him. After removing the sights and breech locks on the remaining guns, rendering them useless, the task force organized a convoy and headed south. However heroic the stand, it was a futile confrontation. About 115 men were killed or wounded, while 70 others were captured. The wounded Perry reported to Gen. Barth at headquarters: "I'm sorry, sir. We couldn't stop them."

The first American death documented by the media was Pvt. Kenneth Shadrick, who was firing his bazooka in a graveyard on the outskirts of Sojong. An Army Signal Corps photographer wanted to get pictures of the flame coming out the back end of Shadrick's bazooka when he fired. So Shadrick would count one, two, three and then jump up and pull the trigger. After one sequence, Shadrick raised up to see where his projectile went. He was machine gunned in the chest and right arm. "What a place to die," muttered a passing medic. The 19-year-old Shadrick, one of 10 children of a Skin Fork, West Virginia, coal miner, had quit high school in 1948 to join the Army. "He just wanted to see the world, " said his brother, Roy.

It took five days for all the stragglers to reach Taejon. By that time, the North Koreans had coerced a tortured prisoner of the opening battle, artillery Capt. Ambrose Nugent, to read a 1,000-word statement over the radio. In clumsy, stilted language, Nugent blamed U.S. involvement on Wall Street warmongers.

The opening defeat was a bit like the U.S. Army's first encounter with the German Wehrmacht in World War II. At the Kasserine Pass in North Africa, Rommel's panzers pushed the untested Americans back 50 miles. Like them, the Americans in Korea needed experience, hardening and more and bigger guns. Douglas MacArthur admitted he was buying time, hoping "by the arrogant display of strength to fool the enemy into belief that I had a much greater resource at my disposal than I did." Arrogance wasn't much of a deterrent for tanks, though. The opening encounter not only failed to put a stopper in the bottle, it barely interrupted the North Korean tide.

Soldiers on the next line of defense heard of Task Force Smith's fate through the grapevine. Said one member of the 24th Division: "It planted a doubt in

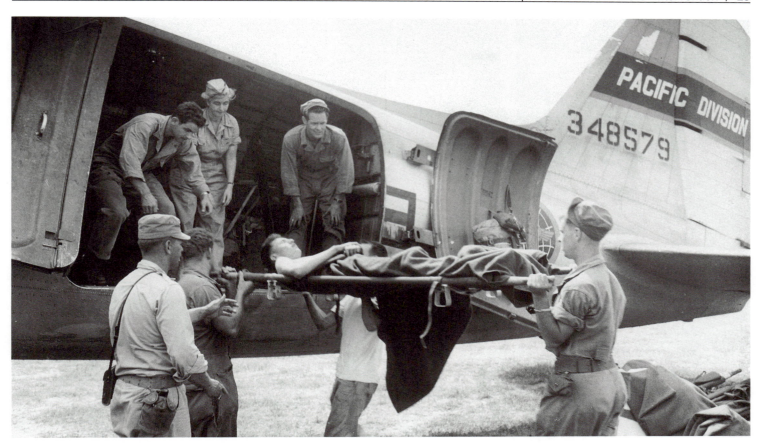

An ambulance plane takes aboard a wounded GI. Some wounded are cared for in MASH units, other more seriously hurt are air-lifted to Japan.

many minds about the effectiveness of our tactics and weapons...the doubt ate like a cancer into the combat morale of all troops moving to the front." It also should have jolted anyone—in Washington, Tokyo or the frontlines—from the notion that this would be a quick, tidy police action.

Now the burden of stopping the North Koreans fell on the 34th Regiment, whose two understrength battalions set up blocking positions about 10 miles south of Task Force Smith's temporary stand. These soldiers, too, were confident they'd soon be back on garrison duty in Japan. But they fared much worse than the infantrymen in the first battle. The regiment was given the job of holding a line from Asan Bay to Ansong, 12 miles to the east, by blocking two roads leading south. Once again, the battalions were outgunned and outnumbered, flung stopgap into battle without reserves or support. Because of what happened to Smith's men, the 1st Battalion of the 34th Regiment was told to hold only until the North Koreans threatened to envelop them, then fight delaying actions in retreat. A bridge over a small stream to their front was blown in the wee hours of July 6, and in the fog and rain of dawn, the 1st Battalion saw 13 T-34s lined up in a single column. The Americans fired their mortars, and North Korean infantry deployed

to move quickly around the American positions. The 1st Battalion's response was slow and erratic. One company fell back, leaving its weapons and radios behind. The withdrawal was so disorderly it turned into a panic. It wouldn't be the last time, in the early stages of the war, that green troops fled when threatened. The condition was common enough to earn the name "bug out fever."

No delaying actions were fought; the Americans just kept moving south to the town of Chonan. To the east, the 3rd Battalion also fell back without putting up a fight. Division commander Gen. William Dean was so upset with the regiment's poor performance that he sacked Col. Jay B. Lovless and replaced him with Col. Robert Martin. Within two days, the North Koreans ripped into Chonan with their tanks. In the terrible street fighting that followed on July 8, Martin was killed when he fired a bazooka at a tank at the same time the T-34 fired at him. He was the first soldier in Korea to win the Distinguished Service Cross. Less than 200 men of the 3rd Battalion got out of Chonan. Two-thirds of the battalion died or surrendered.

At least air power was having some effect. On July 10, some F-80 jet fighters discovered a convoy of tanks lined up in front of the bridge blown by the 34th

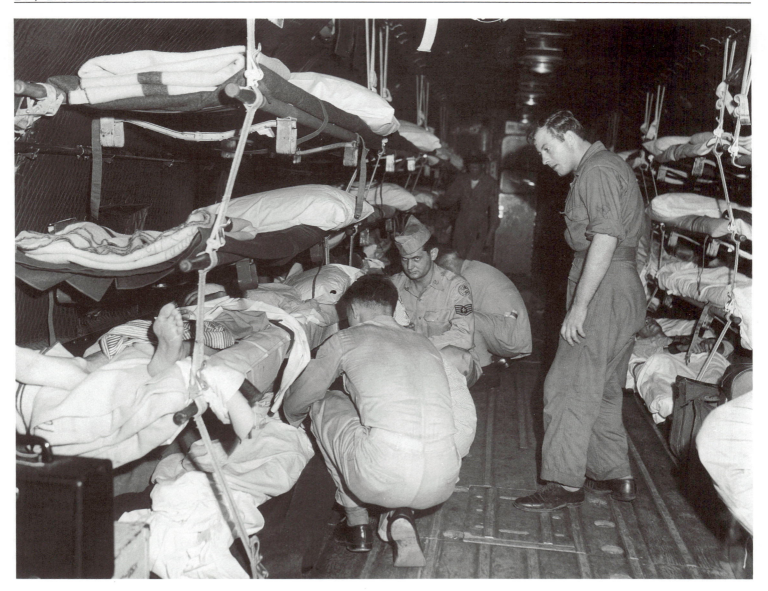

The wounded are loaded aboard Air Force transports for the long flight home. An Air Force sergeant oversees the adjustment of one of the bunks at Haneda Airport, Japan, July 1950.

Regiment. The Fifth Air Force launched everything that could fly, and the reported score was 38 tanks, seven half-tracks and 117 trucks. The raid was so effective that the North Koreans changed their tactics. They holed up in daylight and moved only at night to escape American planes, which slowed their race to the south. On the downside, the Air Force was severely criticized for firing on friendly forces. Target identification and air-ground coordination needed practice too.

The first mass atrocity against Americans was also discovered July 10. Six GIs were found with their hands tied behind their backs, shot through the back of the head. The ferocity of this war was hitting home hard. And the Americans had trouble distinguishing friend from foe among the North and South Koreans. The invaders had perfected the tactic of hiding soldiers among the streams of refugees, which allowed

them to infiltrate defensive positions.

The new defensive line melted back to the natural barrier of the Kum River, about 25 miles south of Chonan. But there were two roads the North Koreans could take from the river to the communications and railroad center of Taejon. Dean had a tiny force as it was; now he had to split it to cover both routes. Some

Above right: The cameraman says this is one of four American soldiers of the 21st Infantry Regiment, 24th Division, captured by North Koreans the night of July 9, 1950, and shot through the head. Their hands were bound behind their backs. They were found midway between a forward observation post and the front line.

Below right: Unidentified American soldiers, wounded by North Korean fire, wait for air evacuation at an air strip somewhere in South Korea, July 1950.

155-millimeter howitzers had arrived, greatly increasing American firepower. And a combat engineer battalion constructed some roadblocks. But the North Koreans were coming with two divisions of about 6,000 men each, supported by 50 tanks.

July 14 was another disaster for the 34th Regiment, which was already shaken after its debut a week earlier. It was again overrun, and one unit, the 11th Field Artillery Battalion, lost all 10 howitzers and 136 men. That meant the 19th Regiment, as yet untried, was all alone on the right flank, covering 30 miles of river with two battalions. The North Koreans exploited their exposed position with a double envelopment. The main assault came at 3 a.m. on July 16 when tanks covered an infantry assault across the Kum River. It was like being held by the nose and being kicked in the sides. Cooks, clerks and mechanics were thrown into a counterattack that was a temporary success. But the regiment had to withdraw as the North Koreans sprung their trap.

In a day of calamity, the 19th Regiment lost 650 of its 3,400 infantrymen and artillerymen. The 785-man 1st Battalion was nearly cut in half. The Kum River line had broken.

American reinforcements were now arriving in quantity. Walton "Bulldog" Walker had moved his Eighth Army headquarters to Korea, and the 1st Cavalry, 25th and 7th Divisions were streaming in by ship from Japan. But it took time to move men and equipment, not to mention getting them in position in the field. Walker had to make a stand at Taejon, which had an airstrip and five roads leading into it. The only force available was the battered 24th Division, and Walker told it to hold Taejon for two days until he could bring up the 1st Cavalry as relief.

It was asking a lot for a unit already thrown into the breach, with no time to lick its wounds while it was losing men, guns and equipment at an alarming rate. The 19th and 21st Regiments could muster little more than a battalion of troops each, making them

GI rations are off-loaded and packed aboard trucks bound for the front at a rail-head in South Korea.

Under the eyes of the enemy, combat engineers pour fire into the sniper-infested hills in the Yongdong area, while a convoy of trucks races across a bridge.

combat ineffective. The main burden fell to the 34th Regiment plus two battalions of artillery. The battle for Taejon began on July 19, with the North Koreans mounting a frontal assault and sending forces along an exposed left flank so it could also attack the Americans from behind. Within a day, they had smashed through and their tanks were ripping apart Taejon.

However, the Americans finally had received a weapon to slow the T-34s. It was the new 3.5-inch super bazooka, which resembled a stove pipe. The bazooka, only recently produced, fired a shaped charge that had an inverted metal cone at the front end. On detonation, the cone drove forward like a liquefied metal jet that could burn through the armor of any tank then known. In the street fighting for Taejon, it worked wonders on its first day in the field. As many as 10 T-34s were killed by the new rockets, and two more were damaged. Gen. Dean himself led tank-hunting expeditions inside Taejon, but nothing

stopped an assault that was now coming from three sides.

As Taejon burned and was being overrun, there were acts of heroism. Sgt. George D. Libby, a combat engineer, twice crossed a heavily shelled road to help wounded soldiers. He piled them onto an artillery tractor passing south, and was wounded several times. The tractor made it, but Libby died from loss of blood. He was posthumously awarded the Congressional Medal of Honor, one of 131 presented in the Korean War.

Taejon was another catastrophe. Of the 4,000 Americans engaged there on July 19-20, one in three was dead, wounded or missing. At noon on July 22, the beleaguered 24th Division turned over the front line position to the 1st Cavalry Division. In 17 days since Task Force Smith first engaged the North Koreans at Osan, two North Korean divisions had pushed the 24th back 100 miles and had killed, wounded or cap-

GENERAL DEAN

Maj. Gen. William Frishe Dean, commander of the U.S. 24th Division in Korea in the summer of 1950, wrote a brave new page in the annals of the U.S. Army. As commander of green troops hurriedly thrown against North Korean invaders, he succeeded in upsetting their timetable and buying time for the Eighth Army to build a bridgehead.

It cost him more than 37 1/2 months in prisoner of war camps.

On July 2, 1950, when U.S. forces were rushed to Korea after the surprise invasion, Dean was sent as commander of the 24th Division, the United Nations' main hope to hold the line against the aggressors. Many of the American troops in the 24th were youngsters barely out of basic training. They were also outnumbered, out-trained, and out-equipped in their fight to defend Taejon. Until Lt. Gen. Walton Walker arrived, Dean was in charge of all U.S. troops there.

He was forced out of the war within a month.

On July 20, 1950, he had set out to check personally on reports that T-34s had broken into Taejon. After entering the town, he and a small group of men gave chase to a tank that parked at an intersection near some stores. Enemy rifle fire made them take cover.

"We withdrew through the stores and tried again at a different spot. But again the rifles found us. One of the soldiers wanted to shoot her, but I couldn't be sure enough that she wasn't a lookout.

"On the third attempt at the tank, we moved directly behind the building at the corner, so the tank should have been just on the other side of it. To get to the second floor of that store building from that back courtyard, I had to chin myself on a window ledge, then clamber in. Moving very quietly, the bazooka man and I entered a plastered room about 7-by-8 feet.

"Very cautiously, I slipped up to the window and looked around the side of it with one eye—directly

into the muzzle of the tank's cannon, not a dozen feet away. I could have spit down the barrel. I signaled to the bazooka man and pointed to a spot just at the base of the cannon where the turret and tank body joined. The bazooka went off beside my ear.

"From the tank came the most horrible screaming I'd ever heard—although I heard its equal later and under different circumstances—but the tank still was not on fire. I think I said, 'Hit 'em again' and pointed to another spot at the side of the turret. The bazooka fired and more plaster cascaded.

"A third time the bazooka fired and the screaming stopped while smoke rose from the tanks.

"I wasn't silly enough to expect to do anything with a pistol," he said. "That was just plain rage and frustration—just Dean losing his temper again and doing something foolish."

On that day, Dean was separated from his division about a mile south

A Korean child is dwarfed by the disabled T-34 tank which carries the inscription "Knocked out 20 July 50 Under The Supervision of Maj. Gen. W.F. Dean." The tank is a memorial to the general.

of Taejon on the Kumsan Road. As darkness fell and Dean set out in search of water, he fell down a steep slope. He lost consciousness and when he came to, he was alone, with a broken shoulder, bruises and a gash on his head.

Then started his long wandering, traveling by night and hiding by day, as he tried to make his way back to friendly troops. He wandered for a month—20 days of that time without food—eluding North Korean troops and local home guards five times. He was finally captured on August 26. On that day—his 24th wedding anniversary—he met a Korean civilian who promised to help him get back to American lines.

The Korean got a truck, but had hardly started when a group of North Koreans came around a bend and started shooting.

"I reached for my pistol," Dean later recounted. The Korean grabbed his arm.

"I thought I was a good wrestler," Dean said, "but before I was able to get my hands free, about 20 Koreans were on me. That night they took me to the local jail and put me in a box about the size of a table, where I spent the night."

Later, when his captors learned he was an officer, he got more commodious quarters.

Shorty after Dean was reported missing in action—the Koreans did not let it be known for more than a year that he was a prisoner of war—he was awarded the Medal of Honor, the first time that highest award had been given in the Korean War.

As the North Koreans' prime prisoner of war, he underwent severe grillings and threats of torture before his release on September 4, 1953.

Dean had been born in Carlyle, Illinois, and attended the University of California where he got a commission as second lieutenant in the Infantry Reserve before joining the Regular Army. His first assignment was with the 38th Infantry at Fort Douglas, Utah.

In World War II, Dean commanded the 4th Infantry Division in its drive through Germany and Austria. His troops were credited with capturing 30,000 prisoners and helping to force the surrender of the 19th German Army. His services earned him the Distinguished Service Medal.

He also received the Distinguished Service Cross, the nation's second highest award for valor, for leading an infantry platoon through a barrage of fire and silencing an enemy battery in France. Other World War II decorations were the Legion of Merit and the Bronze Star.

After the war, he was military governor of South Korea for 14 months, then became military commander of the U.S. 7th Division in Tokyo and later chief of staff of the Eighth Army in Japan.

Dean retired in 1955 at the age of 56 as Deputy Commander of the Sixth Army. He received the Combat Infantryman's Badge on his last day as an American fighting man, after serving 32 years in the military. He died in 1981.

---

tured three out of 10 of the division's 12,200 soldiers.

The 24th had also lost its commanding general. On July 23, Gen. Dean had loaded wounded men onto his jeep a mile south of Taejon. When he went to get water for the wounded, he fell down a steep slope and was knocked unconscious with a broken shoulder and a head gash. Dean wandered for 36 days before the North Koreans found him and imprisoned him for the remaining three years of the war. He, too, won the Medal of Honor.

The division had given Eighth Army the two days it needed, but it failed to accomplish as much as it could have and as much as possible.

Roy Appleman, who chronicled the first five months of the war for the U.S. military, noted that the 24th performed many heroic actions but many unsoldierly ones as well. The division, standing alone, had slowed the North Koreans just enough to allow Americans to reinforce and give them a fighting chance at stabilizing a front. It probably performed as well as any other division would have.

"A basic fact is that the occupation divisions were not trained, equipped or ready for battle. The great majority of the enlisted men were young and not really interested in being soldiers. The recruiting posters that had induced most of the men to enter the army mentioned all conceivable advantages and promised many good things, but never suggested that the principal business of an army is to fight," Appleman said.

In "America's First Battles," Roy K. Flint noted the lack of battlefield preparation, and in particular, the poor performance of the 34th Regiment in the opening battles. "Nowhere were the failures of the prewar Army more evident. In the end, all seemed more concerned with escape than with fighting. The 34th never really made a fight. In time, the 24th Division fought with distinction. But to a man, they regretted the wasted years in Japan. There were no stronger advocates of a combat-ready peacetime army than the veterans of Task Force Smith and their comrades in the 24th Division."

Despite the loss of men and territory, MacArthur proclaimed the North Koreans had lost their chance

The General Pershing tank, the M-26, is an intermediate answer to the T-34 with a lower silhouette, more fire-power and better speed than the old General Sherman which gave away 15 miles an hour to the wider-tracked Russian behemoth. Here, the Pershing's 90 mm high velocity gun is tested.

for victory. The invaders took their share of casualties in their frontal assaults. Their supply lines had lengthened precariously. And they were consuming more ammunition than could be replaced. U.N. air power relentlessly hammered their convoys. The 5th Regimental Combat Team arrived from Hawaii, with 14 M-26 Pershing tanks equipped with 90-millimeter guns. The 4,700-man 1st Provisional Marine Brigade (5th Marines) also landed with a whole battalion of M-26s. At last, there was something to counter the T-34s. And more troops and equipment were in the "Pipeline," the so-called system of delivering goods from America.

To hold southern Korea, the Eighth Army set its sights on a no-retreat position along the Naktong River. More time needed to be bought, but the Americans had less territory to defend and more men and equipment to defend it with. The Pusan perimeter faced its supreme test.

2

Pusan Perimeter

The darkest days of the Korean War were fought in the fierce heat of late summer 1950.

The dawn of a military breakout was approaching, but first a United Nations force had to cling to a precarious toehold that was hardly more than an expanded beachhead. The six-week period of daily crises and sharp fighting was necessary to defend the Pusan perimeter, a box at the lower end of the peninsula protecting the only port and airfield the Americans had left where they could land reinforcements and supplies. The perimeter—100 miles long and 50 miles wide—ran along the last

Above: Credit paid for credit due, Cpl. Ivan Burgess of Rock Hill, Missouri, paints his outfit's trade mark on a dead North Korean tank with its spiked gun while Cpl. Kenneth E. Taylor of Rochester, Massachusetts, offers critical advice.

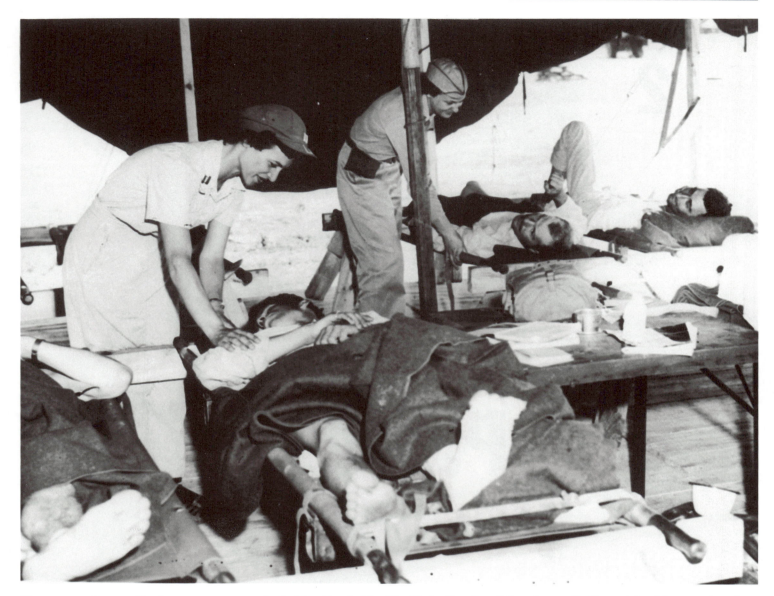

Nurses make medical evacuees comfortable. Capt. Phyllis M. LaConte of the Army (left) and Lt. Marguerite J. Liebold, flight nurse, ready the men for the flight to hospitals in Japan, August 1950.

remaining natural barrier before the sea, the Naktong River. The north-to-south waterway was a quarter to half-mile wide in spots, but shallow enough to be forded in many other places. Around both banks were steep hills that posed a barricade for the North Koreans. The hills made good observation and listening posts for the defenders.

The last of Maj. Gen. Walton Walker's retreating and badly mauled Eighth Army crossed the Naktong River on July 31. This dynamic Texan issued a stand-or-die order, and through sheer force of bulldog will, he hounded and goaded his demoralized troops to make a fight of it.

"There will be no more retreating, withdrawal, re-

GIs dig in along a hillside in the central sector of the front to face the advancing North Koreans.

adjustment of lines or whatever you call it. There are no lines behind which we can retreat. This is not going to be a Dunkirk or Bataan. A retreat to Pusan would result in one of the greatest butcheries in history. We must fight to the end. We must fight as a team. If some of us die, we will die fighting together," Walker said in a desperate bid to rally his forces.

At the beginning of August, Walker had 47,000 U.S. troops from the 24th, 25th and 1st Cavalry Divisions arrayed on the western length of the Pusan perimeter. On his north front, he deployed the 45,000 remnants of five Republic of Korea divisions; three ROK divisions had been wiped out in five weeks. What was left of the South Korean army was of dubious fighting ability. The foxholes were filled with untrained soldiers who were literally dragged into the military; some had fired as little as 10 rounds from their rifles on practice ranges before they were ordered to halt the invaders. Any South Korean over the age of 18 could be drafted from the rice paddies and find himself on the front line within a week. There, he either became a veteran or a corpse.

Although they pressed forward with the attack, the North Koreans were actually outnumbered—something that seemed impossible to believe for men on the defensive line. They had 70,000 men in 11 divisions but had lost 58,000 men in their head-long rush down the peninsula. Among their reinforcements were South Koreans dragooned into their ranks. The invaders were also down to about 40 tanks, fewer than the number in a single U.S. battalion. But they flung themselves forward in a fanatical bid to drive to the sea by August 15—known as Liberation Day in Korea because the country had been freed from Japan's 35-year grip with its defeat in World War II.

The Americans had some advantages, even if they did not have the initiative or any more room to maneuver. They still controlled the skies and seas, which prohibited the North Koreans from moving in daylight if they wanted to escape jet fighters and naval batteries. The North Korean supply lines—the distance from the tail to the tooth—were at their maximum distance and vulnerable to attack. Barring a breakthrough, the U.S. and South Korean positions were difficult to flank because their lines were bordered on the south and west by the sea. Traditionally, Americans disdained defensive fighting and preferred combat on the move. But while their front wasn't a continuous line, they did enjoy artillery support. The big guns provided interlocking fields of fire, which meant more than one unit could pour in fire if lines were broken. This was the kind of fighting the U.S. Army did in Europe in World War II. The familiar

calls for fire missions provided a security blanket for rattled troops. If there was none of the excitement of moving forward, at least the infantry wasn't surrendering territory in big chunks anymore. There was also less territory to defend and more troops to defend it with.

A basic law of combat is that interior lines are more flexible than exterior ones. Gen. Walker was able to form fire brigades of his reserves. If the North Koreans threatened to break through in one area, Walker sent a mobile unit into the breach to counterattack. Units that were flanked had to hold on until reinforcements arrived, which they began to do with trusting regularity. An essential trick of survival was learning to fight from all sides of a foxhole—front, back, left and right. Overall, the lines were sufficient enough to hold—barely—as the North Koreans exhausted themselves in their all-out fury. And everyone was told help was on the way.

Congress was neither asked to provide or took it upon itself to give a declaration of war. But it did provide President Truman with an $11 billion emergency appropriation and extended the Selective Service. Draft orders were sent to 50,000 civilians in September and again in October; 70,000 more were conscripted in November. These new GIs were supposed to get three to four months of extensive field training, but some found themselves on the front lines 10 days after induction and having never zeroed in their rifles. In addition to the Army's 5th Regimental Combat Team and the 5th Marine Regiment, the U.S. Army's 2nd Division landed in Pusan during August. In the meantime, U.S. allies searched their arsenals for combat units and equipment to ship to Korea. Great Britain dispatched its 1,600-man 27th Brigade from Hong Kong, the first of two brigades and five infantry battalions, one aircraft carrier, supporting ships and elements of its air force it mustered for Korean duty. Australia sent ground forces garrisoned in Japan, an aircraft carrier and an air squadron. Canada shipped ground troops, three destroyers and an air squadron. By September, ground forces had also been sent from Belgium, France, Greece, the Netherlands, New Zealand, the Philippines, Thailand and Turkey. In all, more than 300,000 tons of material was offloaded in July at Pusan.

Still, this was largely a United States show. But the army in the field was perhaps the most poorly trained and poorly motivated in U.S. history. It had no grand score to settle such as Japan's sneak attack on Pearl Harbor. There were no strong ancestral links to Korea as there were to Europe. The fighting began as another country's civil war, but the United States viewed it as

TANKS, VERY MUCH

The Russians built more than 53,000 of their workhorse tanks, the T-34, during World War II. One war later, the North Koreans needed just 150 of them to come close to overrunning the entire Korean peninsula.

When the northerners struck across the 38th parallel, tanks in the lead, the South Korean army had no armor at all. American military planners considered the Korean terrain—mountains interspersed with muddy rice paddies—ill-suited to tank warfare.

But the invaders proved otherwise. The wide treads on the 35-ton T-34, the tank that stopped the Nazis outside Moscow in 1941, gave it maneuverability in the mud. Its high-velocity 85mm gun and 32-mph speed made it the dominant weapon of the war's first weeks. In a typical engagement, North Korean tankers, advancing down a road, would pin down a defense line while their foot-soldier comrades slipped around the flanks in a double envelopment.

At first, the South Koreans and

their American allies had little to throw against the T-34s. Both their 57mm anti-tank guns and 2.36-inch bazookas did little damage against the Soviet-made tank's heavy armor. The first American tanks in action were two companies of M-24 Chaffees rushed in from Japan. But the light tanks were disastrously outgunned. In one early engagement, in fact, two Chaffees lost their turrets when their poorly maintained 75mm guns misfired.

Back in Japan, U.S. commanders hurriedly organized a battalion of rebuilt M-4 Shermans, "the tank that won World War II." The Shermans' high-velocity 76mm guns still did not match the T-34's firepower, but at least they could penetrate the enemy armor when in range. At the same time, by late July 1950, the hard-pressed defense forces were supplied with new 3.5-inch bazookas, whose rockets also could stop a T-34.

Other tank units were in transit across the Pacific. As U.N. forces held the Pusan perimeter, more than

500 Shermans, M-26 Pershings and M-46 Pattons—the most advanced U.S. tank—were unloaded in Pusan harbor. The low-slung Pershing, developed late in World War II, was heavily armored and carried a 90mm gun. The Patton was essentially a Pershing with wider treads and a more powerful engine.

By the end of August 1950, six U.S. tank battalions were in Korea. They quickly made a difference. Tanks supported the Inchon landing on September 15, and the 70th Tank Battalion led the 1st Cavalry Division on an 11-hour, 106-mile dash from the Pusan perimeter to link up with the Inchon-Seoul force on September 29.

The T-34s had more than met their match. After Inchon and the Pusan breakout, U.S. military survey teams found 239 of the North Korean tanks destroyed or abandoned on battlefields across the peninsula.

part of communism's scheme to dominate the world. It led to the U.S. policy of containment, which was being made up as it went along. Three months after the war began, President Truman signed National Security Council paper No. 68, becoming the first American commander-in-chief to note that "the nation must be determined, at whatever cost or sacrifice," to defend democracy "at home or abroad."

South Koreans had the promise of self-government, although the government of the autocratic Syngman Rhee bore little resemblance to democracy. But corruption and injustices in Rhee's government paled by comparison to the bloody abuses taken by dictator Kim Il Sung. South Koreans and Americans uncovered shocking examples of executions by anyone who claimed to have opposed the North. The United Nations estimated that 26,000 South Koreans were killed

in cold blood by the invading army; 5,000 of those bodies were found in Taejon. Any question of which side to be on was answered by rivers of refugees straggling south through the American lines. For these ragtag peasants voting with their feet, the South held the moral high ground.

For U.S. troops, their first impression of Korea came through their nostrils. Korea was literally a stinking place, especially in the 105-degree heat of August. GIs got a whiff of kimchi, fermenting cabbage, buried along roadsides. But that aroma was downright tame compared with the stench that came from honey wagons, which were ox-pulled carts of human excrement that fertilized Korean rice paddies. And, of course, the Americans had difficulty distinguishing between North and South Koreans or any other Asians. GIs corrupted the native term han'guk saram, which means Korean, into the derisive slang "gook," which was indelicately applied to all Asians, even in later undeclared wars.

Not surprisingly, North Korea's major attempt to

Left: U.S. Marines prepare their freshly unloaded 45-ton Pershing tanks for battle, reinforcements to face the North Korean advance, August 1950.

crack the Pusan perimeter was thrown against the ROK division on the northern flank. They lacked the armor, the artillery and the traditions of their American allies. Knowing that they were running out of time, the North Koreans crossed the Naktong on August 4 and aimed at Taegu. The assault was led by the *3rd Division*, the first unit to march into Seoul—earning it the distinction from Kim Il Sung as "Seoul's Third." It was also the division that had routed Task Force Smith and battered the Americans on its way south.

The North Koreans borrowed a Russian trick used against the Germans in World War II. Using forced peasant labor, they built up the Naktong's bottom with sandbags and oil drums, creating underwater bridges that were hard to detect from the air. Their T-34s crossed the water barrier on August 8.

Arrayed against them were the 7,000-men of the 1st ROK Division, spread thinly without tanks or howitzers to buttress their defenses. The North Koreans penetrated to within 12 miles of Taegu, whose population had more than doubled to 700,000 with

North Korean Offensive and Pusan Perimeter

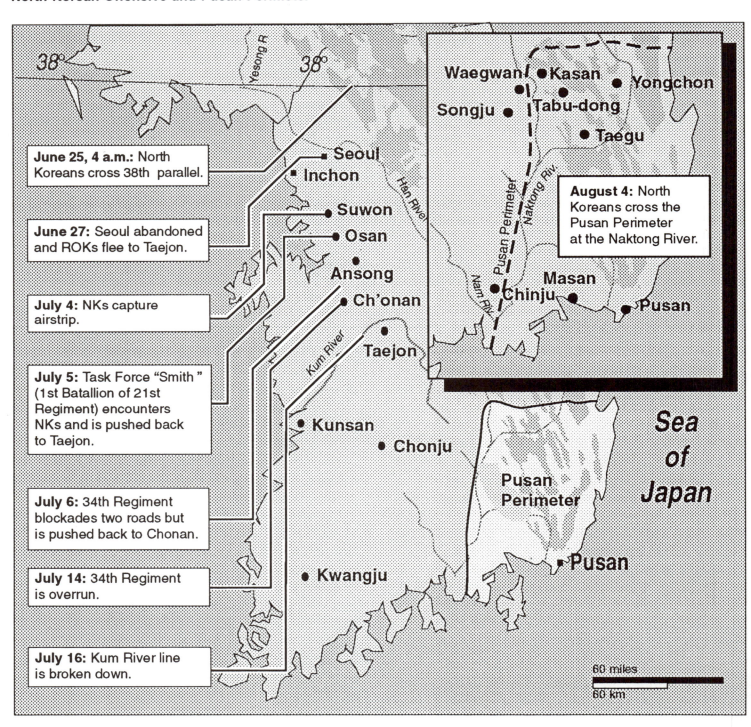

June 25, 4 a.m.: North Koreans cross 38th parallel.

June 27: Seoul abandoned and ROKs flee to Taejon.

July 4: NKs capture airstrip.

July 5: Task Force "Smith" (1st Batallion of 21st Regiment) encounters NKs and is pushed back to Taejon.

July 6: 34th Regiment blockades two roads but is pushed back to Chonan.

July 14: 34th Regiment is overrun.

July 16: Kum River line is broken down.

August 4: North Koreans cross the Pusan Perimeter at the Naktong River.

A wounded Marine is carried away from the fighting in the Chinju area.

the flood of refugees and the core of Syngman Rhee's government. The ROKs were issued some 3.5-inch super bazookas, but they were under strict control of the division commander lest they fall into North Korean hands. The stove-pipe bazookas provided a remedy for T-34 disease. And Gen. Paik Sun Yup, commander of the 1st ROK Division, issued a Walker-like rallying plea to shaken troops literally fighting with the sea at their backs.

"This will be our final defense line. If we can't hold this line, Taegu will fall. If that happens, the U.S. Army defense line along the Naktong will collapse. That means the fate of the nation itself rests squarely on the back of the ROK 1st Division. I chose this line personally and will take full responsibility for failure," Paik said.

The South Koreans moved into their last line of defense on August 12. If they got into trouble, the U.S. Air Force could arrive in 30 minutes from Itazuke Air Base in Japan. The jets could stay over a target for

Happy South Korean officers hold shells they have cleaned out from the disabled North Korean tank behind them.

two hours, which kept the North Korean tanks and supply column hidden in the area's apple orchards except at night and in poor weather. After two days of heavy fighting, the battle reached a crisis on August 15—Liberation Day. The 1st ROK Division was fighting on three fronts covering a 12-mile stretch. The hand-to-hand combat came at such close quarters that rifles were ineffective. Much of the damage was done by exchanging hand grenades. The dead piled up so fast they were used as shields by survivors. Paik asked for and received emergency reinforcements from the 10th ROK Division and the 27th Regiment of the U.S. 25th Division, in what would be the first joint U.S.-Korea action. It was also the toughest action along the Pusan perimeter.

But first, Supreme Commander Douglas Mac-Arthur ordered his Air Force to carpet-bomb an area west of the Naktong River where he thought the

North Koreans were massing. On a target covering 26 square miles, 90 B-29s released 3,084 bombs weighing 500 pounds each and 150 bombs weighing 1,000 pounds each. It was equivalent to 30,000 rounds of artillery. But the North Koreans had already crossed to the east side of the Naktong, and the bombs fell in craggy hills and hollows. Later intelligence failed to determine if the carpet-bombing killed a single North Korean soldier, but it did keep their heads down for a day. Heavy bombing may have damaged German factories and Japanese cities, but it was of dubious value in Korea's backwoods areas. It was as practical as bombing large areas of triple-canopy jungle.

Meanwhile, the fire brigade of the 27th Regiment came to the rescue under the command of Lt. Col. John "Iron Mike" Michaelis. He offered the ROK 1st Division three infantry battalions, 18 105-millimeter howitzers, six 155-millimeter cannons, a tank company, an air-ground liaison team and all the ammunition his men could shoot. The 1936 graduate of West Point also brought experience and candor to the battlefield. An outstanding combat paratrooper in World War II, Michaelis commanded the 502nd Airborne Regiment and was wounded at Normandy and Arnhem. Eventually, he rose in the ranks to become a

Left: At a Pusan dance hall, a grinning newly arrived GI takes a break before facing the war.

Below: A Marine helicopter flies off from a forward command post en route as an aerial messenger to the 1st Marine Division base.

On the attack, U.S. B-29 Superfortresses unleash their deadly cargo on a chemical plant at Konan, North Korea, August 1950.

general officer and in 1971 returned as commander of U.S. forces in Korea. But in 1950 when he assumed command of the Wolfhounds of the 27th Regiment, he found his ranks filled with green, frightened men who had to be molded into soldiers on the battlefield. Michaelis frankly addressed the shortcomings of the moment and the effect of neglect on the U.S. Army when he told *The Saturday Evening Post*: "In peacetime training, we've gone for too damn much folderol. We've put too much stress on information and education and not enough stress on rifle marksmanship and scouting and patrolling and the organization of a defensive position. These kids of mine have all the guts in the world and I can count on them to fight. But when they started out, they couldn't shoot. They didn't know their weapons. They have not had enough training in plain, old-fashioned musketry. They'd spent a lot of time listening to lectures on the

difference between communism and Americanism and not enough time crawling on their bellies on maneuvers with live ammunition singing over them. They'd been nursed and coddled, told to drive safely, to buy War Bonds, to give to the Red Cross, to avoid VD, to write home to mother—when somebody ought to have been telling them how to clear a machine gun when it jams....The U.S. Army is so damn roadbound that the soldiers have almost lost the use of their legs. Send out a patrol on a scouting mission and they load up in a three-quarter-ton truck and start riding down the highway."

Michaelis deployed his men on a defensive line in a valley near Tabu-dong, with the ROKs holding the high hills on either side. The battleground was called the Bowling Alley, because of the sights and sounds of a noisy engagement along a 2.5-mile-long road hemmed in by mountains. On August 18, the North

Newly organized and equipped, ROK soldiers move up to defend their homeland against the North Koreans.

Koreans came south with tanks and infantry in a night assault. Bazookas knocked out the lead tank; then U.S. tanks and preregistered artillery and mortars opened up under the light of flares. From the heights, the projectiles from the tank muzzles were visible red balls as they zoomed through the chute. When the

shells exploded, the blasts echoed off the hills like bowling pins rattling off a wall. The battle played out the same way over the next six nights as the North Koreans repeatedly maneuvered into an American trap. Finally, the North Koreans reverted to their tried and tested method of moving around the flanks and

Combat engineers of the 1st Cavalry Division blow a hole in a rocky mountain road to plant mines to intercept the advancing enemy.

setting up a roadblock in the rear. In the opening days of the war, it would have been enough to scatter the defenders. The North Koreans actually fired seven mortar rounds into Taegu, triggering a panic because residents thought they were surrounded. Syngman Rhee's government pulled back to Pusan, the absolutely last place to run.

Things really looked bleak on August 20. A ROK battalion was forced to retreat, exposing the left flank of Michaelis' 27th Regiment. It looked like a ROK "bug out," the tendency to retreat at the slightest indication flanks were threatened. Michaelis told the battalion commander: "If we lose this battle, we may

Left: Enemy mortar shells send troops at an Army-Marine motor pool scurrying for cover near Masan, South Korea. When it's over, two Marines are dead and five wounded. August 1950.

not have a Korea. We have nowhere else to go. We must stand and fight." With his position in jeopardy, Michaelis ordered his men to withdraw before they were trapped in the valley. But Gen. Paik convinced him to stay while he inspired his men.

"We just don't have room to retreat anymore," Paik told his bloodied division. "The only place left to go now is the ocean. If we run now, Korea is done for. Look at those American troops over there. They're fighting because they trust the ROK Army, and if we retreat, we bring shame down on the entire ROK Army. We are men of Korea; let us fight for this land. We're going to turn around and kick the enemy off our ridge, and I shall be at the front. If I turn back, shoot me."

Led by the yells of charging men, the division retook the hill. Then on the night of August 21, in a five-hour assault aimed straight at the 27th Regiment, the Americans absorbed a blow and turned back the North Koreans. By August 24, the South Koreans again occupied all of its last line of defense. All important hills and ridges were in friendly hands, so Michaelis went south to respond to another North Korean offensive. In the fighting, the ROK 1st Division lost 2,300 killed and wounded—one-third of its force. Most of the men who had dug the fighting holes at the start weren't there at the end. But the North Koreans suffered far worse—5,700 of the invaders were killed.

Instead of massing for a single blow to punch a hole through the perimeter, the North Koreans mounted a series of assaults along the line. One of the last places left for any kind of maneuver was the extreme south of the peninsula near the port of Masan. About 15 miles north of Masan, the Naktong River turns abruptly east and flows to Pusan. So without the natural barrier of a river, the North Korean *6th Division* attempted to loop under the southernmost reaches of the perimeter and cut the windpipe of the United Nations command. The communists were just 33 air miles from Pusan, pushing forward with 7,500 men, 36 artillery tubes and 25 tanks. To block their path, Gen. Walker pulled the U.S. 25th Division out of the line in the north and rushed them to Masan.

A U.S. tank dares North Korean shellfire to trade blows up close.

The division was reinforced with the 5th Regimental Combat Team, the 5th Marine Regiment and a regi-

U.S. sailors form a cross and Marines fire a salute in a memorial service for their dead. Aboard a U.S. carrier in Korean waters, August 1950.

ment-sized group of survivors from the ROK 7th Division. The blocking force totaled 20,000 men and was reinforced with two tank battalions of 50 tanks each. The Marines also brought with them two close-support squadrons of Corsairs from the escort carriers USS *Sicily* and *Baedong Strait* just off shore. After blocking the path, Eighth Army planned a counterattack that would recapture Chinju, then wheel north to the Kum River and relieve pressure on the line. The counterthrust began August 7 with the 35th Regiment of the 25th Division. But America's garrison soldiers were bothered by the 105-degree heat, which made it a lot tougher to hump it over craggy countryside. Coordination was also a problem; the 5th Regimental Combat Team made a wrong turn, going south instead of north to hook up with the 35th Regiment. Air power took a heavy enemy toll on August 11 when jets got 31 trucks, 24 jeeps, 45 motorcycles plus most of the ammunition of a North Korean motorized regiment.

Two things that most Americans associate with Vietnam debuted in Korea. The Air Force dropped bombs of napalm, which is naphthene and palmitate, or gasoline in a jellied state. American wounded were also whisked from the battlefield by an ungainly craft called the helicopter, such as the Bell H-13 Sioux.

The counterattack stopped in its tracks, however. The Americans controlled the roads, but the North Koreans controlled the countryside. It would take dirty fighting to flush them off the hills. A place called Battle Mountain changed hands 19 times, sometimes two of three times in a single day.

Farther north, the North Korean *4th Division* assaulted a place called the Naktong Bulge, seven miles north of where the Nam River flows into the Naktong. Six days after the August 5 attack began against the 34th Regiment of the U.S. 24th Division, the *4th Division* had crossed the Naktong via underwater bridges. The communists established a roadblock, which in preceding weeks would have meant victory as Americans abandoned vehicles and equipment. It was different now. Eighth Army sent in the 27th Regiment of the 25th Division, the 9th Regiment of the 2nd Division and the 5th Marine Regiment to counterattack. Marine Corsairs provided air-ground support, the kind they practiced in the island-hopping campaigns of World War II. And when North Koreans burrowed deep foxholes, U.S. artillery fired air bursts—which exploded before hitting the ground and rained down shrapnel. Finally, the North Koreans

Under Marine guns, a wounded North Korean, flushed from a rice paddy, hoists himself onto a stretcher. In his pockets were an American watch and lighter and other items, the fruits of battle. August 1950.

Along the Naktong River front, Marine tanks return enemy fire from nearby ridges as North Koreans try to impede the Marine advance.

brought up their tanks, which were neutralized by M-26 tanks, recoilless rifles and 3.5-inch bazookas. By the morning of August 19, Marines and soldiers linked up at the river. The *4th Division*, in full flight, was virtually eliminated as a fighting force.

The U.S. 1st Cavalry Division was assigned 35 miles of front south of Waegwan. It had taken up defensive positions on the eastern side of the Naktong, then destroyed a bridge to deny the North Koreans access. Unfortunately, some Korean refugees refused to heed warnings and kept pouring across; scores of them were blown up with the span. At Yongpo, the 1st Cavalry met and stopped an attack from the North Korean *10th Division*. Of the 1,700 who crossed the Naktong, only 200 made it back alive.

The Americans also got further evidence of how ugly this war would be. On August 17, 26 dead U.S. soldiers were found above Waegwan, their hands tied at the back with wire and their bodies sprayed with burp guns. Survivors of the massacre had burrowed under the dead. Even veterans of the fanatical campaigns fought by the Japanese were appalled by North Korean tactics. The communists made no hesitations about dressing up as fleeing refugees, then emptying their burp guns into unsuspecting road guards. They also used refugees as human screens to sneak into and throw hand grenades into American ranks. The rules of war were being redefined.

During the last days of August, a lull in the fighting developed. The North Koreans regrouped for one final shot at a breakthrough. It would be the high water mark of their advance. An attack launched on September 2 gained six miles and pushed the U.S. 1st Cavalry out of Tabu-dong, the place that the ROK 1st Division had held in August. On September 6, the North Koreans also broke through at Yongchon. That same day, the ROK Army Headquarters evacuated Taegu and moved to Pusan, and contingency plans were drawn up to flee to Japan. But the North Koreans had shot their bolt and could no longer exploit their breakthroughs. Their offensive was like the September weather; it was still hot, but it lacked the persistence of summer. The T-34s had literally run out of gas. Yongchon was retaken, lost again and retaken again in counterattacks. Gen. Walker proclaimed on September 7: "Our lines will hold."

Something else was in the wind. Rumors had run through the ranks about a giant operation to relieve the Pusan defenders by landing a force behind the North Koreans and cutting them off. Such a force would cut supply lines and isolate the invaders in the south. It would also act as an anvil, against which the Eighth Army could serve as a hammer to bludgeon what was in between. The U.S. Army had plenty of wounds to lick, but it still had a superpower's land, air and sea resources to pull off such a maneuver. Supreme Commander Douglas MacArthur first envisioned such a bold stroke in the chaos of late June when friend and foe alike were streaming south. His plan had simple genius. Three-fourths of Korea is surrounded by water, and the United Nations controlled the seas. If the communists kept driving south,

A seriously wounded American soldier is loaded into an ambulance after being flown from the front in an L-5 observation plane converted to a one-patient ambulance.

Below: A North Korean tank with its top blown off by U.N. fire is photographed by a GI camera.

they were in essence plunging headlong into a sack. If a drawstring were pulled tight behind them, they were trapped. MacArthur drew it up as Operation Chromite; it belongs to history as Inchon. To pull it off, he needed to reassemble the 1st Marine Division and team it with the U.S. Army's 7th Division, the last of the four occupation units in Japan. "If I had the 1st Marine Division, I would make a landing here at Inchon, and reverse the war," MacArthur told Pacific Fleet Marine commander Gen. Lemuel Shepherd in July. There were weeks of heated arguments against Inchon as generals, admirals, staff officers and the Joint Chiefs of Staff tried to convince MacArthur it was a bad idea. The 5th Marine Regiment was already inside the Pusan perimeter, which meant it would have to be pulled out of the defensive line and put aboard ships.

Walton Walker was so hesitant to give up the Marines he said he could not guarantee successful defense if he lost them. The safe play would be to land the two divisions at Pusan and break out from the perimeter on the ground. But MacArthur was an old warhorse whose Pacific strategy in World War II was to bypass strongpoints with amphibious assaults, then let the garrisons die on the vine. He was sold on the idea of a grand strike to bring the war to a dramatic conclusion. "It will be like an electric fan. You get to the wall and pull the plug out and the fan will stop. When we get well ashore at Inchon, the North Koreans will have no choice but to pull out, or surrender,"

Checking it out, a 25th Division rifleman searches a Korean straw hut for snipers on the southwestern front, September 1950.

MacArthur told his staff officers.

Inside the Pusan perimeter, the ROK 1st Division was told it would be assigned to the new U.S. I Corps with the 1st Cavalry and 24th Divisions. Gen. Paik had one overwhelming thought: "Now we finally get to kick some butt."

A fatigued GI rests his weary head at his machine gun nest along the small Pusan perimeter, August 1950.

3

Inchon

Of all the operations in combat, nothing quite captures the imagination as an amphibious assault. The armada of warships laden with men and stores. Waves of air strikes to soften up shore defenses. The thud of naval guns laying down a curtain of cover. Grim-faced troops emerging from the bellies of transports and going over the side. The air thick with the smell of cordite from spent shells. Landing craft circling in the chop until a prearranged signal sends them across a line of departure. Men with rifles, wondering what awaits on land, scurrying ashore when the gates drop.

So it was at Inchon, Douglas MacArthur's master stroke, the last great sea-air-land operation, the signature moment of American can-do achievement in Korea.

Above: Gen. MacArthur and staff watch the naval and aerial bombardment of Inchon from the flag bridge of the U.S.S. *McKinley* as a new American offensive kicks off. September 1950.

Inchon also stands as a postscript to the previous war, recalling a time of idealism when America and its allies stood up to the forces of evil. It echoed operations such as Tarawa, Iwo Jima, Normandy and Okinawa—the Easter Sunday landing in 1945 that was the final amphibious assault of World War II.

Some felt assaults from the sea were already a military anachronism; Omar Bradley, chairman of the Joint Chiefs of Staff, had indicated in 1949 that such operations were obsolete. But in the desperate early months of the Korean War, an amphibious landing was practically demanded.

Tired GIs of the 25th Division's 24th Regiment trudge to the rear to make way for fresh counterattacking troops near Haman on the southern front, September 1950.

MacArthur wanted a single September thunderclap to dispel all the heat of summer. Instead of evicting the invaders, he wanted to crush them. MacArthur's aim was to deliver a fatal blow to an invading army and recapture Seoul, with all of its psychological and symbolic value. Nothing on the east coast of Korea was as attractive a target because most of North Korea's supplies were flowing down the rail lines on the western side of the peninsula. Chinnampo, the port city of the North Korean capital of Pyongyang, was too far north. Kunsan, 100 miles south of Inchon and 70 miles west of the Naktong, was too close to Pusan to fit MacArthur's strategy.

The U.S. Navy, which had to deliver this force, favored Pusong-myon, 50 miles south of Inchon and southwest of Osan, because it had favorable beach conditions and was within striking distance of North Korean supply lines. But in MacArthur's mind, the target had to be Inchon, just 20 miles from Seoul, with its airfields, roadways and railroads.

Yet Inchon posed some of the most challenging geographical barriers ever to confront military planners. The swing of its harbor tides were among the greatest in the world—a difference of 32 feet between the high and lower water marks. Navy planners figured they needed 23 feet of water to land craft, so it would have three hours to put ships ashore, then it would have to wait 12 hours to go back. During slack tide, those ashore would be stranded, separated from their lifeline of ships by giant expanses of mud flats that could swallow men and vehicles. The first time the seas would be high enough, following the dry

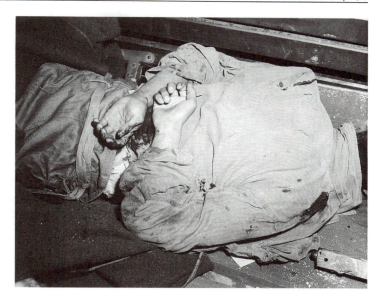

One of a group of murdered American soldiers on the Masan front. Their hands were bound behind their backs.

periods of summer, was at mid-September. And the water levels would be suitable on only four days, September 15-18. If MacArthur waited until October or November, the weather would be turning bad. It would make a breakout more difficult if Pusan could hold out.

There were other drawbacks. The approach to Inchon was a narrow and treacherous seaway called Flying Fish Channel, which mammoth warships would have to negotiate with care. A 1,000-foot wide island called Wolmi-do commanded the approaches to the harbor; it would have to be neutralized in a morning assault and seized before the main landing

2nd Division infantry root out snipers at burning Yongsan on the Naktong River front. North Koreans held the town one day before they were driven out by counterattack. September 1950.

force could come ashore. That meant the main landing must take place in evening, giving assault forces just two hours of daylight to gain a toehold. Because of the swing of its tides, Inchon had no beach but a 15-foot high gray seawall that would have to be scaled or blown apart. And finally, the force would be landing in the heart of a city of 250,000 people held by an opposing army.

"I had to agree that it was the riskiest military proposal I had ever heard of," Omar Bradley said in his autobiography. "Inchon was probably the worst possible place ever selected for an amphibious landing."

Lt. Gen. Matthew Ridgway, deputy chief of staff for the U.S. Army, called Inchon a "5,000-to-1 gamble." The Joint Chiefs of Staff, those great strategists

Pvt. Joseph Vassallo of Chattanooga, Tennessee, heats field rations over an improvised rock stove for a rare luxury, a hot meal.

South Koreans carry murdered GIs from their radio relay post near Masan where they were captured, tied up and shot in cold blood by a woman guerrilla.

who were supposed to look at the bigger picture of war, liked the concept of an amphibious landing but were skeptical about Inchon. Downright dubious was the Marine Corps that would have to go ashore there and the Navy that had to negotiate those treacherous tides.

It was August 23 at the Dai Ichi building, Mac-Arthur's headquarters in Tokyo, where the top brass of the American military gathered to listen to the supreme commander. Gen. J. Lawton Collins, Army chief of staff, and Adm. Forrest P. Sherman, chief of naval operations, both favored Kunsan. Others spoke about the overwhelming difficulty of an Inchon landing. Rear Adm. James Doyle said pointblank: "The best I can say is that Inchon is not possible."

But it was impossible to shake MacArthur, who had been pushed off the Philippines by the Japanese but accepted their unconditional surrender four years

later in Tokyo Bay. At the meeting, he laid aside his trademark corncob pipe and spoke in a resonant, conversational tone for 45 minutes. With the themes he covered, those in the room got the impression he was addressing a larger, unseen audience. He invoked the spirit of one of his military heroes, British commander James Wolfe, who had his army scale a seemingly impregnable Quebec cliff to defeat the French under the Marquis de Montcalm in 1759 and win British control of Canada. And by MacArthur's logic, the very problems of Inchon made it a more attractive target.

"It is plainly apparent that here in Asia is where the communist conspirators have elected to make their play for global conquest. The test is not in Berlin or Vienna, in London, Paris, or Washington. It is here and now—it is along the Naktong River South Korea," the general said. "The very arguments you have made as to the impracticalities involved will tend to ensure for the element of surprise. For the enemy commander will reason that no one would be so brash as to make such an attempt....I can almost hear the ticking of the second hand of destiny. We must act now or we will die....We shall land at Inchon, and I shall crush them."

Still, the Joint Chiefs wanted to see concrete details before they gave approval. The generals sensed a military disaster in the making and didn't want their butts sticking out too far, but Inchon already had the support of three heavyweight civilians—President Truman, Defense Secretary Louis Johnson and presidential advisor Averell Harriman. The Joint Chiefs approved the landing site on September 9, just a day before the preparatory shelling began and six days before the invasion. And they hadn't yet seen the final plans being brought by a courier, Lt. Col. Lynn D. Smith. MacArthur had dispatched Smith with the

plans and this message: "If they say it is too big a gamble, tell them I said this is throwing a nickel in the pot after it has been opened for a dollar. The big gamble was Washington's decision to put American troops on the Asiatic mainland."

The first troops to hit the shore would be from the legendary 1st Marine Division, the leathernecks who had mounted the first counterattack of World War II when they landed on and held Guadalcanal just seven months after Pearl Harbor. The 5th Marine Regiment was inside the Pusan perimeter fighting off the ferocious North Koreans. They were taken out of the line at the last possible moment on September 12, over the heated objections of Eighth Army's Walton Walker. The 1st and 7th Marine Regiments were being created almost from scratch in the United States. The 1st Marines, under the command of Col. Lewis "Chesty" Puller, the most decorated man in the Ma-

Moping North Korean prisoners languish in a hastily set up barbed wire enclosure under the watchful eyes of American MPs. Tanks move along a road near Yongsan on the Naktong River front.

A North Korean T-34 tank burns, knocked out by advancing Marine tanks.

rine Corps, didn't leave the United States until September 1 and didn't know for sure where they were going.

The landing force also included the U.S. Army's 7th Division, which was the last of the occupation army in Japan. It was down to about 9,000 men, because much of the 7th had been cannibalized to feed the divisions fighting in Korea. During August, the pipeline flowing with men and material from the United States was diverted to Japan to build up the 7th to a landing strength of 25,000 soldiers. A curious experiment fleshed out its ranks. Draftees from South Korea were assigned to its ranks under a buddy system. They were called Korean Augmentation to the United States Army, or in military jargon, KATUSAs. The theory was that rice farmers and villagers could learn soldiering if they were paired with Americans. Language barriers and cultural differences posed big problems, however. About 8,600 stunned and confused KATUSAs joined the 7th Division, but putting

Waiting for the Reds, 25th Division tanks line up against a rail embankment northwest of Masan, September 1950.

25th Division riflemen take cover behind their jeeps as U.S. planes dislodge snipers in the adjacent hills.

South Korean Women's Army Corps parade through the streets of Pusan, ready to take their place beside their menfolk against the invaders.

foreigners into the U.S. Army met with only limited success. A motley group of bankers, clerks, bakers and farmers were hustled to Japan for eight days of U.S. Army training at Mount Fuji. At most, they fired five rounds of live ammo. No grenades were issued to KATUSAs until they got into actual combat because the Army was afraid they would blow themselves up beforehand. Some of the Koreans had to be forcibly kept away from Japanese cooks. The Japanese were considered mortal enemies for invading Korea, and fights beween the two nationalities were common.

The invading force was organized as X Corps, which was separate and apart from Eighth Army. Essentially, MacArthur was splitting his command, which would pose serious problems later. MacArthur's own chief of staff, Lt. Gen. Edward M. Almond, commanded the Inchon landing force. Almond was a division commander in Italy but inspired little affection among his subordinates. There was instant friction between him and the 1st Marine Division commander, Oliver P. Smith, a 57-year-old white-haired Texan whose personal philosophy was "You do it slow, you do it right." The plan for Operation Chromite called for the 1st Marine Division to assault Inchon, then seize Kimpo airfield, the south side of the Han River and the Seoul suburb of Yongdungpo before crossing the river to seize the capital and the high ground to the north. The 7th Division would secure the Marines' right flank and link up with the Eighth Army pushing north after it broke out of its defensive positions. MacArthur wanted some para-troopers, the 187th Airborne Regimental Combat Team, to drop behind the targets to block North Korean reinforcements from moving up. But they didn't arrive in time for the invasion, and it fell upon the umbrella of air cover and naval guns to stop communist troops from approaching Inchon.

The expeditionary force encountered a surprise natural obstacle. Typhoon Kezia spawned in the Yellow Sea, scattering some ships with its 125 mph winds and contributing to some severe seasickness among the infantry. The savvy of the U.S. Navy held the fleet together and got it to Inchon. The 230-ship armada included cruisers, destroyers, minesweepers, three U.S. attack carriers, two Marine escort carriers, a light British carrier and Canadian, Australian, and Dutch

The low slanting sun catches the determination in the faces of 2nd Division GIs toting their machine gun to the front.

destroyers. The transports carried 25,000 Marines, 25,000 soldiers, a regiment of ROKs, plus U.S. engineers, tanks and artillery. Military intelligence told them to expect 500 North Koreans on Wolmi-do Island, 1,500 more in Inchon, 500 at Kimpo and 5,000 in Seoul.

To hide their intentions at Inchon, the Americans

Life goes on as these GIs mount a defensive position in Kyongju. On the telephone pole in the background is a sign announcing Tax Day for a house-to-house collection. In the left background a policeman directs traffic.

positioned the battleship *Missouri*—on whose deck the Japanese had capitulated in 1945—on the eastern and opposite coast of Korea. Its 16-inch guns thundered diversionary salvos. The British also carried off feints at Chinnampo and Kunsan. The assault force entertained the notion of not shelling Wolmi-do Island until the morning of the landing. But the Navy and Marines learned in World War II that it took more than one day to damage Japanese bunkers. So for five days, Wolmi-do was shelled, bombed, napalmed and strafed into a moonscape. All buildings were destroyed and it was denuded of vegetation. Yet the Americans knew the North Koreans had 75-millimeter guns in deep revetments that could pierce the thin hulls of the landing craft.

Earlier, U.S. Navy Lt. Eugene Clark had been put ashore at Yonghung-do, 15 miles to the south of Wolmi-do. He confirmed planners' worst fears: about waist deep mud, shallow water and the harbor wall; now he helped direct fire onto the target. Finally, five

Left: U.S. Marines advance through Inchon as they widen the bridgehead near Seoul.

Below: U.S. and ROK infantry take cover from enemy shells along the River Road that runs alongside the Naktong.

U.S. 1st Cavalry troops fire their recoiless weapons at a Red position.

U.S. warships inched closer to the island and opened up. The North Korean commander had two grim choices. To do nothing meant he would be pulverized. But to pull the lanyard on the guns was to die because he would be giving away his positions. The guns did open up, and Navy gunners zeroed in and silenced them. One U.S. sailor was killed in the exchange. MacArthur's command ship *Mount McKinley* had set sail for Inchon on September 13.

On D Day, MacArthur was there in all his grandeur, cap braided in gold, sunglasses, corncob pipe and a coterie of news photographers. This was his creation. A third-rate power was now going to be taught the lessons of war. His forces had as many planes as the airspace could hold; the North Koreans had a total of 19 piston-driven Yaks in their entire air force. There wasn't a single North Korean ship to challenge them.

How this massive operation could remain a secret was mystifying. Talk of the operation was heard from the fighting lines to the GI bars of Tokyo. AP correspondent Billy Shin had it confirmed two days before D Day. After a September 13 staff meeting of ROK officers, Shin encountered Maj. Kim Kun-bae and the two went to a bar. When Shin speculated the landing would come at Kunsan, the officer told him, "Not Kunsan. It's Inchon." Kim knew he had talked too much and became edgy. Don't worry, Shin told him, it'll all be public in three days. "Stupid! It's going to be the day after tomorrow!" Kim said. Shin passed along the information to AP's Tokyo office. But the North Koreans were caught so off-guard the navigational lights were still on in Flying Fish Channel when the invasion fleet moved in. Col. Wong Lichan, a Chinese liaison officer who had been at North Korean

Above left: Gen. MacArthur and staff stop their convoy to inspect two knocked-out North Korean tanks.

Below left: A North Korean soldier is flushed from his position, his clothes afire, as Marines move in guns at the ready in the fight to recapture the South Korean capital of Seoul. September 1950.

headquarters 200 miles away in Pusan, was in Seoul on September 15. A hotel clerk hammered at his door and the ground shuddered that morning.

"The Americans! The Americans!" the clerk said.

"What are you talking about? What Americans?" Wong said.

"The Americans are attacking Seoul," the clerk answered.

"Attacking Seoul? The Americans are in Pusan. How can they be attacking Seoul?" the colonel asked.

After a hasty visit to army headquarters, Wong was ordered to evacuate Pyongyang by train. As dawn's light broke on September 15, the final shower of rockets, bombs, napalm and cruiser shells fell on the wreckage of Wolmi-do, also known as Moon Peak island. Corsairs spit out a final blanket of machine gun fire just before the first of 17 landing craft in the first wave crunched against the shore on Green Beach

Below: Pfc. Paul Rivers of Watertown, New York, stalks enemy snipers in a Korean village as U.N. forces take the offensive near Yongsan.

at 6:33 a.m. Yet the operation had its slapdash elements. The LSTs (landing ship, tank) were World War II vintage that had been salvaged from Japanese fishermen. One LST was steered by a reservist who was driving a bus in San Francisco just two weeks earlier. But once ashore, the Marines killed 108 defenders, sealed 100 others into their caves and captured 136 North Koreans. In return, 17 Marines were wounded but none were killed. Within 77 minutes, the island was secure and leathernecks of the 3rd Battalion, 5th Marine Regiment had raised the Stars and Stripes on 350-foot Radio Hill.

When Vice Adm. Arthur D. Struble, commander of the U.S. Seventh Fleet and boss of the invasion, told MacArthur the landing party was ashore, the general clapped his hands and said: "Good, now let's go down and have a cup of coffee." He ordered a message be sent to the fleet: "The Navy and the Marines have never shone more brightly than this morning."

Then the tide swept back and throats got dry again. The isolated Marines and the men on the assault ships waited for the water to return over miles of dull, flat, stinking mud. A swarm of fighter planes buzzed in the skies and Navy gunners sat at the ready to repel any counterattack. None came.

When the sea returned in the afternoon, so did the guns. The first heavy thuds sounded at 2:30 p.m., sporadically at first until they built to a solid chorus of booms, landing on the main shore behind Wolmi-do. More than 2,000 rockets exploded. Two regiments had to be landed, and at 4:55 p.m., the LSTs pushed off from the transports. The 1st Marines hit Red Beach at 5:32 p.m., the remainder of the 5th Marines touched Blue Beach one minute later. "Beach" was a misnomer. Facing the Marines was a 15-foot high gray stone seawall.

The obstacle was scaled with ladders made aboard the transports or blasted away with explosives. It struck regimental commander Chesty Puller that the Marines hadn't used ladders since they scaled the heights of Chapultepec, a fortress outside Mexico City captured in 1847 in the Mexican War. Tanks, trucks, jeeps, supplies and combat troops stormed ashore with a cost of 20 Marines killed and 170 wounded. A light rain fell in the early darkness as Marines stumbled, clawed and cursed to find their units. A jittery Marine reported poisonous gas at his position; it turned out to be the exotic aroma of Korean garlic.

By midnight, the Marines had reached all of their first-day objectives. The two regiments linked up at 7:30 a.m. on September 16, sealing off Inchon and ensuring victory. MacArthur had plunged his sword of vengeance deep into his enemy's ribs. Later that

Above: High casualties on both sides in the battle for Seoul. A Marine helicopter airlifts one wounded leather-neck to safety as others wait for evacuation. September 1950.

Below: Although fire menaces their homes, Seoul residents stop their firefighting efforts to greet advancing leathernecks.

As American troops move past a roadblock, Seoul falls to the United Nations advance. The North Koreans move toward the 38th parallel.

day, the North Koreans moved up six T-34s and some infantry on a highway. Six Corsairs spotted them, obliterating three of them. American tanks took out the remainder and mopped up the foot soldiers. That was the extent of the North Korean counterthrust. MacArthur came ashore on September 17 to relish the moment and decorate his troops; he wanted Seoul taken by September 25 to coincide with the three-month anniversary of the North Korean invasion. Leaving the ROK regiment to mop up Inchon, street by street, the 5th Marines moved to Kimpo with its 6,000-foot runway—perfect for transports and fighter-bombers. The entire airfield was seized by the morning of September 18, and the 5th Marines reached the south banks of the Han River later that day. Meanwhile, the 1st Marines rolled into Seoul's industrial suburb of Yongdungpo. A decisive thrust came from a quick-thinking and gutsy company commander, Capt. Robert Barrow. Barrow moved his Ma-

Marine tank "DeadEye Dick" moves past a barricade while a spotter shouts directions to the crew inside.

A U.S. Marine prepares to throw a hand grenade into a tunnel and a machine gunner and rifleman set up shop. Civilians reported that North Koreans had taken cover inside.

rines along a dike into the heart of Yongdungpo. Undetected, they were in a perfect blocking position to hit the North Korean rear and block the best exit routes out of the city. Although the company was cut off, no amount of North Korean attacks could dislodge them; 275 North Koreans died trying. The North Koreans abandoned Yongdungpo the night of September 21 and fell back to the north bank of the Han River to defend Seoul. Col. Homer Litzenburg's 7th Marine Regiment, which had arrived too late to participate in the amphibious landing, was now ashore and positioned west of Seoul. U.S. forces were in place for the final assault on the South Korean capital.

For the second part of the Inchon landing, the U.S. Army's 7th Division unloaded at Inchon on D Day plus three. By September 22, they had captured the Suwon airfield with its 5,200-foot runway, 21 miles south of Seoul. They were emplaced near Osan—not far from where Task Force Smith had made the first U.S. defensive stand of the war in July. Here, they set up a roadblock to keep North Korean reinforcements from moving toward Seoul and waited for U.S. and South Korean troops to break out from their Pusan perimeter, 200 miles to the southeast.

H Hour for the breakout was 9 a.m. on September 16. It was a rainy and foggy morning, which negated the impact of air power and encouraged the North Koreans to be more active than usual. Both sides attacked at various points, and fighting was so vicious it was impossible to tell who was defending and who was on the offensive. MacArthur's Inchon strategy figured that the North Koreans would cut and run if a force landed behind them. No soldier fights with much commitment if he's looking over his shoulder to cover his rear. For a few days anyway, the North Korean command thwarted the strategy simply by not telling its soldiers they were cut off. They fought as ferociously as ever. The 5th Regimental Combat Team and the 1st Cavalry Division were supposed to seize a bridgehead at Waegwan so the 24th Division could punch through. It got nowhere. However, the 1st ROK Division broke through north of Taegu on September 19 and cut off three North Korean divisions.

When planes got into the air, bombers dropped leaflets with their ordnance to tell the North Koreans of their plight. The message, complete with a map showing the amphibious landing, read:

UNITED NATIONS FORCES HAVE LANDED AT INCHON

Officers and men of North Korea, powerful UN forces have landed at Inchon and are advancing rapidly. You can see from this map how hopeless your situation has become. Your supply lines cannot reach you, nor can you withdraw to the north. The odds against you are tremendous. Fifty-three of the 59 countries in the UN are opposing you. You are outnumbered in equipment, manpower and firepower. Surrender or die. Come over to the UN side and you will get food and prompt medical care.

American units did not cross the Naktong in force until September 19. The 1st Cav didn't retake Tabudong and the old Bowling Alley battleground until September 21. The U.S. 2nd Division encountered stubborn resistance until September 22. But once North Korean lines had been breached, the front faded

At Masan Military Cemetery, Marines hold a memorial service for fellow leathernecks who died in the fighting.

MARGUERITE HIGGINS: WOMAN AT THE FRONT

Marguerite Higgins became the Korean War's most famous correspondent, but she had to fight the military and her own newspaper to cover it. She started out a mere oddity—the only female battlefield reporter—and wound up the first woman to win a Pulitzer Prize for international reporting.

Maggie Higgins wore mud like other women wore makeup. She would never marry, she told friends, "until I find a man who's as exciting as war." In Korea, she found a war that was as difficult as it was exciting. She had to type her stories on the hood of her jeep, sleep on the ground, eat out of cans and dodge countless bullets, all while following a fast-moving, chaotic front. As a result, *The New York Times* wrote many years later, "Marguerite Higgins got stories other reporters didn't get."

When the war began, Higgins already was an experienced correspondent. At the age of 24 she had covered the fall of Germany for the *New York Herald Tribune*, and was one of the first journalists to reach the Dachau concentration camp. When some prisoners were confined by their Allied liberators until they could be screened for typhus, "they flung themselves against the electrically charged fences," she wrote,

"electrocuting themselves before our eyes."

In 1950, Higgins was assigned to what she considered a journalistic backwater—the *Herald Tribune*'s Tokyo bureau. But two months later war erupted in Korea. As the communists raced south, Higgins and several other reporters flew to Seoul, only to flee within hours as it was overrun. When the bridge over the Han River south of the city was destroyed, she squeezed onto a raft; when the raft sank, she swam across. She reached Suwon after a 14-mile hike, but almost immediately that city fell, too.

In 1945 Higgins had joined the last stage of a grand victory march; now she was part of a ragged, frantic retreat—"the most appalling example of panic I have ever seen," she later wrote. She quoted a Signal Corps sergeant as complaining that "those sons of bitches are trying to save their own hides—there are planes coming, but the brass won't talk. They're afraid there won't be room for anybody."

"It was routine" she reported, "to hear comments like, 'Just give me a jeep and I'll know which direction to go in. This mama's boy ain't cut out to be no hero.'" An exhausted, frustrated young lieutenant asked her, "Are you correspondents telling

the people back home the truth? Are you telling them that out of one platoon of 20 men, we have three left? Are you telling them that we have nothing to fight with, and that it is an utterly useless war?"

She was. Her articles often placed the reader—and the author—in the thick of the fray. A typical passage: "A reinforced American patrol, accompanied by this correspondent, barrelled eight miles deep through enemy territory. Snipers picked at the road, but the jeep flew faster than the bullets which nicked just in back of our right rear tire." The old jeep, her regular transportation, had been scavenged by Keyes Beech of the *Chicago Daily News*. He drove; she rode shotgun.

The conditions in Korea were among the worst ever faced by battlefield correspondents. At first, Higgins had to fly to Japan to file her stories; later, reporters had use of a phone, but the entire press corps had as few as two hours a day to file. MacArthur's press chief "apparently regarded the press as natural enemies," Higgins concluded. "He couldn't get rid of us completely, but he could make our reporting life very difficult."

During the battle for Taejon, Higgins slept on a table at command headquarters, waiting for the

like a fog evaporating under the strengthening sun. In their panic and disintegration, the North Koreans, who had already been foraging for their food, threw away their weapons and uniforms to look like refugees. They abandoned their trucks and tanks, mainly because they had no gas. Although some units fought dogged guerrilla actions, many soldiers from the north chose to sit and watch the advancing columns drive by. For the first time in the war, the soldiers of

Marguerite Higgins is probably the most famous of the war correspondents who covered the Korean conflict, not because she was a woman, but because she "got stories other reporters didn't get." Here she interviews General of the Army Douglas MacArthur.

phone. Many other nights she slept on the ground with whatever unit she was following. "Maggie's the only gal you can brag about sleeping with and not be a cad," one soldier said.

Higgins typically wore tennis shoes, baggy fatigues, aviator sunglasses and an oversize cap over her blonde hair. She carried only a few essentials—typewriter, toothbrush, towel, lipstick and flea powder. She endured mud and lice, and often had to use what she called "a friendly bush" in lieu of a bathroom. Minor maladies such as athlete's foot gave way to more serious ones as the war went on. When she finally went home she was hospitalized for bronchitis, acute sinusitis, recurrent malaria, dysentery and jaundice.

The conditions and the communists were not her only problems. Higgins and her *Herald Tribune* colleague, Homer Bigart, became embroiled in a notorious feud after the more experienced correspondent arrived in Korea and told her to return to her post in Japan. She refused, and in the months that followed they competed recklessly for space on page one. Amazingly, both survived. Higgins wasn't sure if it was luck; "whatever it was," she wrote, "I had perhaps more than my share."

But Higgins was expelled from Korea after Lt. Gen. Walton Walker, commander of the Eighth Army, barred women from the theater. "This is just not the type of war where women ought to be running around the front lines," he said. When Higgins went to Walker's headquarters to complain, the general's public relations officer put her on a plane to Japan.

The *Herald Tribune* released Higgins' defiant reply to Walker's exclusion order, and her expulsion became an international issue. A communist publication ran a cartoon depicting Higgins being marched out of Korea at bayonet point with a headline that read "MACARTHUR'S FIRST VICTORY."

Higgins appealed directly to MacArthur, whom she had met earlier in the war. "I walked out of Seoul," she told him. "I want to walk back in." Her logic apparently appealed to a man whose reputation was based on a vow to return. "BAN ON WOMEN IN KOREA BEING LIFTED," he cabled the *Herald Tribune*. "MARGUERITE HIGGINS HELD IN HIGHEST ESTEEM BY EVERYONE." The Trib's own order to leave Korea was forgotten.

Wherever she went, Higgins attracted gaggles of homesick GIs desperate for a look at a pretty American. Riding in a jeep with Higgins, said columnist Jimmy Cannon, "is like being a jockey on Lady Godiva's horse." Because of her contacts with MacArthur and other generals, her feud with Bigart, and her aggressiveness and ambition, "Maggie threatened to replace the war as the chief topic of conversation" Keyes Beech recalled.

It didn't make her job much easier, however. She needed a bureaucratic mistake to sneak aboard a command ship for the Inchon invasion; she waded ashore with the Marines, but was barred from returning to Navy vessels offshore because of her sex; she had to sleep on the beachhead and give her copy to Beech, who filed it for her from a ship.

After China entered the war, reversing the gains that followed Inchon, Higgins walked south in retreat with the Fifth Marines, her landing partners at Inchon. Then she went home, emotionally and physically spent. She published a book, *War in Korea*, and in 1952 she married William Hall, an Air Force general she'd known in Germany. "Bill is the most exciting thing," she told a friend, "next to war."

Maggie Higgins would have other stories and other battles over the next decade, but Korea was her war. Keyes Beech, her colleague, friend, and driver, summed it up: "She was a good man under fire."

---

the Eighth Army were in their element—behind the steering wheels of their advancing trucks and the turning levers of their northward-bound tanks.

The 3rd Battalion of the 1st Cavalry's 7th Regiment, commanded by Lt. Col. James H. Lynch and designated Task Force Lynch, punched through with its tanks and kept going. They passed startled North Koreans, using captured fuel to fill empty tanks on a thrust that covered 106 miles in a single day. With the white star visible on their tanks, they reached 7th Division lines after nightfall on September 26. The linkup between Eighth Army and the 7th Division came at 8:26 a.m. the next day.

The breakout was not without its costs, however. In one of the tragedies produced by the fog of war,

the British 27th Brigade suffered 60 casualties when it was bombed by mistake by American planes. Soldiers of America's strongest ally had taken a hill and called in an air strike against North Korean positions facing them. To identify themselves to pilots, they displayed white panels on the ground. But so did the North Koreans, and three P-51 Mustangs attacked the wrong troops with napalm and machine guns.

During the drive north, Americans and South Koreans discovered more atrocities committed by the communists. At the Taejon airstrip, the bodies of 500 ROK soldiers, their hands tied behind their backs before they were shot, were discovered. In Taejon, about 5,000 to 7,000 political prisoners were rounded up in the city jail and Catholic Mission. Starting on

Hundreds of civilians caught in the crossfire get U.S. medical attention. Lt. Cmdr. Charles Newton of Coronado, California, treats a 2-year-old as a relative looks on.

Marines, one with a bayonet, carry a wounded buddy to help. By September 30, virtually all of Korea was in United Nations hands.

September 23, during the disintegration of the North Korean army, these prisoners were taken out in groups of 100 or more. They were led into shallow trenches, where they were shot and buried. It was like the horrors of the Holocaust. Six survivors had feigned death and were buried alive. They included two American soldiers rescued on September 26 by the 24th Division. The soil was so thin above them they had punched holes through to the surface to get enough air until they were uncovered.

The assault on Seoul—the ultimate target of Mac-Arthur's bold play—began on September 22 with the 5th Marines staging a frontal assault on the western gates of the city. North Korean defenders had set up their strongest positions on the hills, digging trenches and foxholes with interlocking fields of fire for their machine guns. The Marines captured a key northern

hill. Then when their ROK allies bogged down in the center, the leathernecks took a southern hill. But against stubborn resistance, the Marines gained little the next day and were still short of a ridgeline held by the North Koreans. Gen. Almond was eager to capture the city; he had no interest at all in surrounding Seoul and setting up a siege. Almond and Smith, the 1st Marine Division commander, bickered about tactics. Almond gave Smith one more day to take the capital or he would bring up an Army regiment. The 5th Marines pressed their frontal assault on September 24, with the 1st Marines crossing the Han in ferries and attacking from the south. The 7th Marines drove north of the city to block escape routes. During a gruesome series of battles, North Koreans died in their fighting holes. A key position fell late that day, however. Company D of the 5th Marines captured a knob called Hill 56 that was pivotal to the North Korean defense. At the end of the day, 176 of the 206 men in Company D were casualties, including 36 dead. More than 1,200 defenders were killed in place, mostly from air strikes and mortar assaults. On September 25, the day X Corps hoped to control Seoul, the 1st and 5th Marines formed the left and right flanks of a continued assault through the city. The 32nd Regiment of the Army's 7th Division and the 17th ROK Regiment crossed the Han River three miles east of the city's main rail and road bridges to push from the east. The soldiers took an objective called Nam-san, or South Mountain, that pointed like a spear into Seoul's belly. The North Koreans began evacuating their main force, the *18th Division*, that night. The retreating defenders walked into a trap on September 26. On the eastern edges of the city, Company L of the 32nd Regiment's 3rd Battalion spotted a column headed its way. The soldiers killed 500 men and destroyed five tanks, three artillery pieces, dozens of trucks and stores of supplies. Lt. Harry McCaffrey, the company commander, was awarded the Silver Star. Later that afternoon, the 17th ROK Regiment captured the hills east of Seoul. The city was now sealed on the west, south and east with the 7th Marines slamming the door to the north.

The situation prompted MacArthur to proclaim the city freed late on September 26, but it was no such thing. It wasn't the last time the commander in Tokyo put his own interpretation on the realities of the battlefield. Plenty of casualties were to come the next day as Seoul was being liberated. The destruction—begun by U.S. bombers and artillery during the vicious fight—was completed by the tactics of the last

Capt. William Hedberg (with helmet) of Fort Atkinson, Wisconsin, treats a wounded GI near Taegu.

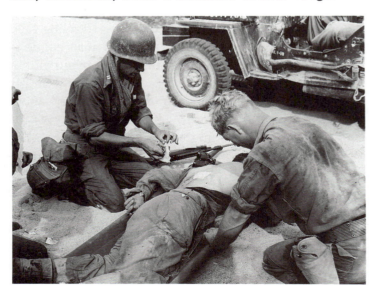

A Marine mounts a shell-splattered barricade in the Seoul business district. North Koreans hold on tenaciously but Marines raise their nation's flag over the Capitol building on September 28.

defenders. The North Koreans erected chest-high barricades throughout Seoul streets, piling up dirt-filled rice bags, laying anti-tank mines and positioning snipers in windows. Each barricade took about an hour to be neutralized. Under covering fire, engineers would explode the mines. Then two or three tanks would plow through the barriers and infantry was deployed to clear out snipers. The destructive scene was replayed over and over and over. Yard by bloody yard, a charred chunk of the 14th century city became a moldering hell. Finally, the end came in the afternoon of September 27 when Company G of the 5th Marines seized the Government House and Changdok Palace, pulled down the North Korean flags and raised the Stars and Stripes.

Elsewhere, the 1st Marines raised the flag over the U.S. ambassador's residence. By evening, it was a total victory. Twelve days after Inchon, North Koreans were streaming north by any unguarded road they could find. The 1st Marine Division had lost 414 dead and sustained 2,430 casualties, the bulk of them in the street fighting in Seoul. North Korean losses were

Upper right: Col. John D. Howe of Benton, Arkansas, deputy operational engineer for the 5th Air Force, inspects a dead Red tank.

Lower right: Pfc. Lundy Fletcher of Columbus, Ohio, looks like he's been hunting ducks, two of which are hanging from his backpack.

A GI mourns the death of a buddy, killed in action, and weeps on a friend's shoulder as a corpsman fills out casualty tags. Somewhere in Korea, September 1950.

Above right: One Seoul resident has had enough. He clips a North Korean sympathizer on the chin, as U.S. Marines and ROK troops reoccupy the capital.

Below right: Dug in and alert, Americans on the lookout for the enemy along the Han River.

13,000 casualties and 4,792 prisoners.

The official celebration in Seoul was held September 29. Immense labor was diverted from battle to build a bridge over the Han River so MacArthur could land at Kimpo and drive into the liberated city. In a solemn ceremony at the capital, MacArthur looked like a kingmaker as he turned over the building to Syngman Rhee.

The capital building smelled of smoke, and artillery booms could still be heard in the distance. Tinkling glass fell from a molded skylight, prompting some officers to scurry for their combat helmets. But the bare-headed MacArthur never flinched. "By the grace of merciful Providence, our forces fighting under the standard of that greatest hope and inspiration of mankind, the United Nations, have liberated this ancient capital city of Korea. ....On behalf of the United Nations Command, I am happy to restore to you, Mr. President, the seat of your government, that from it you may better fulfill your constitutional responsi-

North Koreans abandon tanks everywhere. This T-34 is on a rubble-strewn boulevard in Seoul, parked next to a utility pole. It is one of six blasted by U.N. forces on September 27.

The commander of the United Nations Forces gets a closer look at North Korean armor caught in the American advance.

bilities," MacArthur said. After he had recited the Lord's Prayer, MacArthur said to Rhee: "Mr. President, my officers and I will now resume our military duties and leave you and your government to the discharge of civil responsibilities."

The grateful Rhee clasped MacArthur's hand. "We admire you. We love you as the savior of our race. How can I ever explain to you my own undying gratitude and that of the Korean people?" Rhee told him.

Kim Il Sung had come within miles of overrunning the peninsula. Now his army was shattered. Of the 70,000 troops that had attacked the Pusan perimeter, only 30,000 made it back to North Korea. The battered ragtag remnants had few weapons and almost no

equipment. But it could have been far worse. As stunning as Inchon was, the trap was not completely sprung. When Seoul fell, there was no contingency plan to move the Marines, the 7th Division or Eighth Army eastward across South Korea to block the roads heading north. Perhaps because the American brass considered Inchon such a gamble, nobody planned in advance for stringing the net.

Now, decisions were being made on the fly about the political ramifications of pursuing the North Koreans across the 38th parallel. Flush with victory, Gen. Bradley in Washington had the final word on Inchon.

"In hindsight, the JCS seemed like a bunch of Nervous Nellies to have doubted," he said.

4

Across the 38th Parallel

At the end of September of 1950, the United Nations had largely accomplished what it set out to do: "To repel armed invasion and restore peace and stability in the area." With the exception of some mop-up work, the invading North Koreans had been expelled by the sword. But nobody was of a mind to let the North Koreans withdraw behind their borders when unequivocal victory seemed at hand. The wording of the U.N. resolution was vague enough to allow U.N. forces to carry the fight across the 38th parallel to make sure the North Koreans wouldn't launch another invasion. So the mission of the U.S.-led international force was redefined.

Above: The hunt for snipers goes on as Marine Pfcs. Ralph Clifford of Pittsburgh, Pennsylvania, and Dominic Bulgarella of Grand Rapids, Michigan, ferret out North Korean stragglers amid the ruins. October 1950.

There were basically three options: re-establish the South Korean border at the 38th parallel and go home; allow the South Koreans to carry the fight north so they wouldn't be threatened by aggression again; or continue an all-out drive that essentially would conquer North Korea and remove the scar of partition by unifying the peninsula under one flag. A policy evolved—and continued to evolve—of driving north instead of settling for the status quo. The North Koreans, who in the words of President Harry Truman were guilty of a "bandit incursion," had committed murderous crimes during their invasion. But no one wanted to have the Soviet Union or Red China enter the war to help its communist neighbor. The concept of limited war had its vagaries, upon which the seeds of a tragedy were sown.

The South Koreans didn't wait for U.N. approval to cross the 38th parallel. As early as September 19, President Syngman Rhee had declared the man-made marker to be irrelevant and said: "We will not allow ourselves to stop." His ROK 3rd Division entered

Above left: A Marine fires his bazooka at close range to dig out North Korean troops from a hilltop as mopping up continues south of the 38th parallel.

Below left: Some 400 South Korean civilians are left in and around burial trenches in a prison yard by retreating North Koreans who bound them and shot them in place.

Below: The 31st Regiment of the 7th Infantry Division moves against pockets of resistance south of Seoul. October 1950.

North Korea on September 30 in a drive against limited opposition up the east coast. The ROK 6th Division pushed north of the parallel on October 6 in the central mountains, in hot pursuit of North Korean stragglers regrouping in the Iron Triangle of Chorwon, Kumwha and Pyonggang (not to be confused with the capital of Pyongyang).

A flood of congratulatory telegrams streamed into the Tokyo headquarters of Gen. Douglas MacArthur following the smashing success of Inchon and the liberation of Seoul. Among the cables was a directive from the Joint Chiefs of Staff, who on September 27 passed along a modified form of a U.S. National Security Council resolution for conducting the rest of the war. The directive that arrived at MacArthur's Dai Ichi building read: "Your military objective is the destruction of the North Korean armed forces. In attaining this objective, you are authorized to conduct military operations, including amphibious and airborne landings or ground operations north of the 38th parallel in Korea, provided that at the time of such operations there has been no entry into North Korea by major Soviet or Chinese communist forces, no announcement of intended entry, nor a threat to counter our operations militarily in North Korea. Under no circumstances, however, will your forces cross the Manchurian or U.S.S.R. borders of Korea and, as a matter of policy, no non-Korean ground forces will be used in the northeast provinces bordering the Soviet Union or in the area along the Manchurian border. Furthermore, support of your operations north or south of the 38th parallel will not include air or naval action against Manchuria or against U.S.S.R. territory."

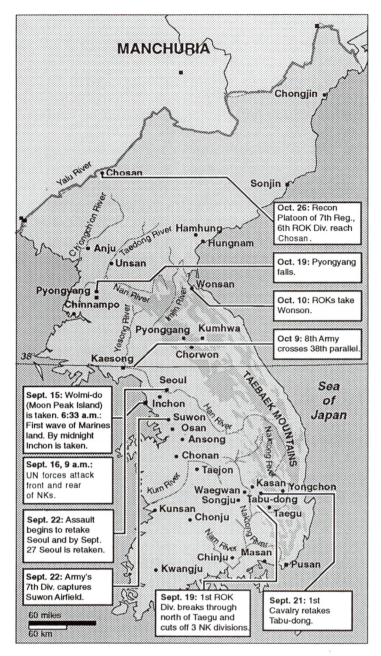

MANCHURIA

Chongjin

Yalu River — Chosan

Sonjin

Oct. 26: Recon Platoon of 7th Reg., 6th ROK Div. reach Chosan.

Chongchon River — Hamhung

Anju — Hungnam

Unsan

Oct. 19: Pyongyang falls.

Pyongyang — Nan River — Wonsan

Chinnampo

Yesong River — Kumhwa

Pyonggang

Oct. 10: ROKs take Wonson.

Oct 9: 8th Army crosses 38th parallel.

38 — Kaesong — Chorwon

Seoul

Sept. 15: Wolmi-do (Moon Peak Island) is taken. 6:33 a.m.: First wave of Marines land. By midnight Inchon is taken.

Inchon — Suwon — Han River — TAEBAEK MOUNTAINS — **Sea of Japan**

Osan

Ansong

Sept. 16, 9 a.m.: UN forces attack front and rear of NKs.

Chonan

Taejon — Naktong River

Sept. 22: Assault begins to retake Seoul and by Sept. 27 Seoul is retaken.

Kum River — Waegwan — Kasan — Yongchon — Songju — Tabu-dong — Chonju — Taegu

Sept. 22: Army's 7th Div. captures Suwon Airfield.

Kunsan

Nam River — Chinju — Masan

Kwangju — Pusan

60 miles

60 km

Sept. 19: 1st ROK Div. breaks through north of Taegu and cuts off 3 NK divisions.

Sept. 21: 1st Cavalry retakes Tabu-dong.

Inchon and U.N. Offensive

The directive contained numerous restraints and caveats, but MacArthur saw the light as green, not cautionary. Direction also came in a September 29 message from George Marshall, recently named by Truman as his new Secretary of Defense. "We want you to feel unhampered tactically and strategically to proceed north of the 38th parallel," Marshall said.

MacArthur replied to his Washington bosses that his only delay in pursuing the North Koreans was logistical. "Unless and until the enemy capitulates, I regard all of Korea open for our military operations," MacArthur said.

Later, he explained his view of the situation by saying: "My mission was to clear out all North Korea, to unify it and liberalize it." In reality, no one had

authorized him to do that. Differences had formed between the supreme commander fighting the war and the administration directing it, although the consequences wouldn't surface until later.

The United Nations, the international body that was overseeing the conflict, added to the muddle with its own vagueness. On October 7, by a vote of 45-7 with seven abstentions, the United Nations resolved that "all appropriate steps be taken to ensure conditions of stability throughout Korea." It advanced the idea of elections to unify the Korean governments, an idea that had failed before. But it did not specify what "appropriate steps" would be.

In the midst of all this, China warned the United States not to cross the 38th parallel. But the warning went unheeded, mostly due to lack of communication. The United States had backed Chiang Kai-shek's Nationalists in the Chinese civil war, and it did not recognize Mao Tse-tung's victorious communists. Therefore, it had no direct relations with China. The communist government had no seat in the United Nations, so it could not voice its intentions directly even if it wanted to. So the Chinese sent word through an intermediary, Indian Ambassador Sardar K. Pannikar. Premier Chou En-lai asked him to forward this message after the South Koreans had moved north—if the United States troops crossed the 38th parallel, China would enter the war. Truman received the message, but he dismissed it as "a bold attempt to blackmail the U.N." The United States was convinced its strategy posed no threat to the Chinese mainland; China was equally convinced the Americans were using the war in North Korea as a pretext of invasion. Its northern plains in Manchuria would be within easy reach of an army camped on the Yalu River, the waterway that separated North Korea from China. For centuries, the Chinese had regarded Korea as a buffer against invasion, and they were not about to give it up now.

Ultimately, the debate was played out on the battlefield. MacArthur broadcast two appeals for the North Koreans to surrender. An October 1 message, drafted by the State Department, received no response. His October 9 broadcast, backed up by leaflets airdropped over North Korea, included the U.N. resolution and served as a final warning to cease resistance "in whatever part of Korea situated." Kim Il Sung responded defiantly the next day, ordering his North Korean troops to fight to the end. And without any public pronouncements, Mao Tse-tung ordered Chinese "volunteers" to resist the attacks of U.S. imperialism.

For the next phase of the war, MacArthur disre-

Pfc. James Freed of Yeagertown, Pennsylvania, looks sadly at the bodies of American soldiers, shot by retreating North Koreans in Taejon's prison yard. The 24th Division discovered 30 American bodies and 1,100 civilians.

South Koreans look for slain relatives and friends among 800 massacre victims in just one of a number of mass graves in Chonju.

garded conventional wisdom and split his ground forces. The battle plan intended to squeeze North Korea in the jaws of a pincer. But Eighth Army commander Walton Walker argued strongly for a single force under his charge. He lost the argument and the two independent forces maneuvered northward.

The immediate goal was the North Korean capital of Pyongyang. The push up the western side of the peninsula was the responsibility of Eighth Army, with the 24th, 1st Cavalry and 1st ROK Divisions making a dash to Pyongyang with the British Commonwealth Brigade. Walker also controlled the ROK II Corps, situated in the middle of Korea and made up of the 6th, 7th and 8th Divisions. The eastern part of the pincer was Lt. Gen. Ned Almond's X Corps, comprised of the 1st Marine Division, the Army's 7th Division and the newly arrived 3rd Division. Mac-

Arthur's plan took into account South Korea's geography. The Taebaek Mountains form a central spine, and roads and railways ran north and south, not east and west over the mountain barrier. A proponent of amphibious war, MacArthur pulled the 1st Marines out through Inchon to sail 830 miles around Korea for an east coast landing at Wonsan. The 7th Division came south by rail to Pusan, where it also sailed to link up with the Marines. The original plan called for X Corps, under MacArthur's direct control, to slash northwest to join the Eighth Army at Pyongyang. But the plan had conceptual and practical flaws. First of all, the liberators of Seoul were removed from the battlefield when circumstances favored hot pursuit of the fleeing North Koreans. And moving troops south clogged traffic when Eighth Army needed troops and supply for a quick strike north. Second of all, the North Koreans had strewn 3,000 Russian-made mines into Wonsan harbor. By the time the Marines could land, ROK ground troops had already taken Wonsan; indeed, Bob Hope arrived ahead of the Marines. In an underground hangar jammed with 3,000 troops, Hope gave a USO show the day before the leathernecks hit an uncontested beach.

On the battlefield, the U.S. Eighth Army crossed the 38th parallel in full force on October 9. Opposition was strong for a week. But after a series of hard fights, the 1st Cavalry Division encircled Kumchon and broke through a thin defensive line north of Kaesong. After that, coordinated North Korean resistance virtually ceased. Only isolated action by individual units opposed U.N. forces.

Seemingly on the brink of victory, Truman summoned MacArthur for a meeting on October 15. The President had never met his Far East military leader before they shook hands on the tarmac at a Wake Island airfield in the Pacific. "I thought that he ought to know his commander-in-chief, and that I ought to know the senior field commander in the Far East," Truman said. They talked alone for an hour in a Quonset hut on the edge of the airstrip, then held a formal meeting inside an airport office. At the Wake Island conference, Truman took off his coat and MacArthur brought out a new briar pipe.

"Do you mind if I smoke, Mr. President?" the general asked. "No. I suppose I've had more smoke blown in my face than any other man alive," Truman answered.

The entire conference lasted 96 minutes. It closed with Truman giving MacArthur his fifth Distinguished Service Medal.

"Formal resistance will end through North and South Korea by Thanksgiving," MacArthur told the

One North Korean tank attacked by 5th Air Force planes ends up in a ditch and when a second comes to its aid the American planes returned for a double kill.

President. When Truman asked about the chances of Chinese or Soviet intervention, MacArthur replied: "Very little. Had they interfered in the first or second month, it would have been decisive. We are no longer fearful of their intervention. We no longer stand hat in hand....Now that we have bases for our air force in Korea, if the Chinese tried to get down to Pyongyang, there would be the greatest slaughter." MacArthur then declined an invitation to go to lunch, pointing out that he had to get back to Tokyo to run his war.

Truman issued a statement that reflected the upbeat mood. "I've never had a more satisfactory conference since I've been President," Truman said. "There is complete unity in the aims and conduct of our foreign policy." In reality, however, Truman and his field commander differed on the conduct of the war. For now, the euphoria in the air masked any problems.

Battlefield successes heightened the perception that the war was just about over. With U.N. forces

Right: 7th Division infantry search through burning brush for North Koreans, thousands of whom are already prisoners.

Below: ROK troops burn communist signs and propaganda posters pulled off buildings in Yangyank, seven miles north of the 38th parallel, captured with virtually no opposition.

attacking on three corridors, Pyongyang fell on October 19. It was the only communist capital ever to be liberated by the West. Gen. Paik Sun Yup's 1st ROK Division won a close race with the U.S. 1st Cavalry Division to get to the city first. For the first time ever, the ROKs were assigned some American tanks for their assault to the north. The South Koreans learned quickly about George Patton's strategy of armored assaults, coordinating attacks using tanks and infantry. With his foot soldiers riding the hulls of tanks, Paik had special reason to celebrate. Pyongyang was his hometown, but for his entire life it had been controlled by either the Japanese or the communists.

"I had left five years earlier as a refugee. Now I was back with 10,000 men, 100 guns and a battalion of M-46 tanks," Paik said. "We thought the war was over. The North Koreans were completely wiped out, throwing away their weapons as we met them." Calling Pyongyang's liberation "the greatest day of my life," Paik showed the American tanks where to ford the Taedong River because he had swum in it as a child.

Unlike Seoul, the capital was spared destruction. Kim Il Sung and his government had already fled for Sinuiju at the mouth of the Yalu, then on to Kanggye, a sanctuary in the north central mountains that was a guerrilla stronghold during Japanese rule. On Sunday, October 20, the first church bells pealed in Pyongyang since the communists took over. But once again, atrocities were uncovered. At a Pyongyang prison, soldiers found hundreds of bodies of murdered political prisoners stuffed inside wells.

MacArthur flew in for a brief ceremony. At the airport on October 21, he inspected Company F of the

Right: ROK troops, 7 miles north of the 38th parallel border with North Korea, continue to pursue their enemies.

A patrol of the 2nd Battalion, 8th Cavalry Regiment, deploys in the hills over the 38th parallel.

A land mine explodes on the outskirts of Pyongyang and temporarily halts an advancing American column.

5th Cavalry Regiment, the first Americans to enter the capital. MacArthur asked those who had landed 96 days earlier in Pusan to take one step forward for special recognition. In a telling sign of how bloody the fighting had been, only five men took the step,

and three of them had been wounded. "The war will soon be over," MacArthur told his troops.

U.N. forces were now 100 miles from the North Korean border, and the cry went up: "On to the Yalu!" The last major terrain feature before the final lunge

Crouching in Indian file, soldiers of the 8th Regiment plant their guidon within sight of enemy forces north of the 38th parallel. The road in the background leads straight to the North Korean capital of Pyongyang.

to the Yalu was the Chongchon River, about 45 miles north of Pyongyang. Eighth Army began its push on October 20, leaving the 1st Cavalry in the capital in reserve. To cut off the fleeing North Koreans, the 4,000-man 187th Airborne Regimental Combat Team parachuted down on two main leads at Sukchon and Sunchon, 26 miles north of Pyongyang. It was the largest airborne operation of the war, and the first time paratroopers were able to drop such heavy cargo as 105-millimeter howitzers.

Max Desfor, an Associated Press photographer who won the Pulitzer Prize for his work in Korea, jumped with the paratroopers and filed this report via courier:

SUKCHON, OCT. 20 (AP) — Thousands of vari-colored parachutes polka-dotted the clear sky this afternoon, quickly dropping men and equipment of the U.S. 187th Airborne Regiment.

It was perfect jump weather—clear, no wind and not too cold. Fighter planes kept a constant cover during the operation and kept firing at targets in the surrounding area.

I stepped out of the plane and a second later I felt a tug and a snap. Another second and I felt as if I were just standing still, suspended in air.

There was very little jar as I hit the springy, paddy ground. About 20 feet away, a paratrooper was trying to undo his gear but was interrupted by a local resident, who embraced him and hugged him.

The soldier untangled himself and quickly took off to join the rest of his unit moving to the assembly area. As the men started off across the rice paddies and cornfields, mortars started firing into the hills against Red positions.

There was extremely light resistance as the paratroopers moved forward to their objectives. Some prisoners were taken and placed under guard.

Only 45 minutes from the time the men spilled out of the planes, their objectives were secured. A patrol moving along a road toward a village was met by a

Left: Maj. Gen. Hobart R. Gay, commanding general of the 1st Cavalry Division, shows a newly knocked out enemy tank to Lt. Gen. Yaegili of the Turkish General Staff, whose troops will join U.N. forces. October 1950.

Above: American paratroopers by the hundreds fill the skies north of fallen Pyongyang and land in a rice paddy to cut off retreating North Koreans. October 1950.

American paratroopers jump behind enemy lines to cut off retreating Reds and then mop up near Sunchon in the drive into North Korea.

British and Australian troops mop up in Hwangju in the drive into North Korea.

cheering group of inhabitants. The group consisted mostly of women and children. They shouted "Manzai"—the Korean equivalent of "ten thousand years life"—as they waved the flag of the Republic of South Korea.

As soon as the hills were secured, the United States' and United Nations' flags were raised on a knoll overlooking the area. Maj. Thomas P. Mulvey of Wenonah, N.J., and Master Sgt. Russell Brahmi of Detroit, Mich., put the flag on a slender pole. There were comparatively few jump injuries. Among those injured was Capt. John Coulter of Washington, Iowa, commanding officer who led my planeload of men in the jump. Two of the eight correspondents who made the jump also suffered leg injuries. By 5:30 p.m., all was quiet in the entire area except for the clanging of shovels and the men dug in for the night.

The airdrop was too late to trap large numbers of communist troops or their leaders. But at Sukchon, the paratroopers routed a 2,500-man North Korean regiment that was the last force to exit Pyongyang. Also, the newly arrived 3rd Battalion of the Royal Australian Regiment confronted some North Koreans scattered in an apple orchard. Because paratrooper positions were so close, no tanks could be used. So the Australians fixed bayonets and charged. In the hand-to-hand infantry fight, 270 North Koreans were killed and 200 were captured; 7 Australians were wounded.

Commanders had hoped that the airborne deploy-

ment would also head off two northbound trains reportedly crammed with American POWs. The venture produced one of the most galling moments of the war. On October 22, just past a railroad tunnel, U.S. troops discovered a mass grave of massacred prisoners. These soldiers had been herded into three groups under the guise of receiving their evening meal when North Koreans murdered them where they sat. In all, 73 Americans were slaughtered. Survivors who crawled to safety in the brush provided details. Two days later, South Koreans found 23 more murdered Americans.

Associated Press writer Tom Lambert spoke to one of the survivors who had been removed to the safety of a hospital cot. Lambert filed this dispatch:

PYONGYANG, Oct. 23 (AP) — A gaunt and weak young American told today of surviving three death marches totaling more than 400 miles. He lived through two Red shootings — including the machine-gun massacre near Sunchon.

The youth was Pfc. Raymond Rindels, who turned 20 last Sept. 28 while still a prisoner of the communists.

The 6-foot-3 former military policeman, a resident of Shell Rock, Iowa, served with the 19th Infantry Regiment of the U.S. 24th Division.

Rindels weighed 235 pounds when he was captured by the North Koreans on July 29, near Chinju in extreme South Korea. Today he weighs about 150 pounds, partly because his captors ruined his false teeth and he was unable to chew the hard crackers he was given.

Rindels was marched from Chinju to Taejon, a walk with death of about 150 miles. There followed a 90-mile forced march to Seoul and a 160-mile march north to Pyongyang. He left this former Red capital about Oct. 14 with a group of other American war prisoners headed north by rail toward the Manchurian border.

About Oct. 18, the Americans were divided into groups of 30 or 40 under the pretext they were going to be fed.

The prisoners were herded into the embankments and told to sit down. As soon as they were seated, the North Korean guards standing on the embankment sprayed them with Russian-type submachine guns. Other Reds walked among the dead and dying, sending final shots into the heads of some.

Rindels was hit in the right shoulder and left elbow by Red machinegunners. As he slumped to the ground, Americans on either side of him fell on top of him.

Korean guards shot the prisoners on top of him in the head, but he was protected by their bodies. Five other Americans in Rindels' group also lived through the Red murder-fire. Two of the survivors were either not hurt or refused to acknowledge their wounds.

"They really saved our lives," Rindels said. They

were Pvt. William Henninger of St. Paul, Minn., and Pvt. James Yeager of Grand Junction, Colo. Henninger and Yeager dragged Rindels and three other wounded Americans from the pile of dead, helped them across the fields and into the hills.

They obtained cooked rice and water for the wounded men and cared for them until Brig. Gen. Frank A. Allen Jr., deputy commander of the 1st Cavalry Division, found them near Sunchon tunnel.

"Take it easy, boys. The war is over for you now," the general told them. Rindels gulped and spoke with great difficulty from his cot in an Army hospital.

When first taken near Chinju, he had tried to escape and was hit twice in the left arm. The Korean Reds tried under the threat of a gun to obtain military information from him, but Rindels didn't talk. His arms were bound to his sides after that. His captors took his New Testament and "tore it up leaf by leaf" in an effort to make him talk.

Rindels said the North Koreans murdered in cold blood the American prisoners who were unable to march north toward Seoul. Civilians, however, gave them candy and biscuits "and were very good to us."

MacArthur, meanwhile, had unleashed his army.

Just a week after he said only ROK forces should operate within 30 to 40 miles of China, MacArthur on October 24 lifted the order and urged an all-out pursuit to the Yalu River. In what MacArthur said was a military necessity, all commanders were "authorized to use any and all ground forces as necessary, to secure all of North Korea." By doing so, he unilaterally changed U.S. policy and ignored the orders he received in late September from the Joint Chiefs of Staff. The JCS said MacArthur's decision "was a matter of concern," but it did not reverse him. "It was really too late for the JCS to do anything about the matter," said Gen. Omar Bradley, chairman of the Joint Chiefs. But the Chinese took notice.

Korea is only 120 miles wide between Pyongyang and Wonsan, but the northern country expands out to 400 miles. So as United Nations troops pushed north, gaps appeared between their own formations. The 1st Cavalry and 24th Divisions with the British 27th Brigade crossed the Chongchon River on October 25 and fanned out north and west. The 1st ROK Di-

Pfcs. Charles Jarvis (center) of Minnora, West Virginia, and Theodore Stamper of Portsmouth, Ohio, rescued from the massacre site at Sunchon, are nursed back to health by Chief Army Nurse Maj. Eileen K. Murphy of Springfield, Massachusetts. The recuperation is at Tokyo's Itazuke Hospital.

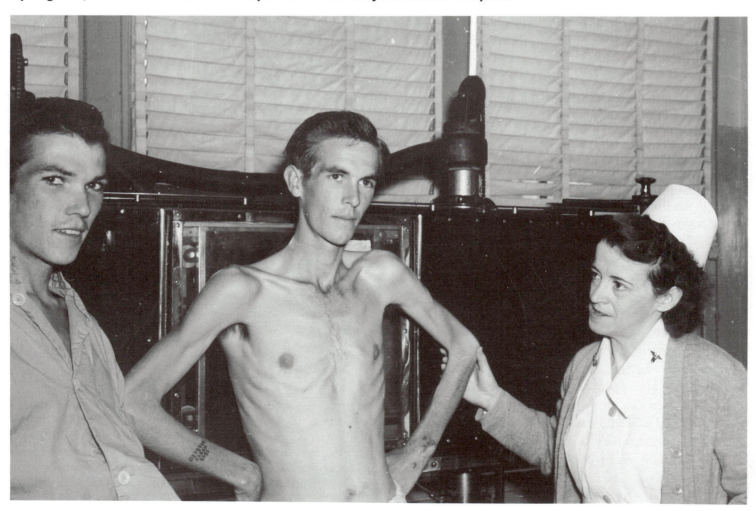

Shot in effigy. Pvt. William Hamilton of Sydney, Australia, gets a little Sten gun practice on portraits of Stalin and North Korean leader Kim Il Sung.

vision, which had captured a bridge at Anju to allow U.S. tanks to ford the Chongchon, attacked northeast toward Unsan. The Yalu was only 55 miles away, a drive of several hours at most. In the peninsula's center, ROK II Corps also advanced. The Reconnaissance Platoon of 7th Regiment, 6th ROK Division, was 30 miles ahead of everyone else. The platoon actually reached Chosan on the Yalu on October 26. The first U.N. forces to reach the border, ROK soldiers ceremoniously filled a bottle with Yalu water for Syngman Rhee, and some urinated into the waterway. Attached to the platoon was Maj. Harry Fleming of the Korean Military Advisory Group; he was the only American in Eighth Army to reach the Yalu. In the northwest, after the British Commonwealth Brigade fought a series of hard battles, the 21st Regiment of the 24th Division passed through into the lead and was 18

miles from the Yalu by the end of the month. It was the farthest penetration of an Eighth Army unit. Ironically, this was the same regiment that was the first to arrive in Korea and contributed to Task Force Smith at the beginning of the war. No one had a clue the advance had reached its high water mark.

On the eastern side of Korea, the mission of X Corps quickly became dated. Because of Russian mines blocking Wonsan harbor, the 1st Marine Division's landing was delayed. The minesweepers USS *Pirate* and *Pledge* were sunk October 12, and it took two weeks—and the loss of two more minesweepers—to clear the way. At sea, a severe outbreak of dysentery afflicted the Marines in their foul-smelling ships. Their convoy sailed up and down the coast so many times the deployment became known as Operation Yo-Yo. Their landing was unopposed because the

Bayonets fixed, British troops keep up the hot pursuit of the enemy north of Sariwon.

South Koreans took Wonsan on October 10 before the Marines had loaded onto their ships. In fact, the ROK Capital Division was 50 miles north when the Marines waded ashore October 25. The Marines' advance party was entertained by Bob Hope's USO troupe the night before the main body disembarked. What's more, Pyongyang had fallen six days earlier, negating the need for the Marines to slash westward or attempt to cut off North Korean troops. Instead, they were

ordered to advance inland up a forbidding plateau to seize four hydroelectric plants along the Chosin Reservoir. From there, they could complete their journey to the Yalu River.

A new role also was given the U.S. 7th Division. Some elements were diverted 150 miles north of Wonsan to Iwon, a port that had been seized by ROK troops. The 17th Regiment, under the command of Col. Herbert B. Powell, moved on a northwest angle

Orphaned by war, two Korean children huddle by the body of their dead mother in a roadside ditch. British and Australian troops took them to safety.

More than 60 South Koreans are found bludgeoned to death in a mine shaft at Kum Bong San near Tubo-ni. They had been held by North Koreans at a prison in Chinnampo.

to the burned-out village of Hysesanjin. At last, a U.S. unit stood on the banks of the Yalu River, where the bleak hills of Manchuria rose on the far bank. Like the ROK units in the west, Powell relieved himself in the Yalu. X Corps commander Ned Almond flew in with Maj. Gen. David G. Barr, commander of the 7th Division, for a picture-taking session. Barr was former chief of the American Military Mission to China. As such, he had witnessed the defeat of the Chinese Nationalists two years before. Now in mid-November, he had provided MacArthur with sweet news. The supreme commander messaged his Army commanders: "Heartiest congratulations, Ned, and tell Dave Barr that the 7th Division hit the jackpot." About 20 miles to the west, a small task force of the 7th

Division's 32nd Regiment under the command of 2nd Lt. Robert Kingston also reached the Yalu's banks. And on the east coast, under cover of U.S. air and naval power, ROK troops approached Chongjin, the last major North Korean city before the Siberian border. Celebrations were premature, however. Dramatically and without warning, the war had already taken an ominous turn.

While the United Nations army was moving north with much fanfare, China secretly shifted a 150,000-man force into North Korea without so much as a ripple. It ranks as one of history's stealthiest troop movements. Although Prime Minister Chou En-lai had warned the Americans not to cross the 38th parallel and the activity of Chinese troop trains had in-

Americans guard salvaged furnishings from burning Kim Il Sung University, named after the North Korean premier. The fire of mysterious origin swept the building, one of North Korea's finest.

creased, the new Central Intelligence Agency failed to perceive a threat. As late as October 12, the CIA said that "despite statements by Chou En-lai, troop movements to Manchuria, and propaganda charges of atrocities and border violations, there are no convincing indications of an actual Chinese communist intention to resort to full-scale intervention in Korea." But, at the time MacArthur was assuring Truman on Wake Island that China would not commit itself, the first trickle of Chinese "volunteers" crossed the Yalu River bridges into North Korea. They marched under cover of darkness without any of the encumbrances of a modern army—no artillery and very few trucks, which made them difficult to detect from the air. These foot soldiers moved by mountain trails, not roads, and without radio chatter. Their march discipline was deadly strict—any soldier moving in daylight could and would be shot by officers. To prevent giving away positions, they hid out under camouflage in the craggy nooks of North Korea. Wearing quilted cotton uniforms and canvas sneakers, these battle-hardened veterans of China's civil war carried everything they needed on their backs—rifle, grenade, 80 rounds of ammunition, foot rags, sewing kit and a week's ration of rice, fish and tea.

Warnings were still unheeded in Washington. Gen. Nieh Yen-jung, China's acting chief of staff, had told India's Ambassador Sardar K. Pannikar that his country did not intend "to sit back with folded hands and let the Americans come to their border. We know what we are in for, but at all costs American aggression has got to be stopped. The Americans can bomb us, they can destroy our industries, but they cannot defeat us on land....They may even drop atom bombs on us. What then? They may kill a few million people. Without sacrifice, a nation's independence cannot be upheld."

Because South Korean troops led the U.N. offen-

Left: A knocked out T-34 tank is a vantage point for American Marines watching artillery bursts march up an enemy-held hill. The tank had been dug in to stop the Marine advance toward Chosin Reservoir. November 1950.

sive, the first Chinese blows landed against the ROKs—and their entry came right after MacArthur lifted all restrictions about going to the Yalu. When the main U.N. assault was roughly 40 miles south of the Yalu, the 1st ROK Division was hit by an unknown force on October 25. Mortar fire by about 300 Chinese stopped the ROKs about a mile-and-a-half north of Unsan. The first Chinese prisoner of the war told a fantastic story of 10,000 Chinese Peoples' Volunteers in the nearby hills, with another 10,000 laying in wait for the three divisions of the ROK II Corps. "Many, many Chinese are coming," Gen. Paik told his corps commander. But the prisoner's story was dismissed as incredible, even though the advance came to an abrupt halt.

Later that same day, the trap was sprung on the ROK 6th Division. Infantrymen in thick, padded uniforms wearing a red star on their caps surrounded two regiments of the 6th Division. After the Chinese attack, not a single company remained intact. South Koreans abandoned their weapons and vehicles, taking backward steps for the first time since Inchon. In the first days of the war, the ROKs fled at the clattering of T-34 tanks. Now they ran at the frightful cacophony of Chinese bugles, whistles, gongs and jabbers. Some felt the noise was raised to scare the wits out of U.N. forces, which it did. But it was also the way Chinese commanders and units communicated orders because the army lacked radios. The ROK 7th Regiment, which had reached the Yalu, was cut off and chewed up. Only 875 men escaped; 2,700 were killed or captured. The American liaison officer who reached the border, Maj. Fleming, was wounded in 15 places and taken prisoner. In a matter of three days, the ROK 6th Division was erased as a combat unit, and the entire ROK II Corps collapsed, exposing the entire right flank of the U.S. Eighth Army.

The Americans figured this was a last-gasp defense by North Korea. Eighth Army commander Walton Walker wrongly thought the Chinese POWs being brought to his headquarters actually lived in Korea. "After all, a lot of Mexicans live in Texas," Walker reasoned.

MacArthur's headquarters was even less concerned, partly because of the very human tendency to see what one wants to see. The top brass looked at the Yalu and the end of the war; it never noticed the Chinese. MacArthur's chief of intelligence, Maj. Gen. Charles Willoughby, told Washington on October 28 that the Chinese had missed their chance. "From a tactical standpoint, with victorious United States divisions in full deployment, it would appear that the auspicious time for intervention has long since passed; it is difficult to believe that such a move, if planned, would have been postponed to a time when remnant North Korean forces have been reduced to a low point of effectiveness," he said.

The situation had changed as suddenly as the weather. GIs who sweated through 100-degree summer days in Korea now felt the frozen blasts of air swooping down from Siberia. Almost overnight, winter gripped northern Korea before anyone had received cold-weather parkas, gloves and boots. Standard-issue overcoats and threadbare fatigues were no match for the frigid blasts that put a heavy strain on troops and equipment. It was the beginning of the coldest Korean winter in a decade, and it took a frightful toll.

A critical situation unfolded at Unsan, an insignificant market town 45 miles south of the Yalu that now became the hinge for the Eighth Army's right flank. Supplies were air-dropped to the 1st ROK Division, which was still puzzled to find nothing but Chinese bodies in their kill zones. The ROKs tried to keep the initiative, but by October 29, the Chinese had stopped them cold. Walton Walker ordered the 1st Cavalry Division, garrisoned in reserve in Pyongyang, to shore up the crumbling front. Maj. Gen. Hobart Gay, the division commander, was George Patton's chief of staff in the U.S. armored drive across France in World War II. He was more accustomed to offense than digging in, so when his 8th Cavalry Regiment arrived on point the defensive lines were skimpy. Entrenching tools dug half-hearted foxholes along lines that were undermanned and poorly sited. Most GIs figured they would be back in Tokyo for Thanksgiving. None of the three battalions patrolled aggressively to their front; they relied on air power and artillery to work on whatever was out there. But two circumstances negated U.S. firepower: the sheer numbers of Chinese and a series of forest fires that were set to mask troop movements. One artillery observer in a spotter plane was overheard by the 1st Cavalry command post as saying: "There are two large columns of enemy infantry moving southeast over the trails. Our shells are landing right in their columns and they keep moving."

The Chinese hoped to deliver a message at Unsan. "Our task is to check the enemy here," said Maj. Gen. Wu Hsiu-chuan of the *39th Field Army*, the most ex-

The weather does more to slow the advance on Chosin Reservoir. Huddled in winter parkas and carrying shovels to free vehicles from the icy mud, Marines cope with sub-freezing temperatures.

M*A*S*H

As a popular movie in 1970 and for 11 years one of television's most-watched series (with its theme song, "Suicide Is Painless"), *M*A*S*H* probably provided American civilians with their strongest image of the Korean War.

The popular entertainment that depicted the antics Hawkeye Pierce, Radar O'Reilly and Hot Lips Houlihan was first a book, written by a real-life MASH surgeon under the pseudonym of Richard Hooker. Dr. H. Richard Hornberger, a New Jersey native who practiced as a chest surgeon in Maine, interrupted his medical internship to serve for a year-and-a-half with the 8055th MASH unit (the fictional 4077th) in Korea. Hornberger wrote his book 12 years after the war, basing it on his own medical-military experiences. By the time it was published, however, after numerous rejections by publishers, it had taken on the anti-Vietnam sentiments of the time and was described as "a displaced substitute for Vietnam," although set in Korea.

Hornberger's unit 8055th, commanded by Dr. Henry Holleman, had 16 surgeons, divided into two crews which worked 12 hours a day or more. When casualties were heavy, the operating room often ran full blast 24 hours a day. One of the 8055th surgeons, Dr. James Secrest, once said, "We recognized the show as a farce. It didn't depict what really went on." But Holleman has said, "In some respects it compares very favorably" with what really happened. "This is especially true in patient care and dedication of the guys when it comes down to treating casualties."

The TV show also accurately depicted the differences in military medicine between World War II and the Korean War. Holleman was a veteran of both wars, having joined the Mississippi National Guard after coming home from World War II and returning to private practice. The Guard unit was activated when the Korean conflict began. Holleman said that in World War II an arterial wound almost certainly meant the loss of a limb for the injured soldier. But in Korea, medical training in vascular surgery helped many to keep their limbs.

Speed played an important part. Those who were wounded in the daytime had a very good chance, as medics lit purple smoke flares to guide the helicopters to the scene. Many of the dead were those who were injured during the night and were hard to find by the air crews.

Mobile Army Surgical Hospital units in Korea provided timely medical care that saved numerous lives, as their mobility made it possible to keep up with combat operations. Located near front-line infantry medical clearing stations, they treated the wounded who needed immediate care and then evacuated them to hospitals in the rear, usually by helicopter. Often, the evacuation began by hand-carrying litters from inaccessible mountain positions and then by truck to the MASH units. The Air Force 801st Medical Air Evacuation Squadron and its successor 6481st Medical Air Evacuation Group provided evacuation for nearly 312,000 sick and wounded between Korea and Japan. Helicopters—the light H-5 and the medium H-19 and H-21 especially—were used extensively for the first time in Korea.

MASH units were instrumental in bringing down the percentage of wounded who died (22 percent in Korea compared to 28 percent in World War II). It was also in MASH units that peripheral vascular surgery was performed during the war for the first time; there were other medical innovations, necessity apparently still mothering invention.

perienced Chinese formation in the field. "As a warning to the imperialists we shall destroy the most vulnerable American advance unit."

By nightfall on November 1, the Americans were surrounded on three sides by Chinese. In their shallow foxholes, soldiers in summer uniforms were more concerned with fighting the cold with sleeping bags and blankets. Unwisely, some had even built camp fires. When the 1st Battalion was attacked and overrun at 7:30 p.m., some GIs were bayonetted in their sleep. The ferocity of the attack shook the lines. A foe moving with catlike quickness under a bright moon was able to probe weaknesses and exploit them. The haunting sound of bugles and gongs was mixed with explosions of grenades and satchel charges. The cry

of every man for himself went up. "We just ran and ran until the bugles grew fainter," said Pvt. Carl Simon. The 2nd Battalion buckled next. The Chinese seemed to be everywhere at once; there were 20,000 of them attacking from the north, northwest and west. Infiltrators had picked up helmets, parkas and fatigues discarded by the fleeing ROKs to march into the middle of American positions. An exhausted cascade of U.S. soldiers lost all sense of organization and retreated pell-mell in the dark. Their escape route was a raised road leading through a checkerboard of frozen rice paddies with hills on each side. A vehicle towing a howitzer was blown up, blocking the road so no more artillery or trucks could get out. Chinese mortars did lethal work on convoys trapped behind the wreckage.

By 3 a.m. on November 2, the Chinese had surrounded the 8th Regiment's 3rd Battalion, under the command of Maj. Robert Ormond and poorly deployed on low ground along the Nammyon River. In something reminiscent of Custer's Last Stand, the battalion was attacked from all sides of a pocket along the Nammyon River. After a melee in which Ormond was mortally wounded, the unit was cut off and at the mercy of the Chinese. When daylight came, the Air Force dropped morphine and bandages but could not chase away the Chinese. The 5th Cavalry Regiment rushed in a relief column of two battalions in an attempt to free the trapped men, but it was stopped at Bugle Hill. More attempts to reach the marooned men failed. And by 3 p.m., with the entire front collapsing, the 1st Cavalry Division was ordered to withdraw and rescue efforts were abandoned. Gen. Gay had to leave his embattled 3rd Battalion to its fate. "A soldier accumulates many sad memories over his lifetime. But I have never before or since made a decision that was more sad or more lonely," Gay said later. A plane dropped a note to the cut-off battalion, giving survivors the bleak order to withdraw as best they could. By dusk, when weakening daylight hampered U.S. air strikes, the Chinese rained mortars on 3rd Battalion. Six times through the night, waves of infantry hit the American lines. The battalion hung on through the night, the next day and the next night, stripping ammunition from dead Chinese as their own supplies ran out. Out of a starting force of 800, less than 200 able-bodied men survived by daylight of November 4. That day, those who could walk moved out in small groups as best they could, moving first to the north and west before cutting south to friendly lines. Prisoners were startled to discover their attackers were Chinese.

"For God's sake! This isn't your war," one POW said.

"It is now," said Capt. Lao Chongkeng, leader of a Chinese assault force.

The thunderous strike inflicted heavy losses. The Chinese pressed the initiative for 10 days, when their supplies began to run low. The Eighth Army, no longer on the offensive, withdrew to the southern banks of the Chongchon River to regroup. But while U.N. units were rebuilt and re-equipped, the Chinese withdrew from the battlefield as efficiently as they appeared. Their columns were seen marching north as strategists pondered the next step.

On the eastern side of the peninsula, the 1st Marine Division never bought the talk that the war was all but won. The leathernecks advanced in battle posture,

and Col. Homer Litzenberg of the 7th Marines told his regiment: "If there is anyone here who expects an easy walk to the Yalu, erase it from your mind now. We're going to have to fight." North of Hungnam, the Chinese stuck to their strategy of attacking South Korean units first, this time stopping the ROK 3rd Division. Liztenberg's 7th Marines passed through the ROKs and killed 700 Chinese in front of them. But as they had on the western side, the Chinese withdrew and moved north again by the end of the first week of November.

MacArthur, who had insisted the Chinese would not intervene, was outraged. He accused China of having "committed one of the most offensive acts of international lawlessness of historic record by moving without any notice of belligerency elements of alien communist forces across the Yalu River into North Korea." And on November 5, the supreme commander ordered the Air Force to bomb the Korean ends of the Yalu bridges. Abruptly, the Joint Chiefs of Staff canceled the operation just hours before it was to start; the generals in Washington wanted a better handle on the situation and feared air strikes would escalate the war. MacArthur agreed grudgingly, but he went over the heads of the JCS and demanded that Truman be consulted on these limits. He messaged the JCS:

Men and materiel in large force are pouring across all bridges over the Yalu from Manchuria. This movement not only jeopardizes but threatens the ultimate destruction of the forces under my command. The actual movement across the river can be accomplished under cover of darkness and the distance between the river and our lines is so short that the forces can be deployed against our troops without being seriously subjected to air interdiction. The only way to stop this reinforcement of the enemy is the destruction of these bridges and the subjection of all installations in the north area supporting the enemy advance to the maximum of our air destruction. Every hour that this is postponed will be paid for dearly in American and other United Nations blood. The main crossing at Sinuiju was to be hit within the next few hours and the mission is actually already being mounted. Under the gravest protest that I can make, I am suspending this strike and carrying out your instructions.

What I have ordered is entirely within the scope of the rules of war and the resolutions and directions which I have received from the United Nations and constitutes no slightest act of belligerency against Chinese territory, in spite of the outrageous international lawlessness emanating therefrom. I cannot overemphasize the disastrous effect, both physical and psychological, that will result from the restrictions which you are imposing.

Marines of the 7th Regiment approach the southern tip of the Chosin Reservoir in freezing weather with no opposition. But a major Red force lurks in the distance.

I trust that the matter be immediately brought to the attention of the President as I believe your instructions may well result in a calamity of major proportion for which I cannot accept the responsibility without his personal and direct understanding of the situation. Time is so essential that I request immediate reconsideration of your decision pending which complete compliance will of course be given your order.

Caught in a dispute between his Joint Chiefs and his field commander, Truman sided with MacArthur and lifted the restrictions. Bombings began November 8, the date of the first all-jet air battle in history. Lt. Russell Brown in a U.S. F-80 shot down a MiG-15, probably piloted by a Chinese. The bombings, however, had moderate success. Pilots were barred from coming in from the Manchurian side, so their approaches were limited. After a month of bombing, only four of the 12 highway and railway bridges linking Korea and China had been broken. By this time, the Yalu had frozen and the Chinese crossed at any number of places.

When he was ordered not to bomb the Yalu bridges, MacArthur threatened to resign. He told his chief of staff, Doyle Hickey: "For the first time in military history, a commander has been denied the use of his military power to safeguard the lives of his soldiers and safety of his army. To me it clearly foreshadows a future tragic situation in the Far East and leaves me with a sense of inexpressible shock." He called the order "the most indefensible and ill-conceived notion ever forced on a field commander in our nation's history."

There was some debate about what to do next. The British favored stopping at the narrow part of Korea, which would have given the Chinese a buffer zone. But MacArthur was adamant about achieving total victory, and his view obscured anything Washington was thinking. "To give up any portion of North Korea to the aggression of the Chinese Communists would be the greatest defeat of the free world in recent times. Indeed, to yield to so immoral a proposition would bankrupt our leadership and influence in Asia and render untenable our position both politically and militarily," MacArthur said on November 9.

His reaction was to keep attacking.

5

An Entirely New War

Having stumbled once into an ambush, Douglas MacArthur did it again. The Chinese presence in Korea was undeniable, but MacArthur believed—wrongly—the Chinese had been beaten because they were withdrawing. From his war room in Tokyo, MacArthur saw only a 60-mile distance between his front lines and the Yalu River. Now he ordered a final offensive to end the Korean War. He wanted the attack to begin November 15, but Eighth Army commander Walton Walker begged for some time to refortify his troops. Such an offensive required 4,000 tons a day of supplies, and Walker was only getting half that over his strained logistics lines. The attack was delayed until November 25, the day after Thanksgiving. Even then, Walker's army was short on ammunition, winter clothes and rations.

Above: U.S. tanks head south in retreat and ROK troops head north to try to stem the Red tide.

OFF LIMITS
CG TEMPEST
出入嚴禁

Left: Gen. MacArthur inspects the advance at the 9th Corps headquarters and personally supervises a new all-out offensive.

An uneasy feeling surfaced among combat troops and political leaders in Washington about the Chinese intervention. Still, no one came forward to confront MacArthur. In retrospect, it was a terrible miscalculation. "This government missed its last chance to halt the march to disaster in Korea. All the President's advisors in this matter, civilian and military, knew that something was badly wrong, though what it was, how to find out, and what to do about it they muffed," Secretary of State Dean Acheson wrote later.

No one on the Joint Chiefs of Staff had the stomach to tell the supreme commander to stop short of the Yalu. "It would have meant a fight with MacArthur, charges by him that they had denied his victory....So they hesitated, wavered, and the chance was lost. While everyone acted correctly, no one, I suspect, was ever quite satisfied with himself afterward," Acheson said.

There was plenty of blame in Washington to go around. "What we should have done is stop at the neck of Korea....But (MacArthur) was commander in the field. You pick your man, you've got to back him up. That's the only way a military organization can work. I got the best advice I could and the man on the spot said this was the thing to do....So I agreed. That was my decision—no matter what hindsight shows," Truman said.

The Chinese, meanwhile, used the delay to restock

Left to right, HM/1 C. J. Sellers of Chesterfield, South Carolina, HN E.L. Frederickson of Omaha, Nebraska, and Pfc H.B. Doane of Grand Rapids, Michigan, get a chuckle from a communist poster near the Chosin Reservoir in North Korea.

A U.S. 7th Division convoy struggles to cross an icy stream near Kapsan on its way to the Manchurian border at Hyesanjin, November 1950.

vital supplies. Supply trains of Mongolian ponies and coolies hauling A-frame packs walked into Korea from Manchuria, again largely undetected by U.N. intelligence. President Truman went to the United Nations to assure the Chinese that the international force had no intention of violating Chinese territory. But the Chinese remained unconvinced because of the troops massing in front of them. Gen. Peng Teh-huai, commander of the *Chinese Peoples' Volunteers*, prepared a counterattack with all available force. "The enemy has learned nothing over the past few weeks. They continue to advance recklessly. China has no alternative but to teach the imperialists a lesson," Peng said.

Eighth Army had 118,000 men in eight divisions and two brigades. They were arrayed from west to east as follows: the U.S. 24th Division and 1st ROK Division with the British Commonwealth Brigade un-

der I Corps; the U.S. 25th and 2nd Divisions with the newly arrived 5,200-man Turkish Brigade under IX Corps; and the ROK 7th and 8th Divisions with the battered 6,000-man 6th Division comprising the ROK II Corps. The U.S. 1st Cavalry, battered at Unsan, was held in general reserve.

In the east, X Corps had the 1st Marine Division and the Army's 7th Division, with the understrength U.S. 3rd Division in reserve at Wonsan. The ROK I Corps, consisting of the 3rd Division and the Capital Division, operated along the east coast. The total U.N. strength was about 270,000 men plus a huge advantage in tanks, artillery, planes and ships.

By this time, the Chinese had moved 300,000 men into Korea—180,000 arrayed against the Eighth Army and 120,000 in the rugged hills who were given the task of annihilating the Marines. The North Koreans mustered about 100,000 men by mid-November.

Korea was introduced to the American feast of Thanksgiving the day before the offensive kicked off. In a miracle of U.S. logistics, troops were treated to roast tom turkey, gravy, cranberry sauce, candied sweet potatoes, buttered corn, fresh bread, pumpkin pie, candy, nuts, oranges and apples. Allies who had never heard of Thanksgiving marveled at the resources of a country that could ship such a feast with all the trimmings halfway around the world. The Siberian-like weather chilled the holiday spirit—it was so cold that hot turkey turned into something like a popsicle by the time it passed from serving tray to a GI's mouth.

MacArthur, as was his custom, visited his corps commanders the following morning to kick off what he believed would be the last maneuver of the war. By doing so, he also tipped off the Chinese that the attack was coming. In a meeting with IX Corps commander, Maj. Gen. John Coulter, MacArthur in his fur-lined cap and winter gear said: "If this operation is successful, I hope we can get the boys back by Christmas." War correspondents had fresh leads for their stories, the end-the-war assault was now christened the Home-by-Christmas Offensive. Seldom has a commander's view been less attuned to reality when war returned.

After the final offensive was launched, MacArthur ordered his plane to fly north so he could view from the air what was in front of his troops. He later wrote: "All that spread before my eyes was an endless expanse of utterly barren countryside, jagged hills, yawning crevices and the black waters of the Yalu locked in the silent death grip of ice and snow. It was a merciless wasteland."

But Walton Walker was nervous about Chinese intentions. He told 24th Division commander Maj. Gen. John Church to advise the officer commanding his lead regiment that "if he smells Chinese chow, pull back immediately."

At 10 a.m. on Friday, November 25, the thunder of a tremendous artillery strike preceded the movement of tanks and trucks northward from the Chongchon River. Ahead lay hill after hill of barren countryside marked with narrow gorges and mountain passes. The 24th Division moved seven miles without opposition, and the ROK 1st Division made similar spectacular gains. IX Corps had no opposition in a three-mile advance. (X Corps' attack in the east was delayed for two days.)

From Tokyo, MacArthur was on Armed Forces Radio broadcasting the battle plan, which infuriated commanders who toiled to keep the plans secret from the Chinese. The communists learned they still had

the element of surprise. In MacArthur's mind, X Corps was already anchoring the eastern side of a vise that Eighth Army could now close in the west.

"The United Nations' massive compression envelopment in North Korea against the new Red armies operating there is now approaching its decisive effort," MacArthur said in his deep, resonant voice. "...This morning the western sector of the pincer moves forward in a general assault in an effort to complete the compression and close the vise. If successful, this should for all practical purposes end the war, restore peace and unity to Korea, enable the prompt withdrawal of United Nations military forces and permit the complete assumption by the Korean people and nation of full sovereignty and international equality. It is that for which we fight."

His grand plan to subdue North Korea went up in smoke that night. The Chinese were waiting with a plan of their own, one rooted in the centuries-old writings of Sun Tzu, advisor to the ancient Chinese warlords. In *The Art of War*, Sun Tzu wrote: "All warfare is based on deception. Hence, when able to attack, we must seem unable; when using our forces, we must seem inactive; when we are near, we must make the enemy believe we are far away; when far away, we must make him believe we are near. Hold out baits to entice the enemy. Feign disorder, and crush him."

Based on the battle at Unsan with the 8th Cavalry, the Chinese prepared a Military Lessons Bulletin. Basically, it was a hasty manual on how to fight in Korea. It read:

> The U.S. Army relies for its main power in combat on the shock effect of coordinated armor and artillery...and their air-to-ground attack capability is exceptional. But their infantry is weak. Their men are afraid to die, and will neither press home a bold attack nor defend to the death. They depend on their planes, tanks and artillery. At the same time, they are afraid of our firepower. They will cringe when, if on the advance, they hear firing...Their habit is to be active during the daylight hours. They are very weak at attacking or approaching an enemy at night...They are afraid when their rear is cut off. When transportation comes to a standstill, the infantry loses the will to fight.

The manual also included a section on the South Koreans, which were the favored targets of any Chinese attack. The Chinese bulletin called them puppets:

> "The Korean Army is deficient in all pertinent aspects. Their training is absolutely insufficient. Three Korean divisions do not equal one American division when it

BUGLES

The Chinese Communists used bugles and whistles to signal their troop movements—a cacophony that often unnerved the allied forces more than the roar of artillery. One British officer said his commando unit was nearly driven mad by the bugles and whistles in their first contact with the Chinese south of Hagaru in late 1950.

A sergeant said: "I fought against the Jerries during the last war, but those damned Chinese with their whistles and bugles were the worst experience I've ever had. It was more upsetting to some of the boys who were having their baptism of fire. Bugles would seem to be blowing all around. But, after a while we got used to them and we would welcome the three long blasts that meant a rest period." Later on in the war, when musical notes appeared on front line battle maps, an American officer explained they marked "places where the Chinese have blown bugles."

U.S. Col. William A. Harris eventually issued bugles to each of his battalions in the Seventh Regiment of the 1st Cavalry Division. He instructed his men to go into battle blowing "Garry Owen," the old Irish drinking song. It was the song of the Seventh "way back when it was Gen. Custer's old regiment," he said. Harris also ordered his buglers to learn Chinese bugle calls—to confuse them.

comes to firepower and overall combat strength. But Koreans do have a measure of fighting spirit."

Not surprisingly, China's crushing blow fell against South Korean units. The 8th Division of the ROK II Corps was enveloped and blocked at Tokchon on the night of November 25-26, 25 miles east of the nearest U.S. position. Using bugles and gongs to start their assault, the Chinese achieved instant and total success. II Corps disintegrated overnight, opening an 80-mile wide chasm in the U.N. lines and exposing the entire right flank of the U.N. western assault.

Under the discipline of a forced march, and disguised in the gear the ROKs abandoned, the Chinese infiltrated the rear of the IX Corps positions by the night of November 26. The communists hit the 2nd and 25th Divisions, but the "Indianheads" of the 2nd Division were the most vulnerable because they held the right shoulder of the deployment after the ROKs collapsed. The 9th Regiment was about 15 air miles northeast of Kunu-ri, once a thriving mining town and now the critical position for the entire Eighth Army. The Chinese hit the regiment on both flanks and the rear. Soldiers were chased from their sleeping bags. They junked their artillery pieces by dumping phosphorous grenades down the barrels, abandoning guns and equipment as they withdrew. The 23rd Regiment passed through the 9th, taking up the fight.

At Kunu-ri, there were two escape routes, including one to the southwest that the 25th Division, with its battered 24th Regiment, took to reach safety in the west. The 2nd Division chose a shorter route to Sunchon that led through the mountains, but the ambitious Chinese had already severed the passage and had dug trenches into the frozen, stony ground. Col.

Gu Teh-hua, a Chinese guerrilla fighter, had told his men below Kunu-ri: "Draw the enemy in deep. Hit them with all available force on ground of your own choosing. Finally, cut the enemy off and destroy them."

By daylight of November 27, IX Corps commander John Coulter committed the 5,200-man Turkish Brigade. The Turks were ordered east of Kunu-ri to protect the 2nd Division's right flank and keep the Chinese from cutting off the Americans. The Turks only got about eight miles before they were encircled. Their officers, colorfully wearing swooping moustaches, flung their caps on the ground and vowed to stand or die. In the bloody battle that developed, only a few Turkish units were able to fight their way out of the trap. The Turks had a reputation as fierce fighters, but they were green and ill-trained. They also faced language barriers. Scores of prisoners they captured turned out to be ROKs rather than Chinese, and the Turks had trouble understanding orders given by U.S. commanders.

By the end of November 27, the 25th Division was retreating across the Chongchon River to Anju. The 24th and ROK 1st Divisions, the only two elements which escaped relatively unscathed in the counterattack, also pulled back across the Chongchon with their train of tanks and guns and trucks. To stem the Chinese attack and to protect escape routes, Walton Walker ordered his reserves—the 1st Cavalry Division and the British Commonwealth Brigade—to assist the withdrawal of 2nd Division from Kunu-ri.

At right: Marine bazooka men of the 2nd Battalion, 7th Marines, pummel a Red troop hideout in the North Korean hills.

Allied casualties rise dramatically as China sends its hordes into North Korea. Injured Americans are brought ashore from a Navy hospital ship for airlift to Japan.

Across the peninsula, the Chinese were also in full combat with Marines and Army troops who were surrounded at the Chosin Reservoir.

Initial reports of U.N. successes now gave way to battlefield reality. MacArthur summoned Walker and X Corps commander Ned Almond to Tokyo for an emergency conference. The inevitable was finally recognized; operations were to go from offense to defense. Until now, MacArthur had low-balled Chinese strength. Now, he overestimated it slightly. "A major

segment of the Chinese continental forces in army, corps and divisional organization of an aggregate strength of over 200,000 men is now arrayed against the United Nations in North Korea. Consequently, we face an entirely new war," MacArthur cabled his bosses in Washington. "Our present strength of force is not sufficient to meet this undeclared war by the Chinese...This command has done everything within its capabilities but now is faced with conditions beyond its control and strength."

Walker ordered a general withdrawal of Eighth Army on November 29. It would be the longest retreat in U.S. Army history. Still out on a limb was the 2nd Division under Maj. Gen. Laurence B. Keiser. He knew he had to fight his way south, but had no idea what awaited him. A patrol of military police sent south was annihilated; a relief column of tanks and trucks sent north from Sunchon was ambushed and stopped. At noon on November 28, Keiser made a break for it with his battered 9th Regiment leading the way. The roadbound army's vehicles were bumper to bumper: towed guns, ambulances, service trucks, mess trucks, jeeps and everything else a modern army drags along.

The Chinese dug in with mortars, machine guns

Left: American bridging material goes up in smoke to keep it from falling into Chinese hands.

Below: Retreating allied tanks retrace their route into Pyongyang before overwhelming Chinese forces.

and rifles on both sides of a narrow defile. They had created a gauntlet, a six-mile long avenue of death and destruction. The road was too narrow to allow the Americans room to deploy and maneuver. In some places, the Chinese were less than a hundred yards from the road, waiting with their satchel charges and grenades. The strategy was simple—let the convoy get deep into the trap, then knock out the lead vehicle and open fire on the stuff stuck in the middle. Lacking radios, the Chinese jury-rigged signal beams from the headlights and batteries of junked U.S. trucks.

Lt. James Mace, commanding the lead tank, was the first to realize this was a trap. The road was blocked by a damaged tank, truck and utility carrier. A mile-long line of vehicles was now exposed to machine-gun fire until Mace could clear the obstruction. Mace's pathfinder tank got through with the front of the convoy, but then the Chinese blocked the road again. They bombed a half-track known as a quad-50, designed as an anti-aircraft weapon with its four .50 caliber machine guns but used in Korea to support infantry. In the gauntlet, the Chinese had 40 machine gun and 10 mortar positions, plus strings of infantry along the ridgelines. They opened fire in full volume. Truckers died in their cabs. Roadside ditches choked with wounded and dead who were left behind. Soldiers ran after fleeing tanks, yelling for them to stop so they could hitch rides to safety. The column became a stalled junkyard. "All hell broke loose," said Cecidio Berberis, a battalion commander in the 9th Regiment.

U.S. planes ranged up and down the road, savaging anything that looked suspicious on either side. Sortie after sortie dropped bombs and napalm, which sometimes spattered the road with orange flicks of flame. Jets with white stars on their wings let loose a hiss and thud from rockets and strafing cannon. But as night fell, the air strikes were limited and the slaughter continued.

The Chinese moved in behind the column with grenades and mortars, blowing up those vehicles last in line and making escape to the rear impossible. With his column blocked front and rear, Gen. Keiser knew his infantry must attack both sides of the pass and clear the roadblock. When he came up to get a look at the situation, Keiser found only one man firing back with a mortar. The general tripped over a body in the middle of the road, which sprang up and yelled at him: "You damned son of a bitch." Replied Keiser: "My friend, I'm sorry."

Keiser organized squads of clerks, cooks and ROKs to send up the slopes to clear the Chinese from their killing positions while wreckage was bulldozed off the pass. Finally, Keiser gave the order to How Able—

military jargon for Haul Ass. Organization broke down, and it became every man for himself. Some fought their way out in small pockets, escaping across country through the hills. Finally, the road was cleared at about 7:30 p.m. and the convoy charged ahead.

The British Commonwealth Brigade made a desperate attempt to break through from the south to free the Americans. Communications were never established with the trapped soldiers because nobody knew the British radio frequency.

The Middlesex Battalion charged with bayonets against dug-in Chinese, but they were unable to open the corridor. When the Americans opened the road and raced south, one of the Australian soldiers said: "Their cigar butts went by like tracer bullets in the night." Into the waiting arms of the 1st Cavalry, the 2nd Division reached Suchon with wounded piled atop trailers, howitzers and truck fenders. In a single day in the gauntlet, it took 3,000 casualties—as many as the Continental Army took in the 1777 winter at Valley Forge.

Back at Kunu-ri, the 2nd Division's 23rd Regiment had covered the retreat. "Without air or artillery, they're making us look a little silly in this godawful country," Col. Paul Freeman said of the Chinese. Tanks and howitzers fired off their reserves of ammunition—3,206 rounds in 22 minutes. Paint blistered off the howitzer tubes barrels when the stocks were exhausted, then the artillerymen destroyed their own guns with thermite grenades. The salvo tricked the Chinese. They dug in, figuring a counterattack was coming. It gave the 23rd Regiment time to escape. The regiment bypassed the road south where 2nd Division was trapped in the gauntlet. Paul Freeman took his unit west to Anju, where it got jammed with the traffic of the 25th Division but ultimately made it to safety.

Since the beginning of the offensive, the 2nd Division suffered 4,940 casualties, or one out of every three men in its ranks. Combat ineffective, it was moved south to Seoul to rest and rebuild while Keiser was removed as commander. The survivors made up a bitter song:

Hear the pitter patter of tiny feet
  It's old Two Div in full retreat
I'm movin' on...back to Inchon
  I'm buggin' out fast
Afore they get my ass
  Yes, I'm movin' on...

The collapse of the Eighth Army's right flank wasn't as bad as it could have been because the Americans were so mobile. The Chinese, on foot, couldn't

Pvt. William M. Robinson of Nashville, Tennessee, adds a tire to burning supplies as his 189th Regimental Combat Team destroys what it can't take in retreat.

The last wounded soldier is flown out of Pyongyang.

keep up with the retreat and couldn't exploit their victory. But because of the disarray, the withdrawal was known as the Big Bugout. When Brig. Basil Coad of the British Commonwealth Brigade went to IX Corps headquarters to get his new orders, he was simply told: "Haul ass." His units marched south to the skirl of bagpipes. Professional soldiers were heartsick at the scene. "Look around here. This is a sight that hasn't been seen for hundreds of years—the men of a whole United States Army fleeing from a battlefield, abandoning their wounded, running for their lives," said Col. Freeman of the 23rd Regiment.

The situation finally became clear in Washington. But President Truman said U.N. forces had "no intention of abandoning their mission in Korea."

Now the question was raised whether America should play its ultimate hole card—the atomic bomb, the technological weapon that Truman authorized to reduce Hiroshima and Nagasaki to radioactive rubble. At a news conference on November 30, Truman said that the United States would take "whatever steps are necessary to meet the military situation."

"Does that include the atomic bomb?" the President was asked.

"That includes every weapon we have," he replied.

The reporters pressed him. "Mr. President, you said every weapon we have. Does that mean that there has

been active consideration of the use of the atomic bomb?" he was asked.

"There has always been active consideration of its use. I don't want to see it used. It is a terrible weapon, and it should not be used on innocent men, women and children who have nothing to do with this military aggression."

He was pressed once more on whether the United Nations must authorize the bomb's use.

"It is one of our weapons," Truman said. "It's a matter that the military will have to decide. I'm not a military authority that passes on these things."

But the British, America's chief ally on the battleground and in the United Nations, adamantly opposed the use of the bomb. They insisted that they be consulted before any were used. And Truman later backed down from talk of dropping the bomb, trying to clarify what he said earlier. By the end of December, however, MacArthur submitted a list of retaliation targets in North Korea and China, requiring 25 atomic bombs. Four were targeted against the communist forces in North Korea, and four others on critical concentrations of enemy air power. The world may never know how close it came to seeing mushroom clouds in war again.

For the immediate crisis, MacArthur demanded more troops to stem the tide. The Chinese had as their

A demolition team readies a bridge over the Taedong River as one of the last convoys heads south. The bridge was destroyed in the face of the Red advance.

objective "the complete destruction of the United Nations forces and the securing of all Korea," MacArthur said. But the only available reserve in the United States was the 82nd Airborne Division, which was the last-line contingency force against any crisis in the world. No other U.N. members were in a position to offer assistance either. MacArthur renewed a suggestion to use three divisions of Chinese Nationalists from Taiwan. They were of dubious value; they were the remnants of Chiang Kai-shek's army that had lost to the communists in China's civil war and had been exiled on Taiwan. Fearing a broadening of the war with China, Washington denied MacArthur's request. It also denied him permission to bomb Chinese sanctuaries in Manchuria.

Now the rift between Truman and MacArthur was readily apparent. MacArthur claimed he was being forced to fight under "an enormous handicap...without precedent in military history."

Truman wrote later of the situation: "I should have relieved General MacArthur then and there. The reason I did not was that I did not wish to have it appear as if he were being relieved because the offensive failed. I have never believed in going back on people when luck is against them, and I did not intend to do it now." He also said: "Now, no one is blaming General MacArthur, and certainly I never did, for the failure of the November offensive...(But) I do blame General MacArthur for the manner in which he tried to excuse his failure."

Refugees from Pyongyang crawl perilously over the twisted steel girders of the city's vehicular bridge, fleeing south over the Taedong River to escape advancing Chinese. This Pulitzer Prize winning picture is by AP photographer Max Desfor. December 1950.

ROK troops of the 2nd Division retreat along a dusty road 10 miles south of Pyongyang.

Truman reassured British Prime Minister Clement Attlee he did not want a war with China; the newest policy reverted to defending Korea at the 38th parallel. Truman also ruled out any possibility of withdrawing from Korea. "We must fight it out. If we failed, we should at least fail honorably," the President said.

On the battlefield, MacArthur told the Joint Chiefs he was "facing the entire Chinese nation in an undeclared war and unless some positive and immediate action is taken, hope for success cannot be justified and speedy attrition leading to final destruction can reasonably be contemplated."

In their December 4 reply, the Joint Chiefs advised him to find a line he could hold so negotiations might begin to end the fighting. "We consider that the preservation of your forces is now the primary consideration. Consolidation of forces into beachheads is concurred on." Army Chief of Staff J. Lawton Collins was also dispatched to get a first-hand view of the situation.

A defensive line was contemplated along the narrow waist of North Korea, just above the capital of Pyongyang. But Walker felt his army was too jittery to make a stand. Within a week of kicking off the offensive, Eighth Army backtracked 50 miles from the Chongchon River. In 10 days, the retreat reached 120 miles. "I will give up any amount of real estate if necessary to prevent this army from being endangered," Walker said.

Left: President Syngman Rhee tries to rally his countrymen in crowded Seoul Municipal Stadium, saying the military situation is no worse than it was five months before. December 1950.

Below: A Korean child is part of the waves of refugees heading south.

Pyongyang was abandoned without a fight. Early on December 5, the last United Nations forces pulled back across the bridges leading south; then the bridges were blown to slow down the pursuing Chinese. Mountains of stockpiled supplies—guns, bullets, helmets, artillery rounds, fuel and food—were blown up to keep them from falling to the Chinese. A mile-high black blossom of smoke from the explosions was the last thing the U.N. army ever saw of Pyongyang. AP correspondent Tom Lambert and Homer Bigart of the New York *Herald Tribune* were among the last to leave the empty streets. "We've been run out," Lambert said ruefully. Still, the Chinese gathered American sleeping bags, overcoats, trucks, M-1 rifles, biscuits and rice as they swooped south. The Joint Chiefs of Staff placed troops in other parts of the world on high alert, because suspicions still persisted that the Soviets would attack in Europe. "The current situation in Korea has greatly increased the probability of general war. Commanders addressed should take such action as is feasible to increase readiness, without creating an atmosphere of panic," the JCS said.

By December 7, the split command in Korea had ended. X Corps was consolidated with Eighth Army. And Lawton Collins' report back to the JCS said the situation "remained serious" but "was no longer critical."

In Pyongyang, meanwhile, Kim Il Sung returned to power with a vengeance. His demand for a victory parade of war booty and American POWs was precluded by fears of air strikes. Instead, he gave a brief speech at city hall in his first public appearance, then reviewed North Korean troops at a soccer stadium. His closing words on December 12 were: "March south." His henchmen were already at work cleaning up graffiti written by some American named Kilroy, who had put his name all over the city telling people he was there.

Truman made a national radio broadcast on December 15, pledging that America would "continue to uphold and if necessary, to defend with arms, the principles of the United Nations—the principles of freedom and justice." The next morning, he declared a state of national emergency. "No nation has ever had a greater responsibility than ours at this moment. We must remember that we are leaders of the free world," Truman said. He also announced that huge sums would be spent to build America's defense, a policy that continued for four decades to the end of the Cold War.

By this time, Eighth Army had crossed south of the 38th parallel to lines along the frozen Imjin River. They didn't stay there long. Before it was over, the retreat covered 275 miles from where Eighth Army had stood during the "Home-by-Christmas" offensive. Total Eighth Army casualties for the offensive were 7,337 killed, wounded or missing.

The Army also endured one more bitter loss. The field commander, Walton Walker, the defender of Pusan, was killed December 23 when his jeep collided with a ROK truck.

6

Frozen Chosin

In northeast Korea, with Eighth Army already withdrawing in the west, a separate ordeal of fire and ice befell Marines and soldiers around the Chosin Reservoir.

About 25,000 troops of X Corps were surrounded—and marked for extermination—by 120,000 Chinese soldiers. An epic battle seethed for two cruel weeks over dozens of miles of forbidding mountain road, at brutal temperatures of 30 degrees below zero and lower. The fighting conjured up references to Xenophon's *Anabasis*, the story set in 400 B.C. of 10,000 Greek soldiers who fought through a terrible winter campaign in Persian mountains until they reached the sea. But nothing compares to the frozen hell of Chosin.

Plans called for the Marines to slice inward and hook up with the right edge of the Eighth Army, then advance to the North Korean sanctuary at Kanggye and ultimately to the Yalu River. But even the rugged geography made this a challenging assignment. X Corps and Eighth Army were separated by 25 to 30 miles of trackless Taebaek

Above: Men of the 1st Marine Division rest on a snow-covered roadside after repulsing an enemy ambush somewhere in Korea.

Mountain ranges that would be difficult to traverse in good weather, let alone in the depths of winter. "It was an insane plan. You couldn't take a picnic lunch in peacetime and go over that terrain in November and December," Nick Ruffner, the X Corps chief of staff, wrote later.

Marine commander Oliver P. Smith was wary of being stuck between the bleak mountains and an open right flank, so he stalled to consolidate his units. He didn't want his men scattered along a flimsy Korean road, which was hardly more than a dirt lane. And he wanted to have reliable supply points.

After the October 26 landing at Wonsan, the Marines had moved north to Hungnam and Hamhung, then northwest into the mountains. They pushed 42 miles to a railhead at Chinhung-ri, where the coastal plain abruptly gives way to a 3,500-foot plateau accessible via a meandering passage. From the railhead, it is 10 miserable miles of crooked road to Koto-ri. And 12 miles beyond Koto-ri is the mountain hamlet of Hagaru-ri at the base of the Chosin Reservoir. Seen another way, the 64 miles from the Sea of Japan to Hagaru-ri is like the stem of a Y; at its fork, the Marines took a road on the left to Yudam-ni while three battalions of the Army's 7th Division split right on the reservoir's eastern shore to protect the Marines' flank. To strengthen his supply capabilities, Smith built airstrips on the frozen ground at Koto-ri and Hagaru-ri. The crude airstrips paid life-saving dividends later. Smith also ordered his engineers to improve the single road, so his tanks and heavy trucks could negotiate its hairpin turns.

Siberian cold descended on the plateau. Marines watched in utter amazement as the thermometer plunged to 10, 20, even 30 degrees below zero. The cold numbed fingers and toes, and it froze motor oil and weapons.

Commanders faced a muddled situation. On the one hand, the 7th Division's 17th Regiment had reached the Yalu at Hyesanjin on November 22. And just to the west, a small task force under 2nd Lt. Robert C. Kingston of the 32nd Regiment reached the Manchurian border. Yet the Marines sensed something was amiss. They had encountered Chinese forces, although the Chinese broke off contact on November 7. Still, prisoners later talked of massive troop buildups.

When Eighth Army launched the November 25 "Home-by-Christmas" offensive the day after Thanksgiving, X Corps was still getting into position around Chosin. From the supply base in Hagaru-ri, where Marines placed a mobile hospital and dumps of fuel and ammunition, the 5th and 7th Marine Regi-

ments moved 14 miles northwest to Yudam-ni on November 25. Meanwhile, the three Army battalions moved 13 miles to the northeast the next day.

The X Corps offensive began at 8:10 a.m. on November 27. At Yudam-ni, the Marines attempted to take the high ground on the road heading west, with the 2nd Battalion of the 5th Marines in the lead. But less than an hour later, spotter planes located heavy concentrations of Chinese ahead of them. The Marines gained 1,500 yards in 16 hours. It was snowing and the wind was whipping at 40 miles per hour, making it feel much colder than minus-20 degrees. Typical dress was worn by Capt. Elmer Dodson, a lawyer and reservist from Charleston, West Virginia, who had been on active duty since August 13. To battle the cold, Dodson wore two pairs of ski socks, heavy rubber and leather boots, cotton drawers, long underwear, two pairs of heavy utility trousers, a shirt, wool sweater, a flannel shirt, one utility jacket, one field jacket, one muffler, a knee-length parka, a pile cap with ear muffs and a steel helmet. "We were pushing ahead of everybody when we ran smack into what seemed like most of the Chinese from China. I'll always wonder why they sent us up into all that," Dodson said.

The Marines organized an all-around defense at Yudam-ni, a tiny huddle of clapboard huts girdled by five imposing ridges. Leathernecks counterattacked to seize the high ground overlooking their positions, and fighting was hand-to-hand on the snow-covered knobs. That night and into the wee hours of November 28, the howl of the wind was drowned out by the frightful sound of Chinese bugles and burp guns. Human waves of attackers from two Chinese divisions charged again and again into Marine positions. A third Chinese division swung south to cut the road and attempted to capture a vital area known as the Toktong Pass, a notch in the road between Yudam-ni and Hagargu-ri. On the strategic hills protecting the Marines' only link to the rear, Company F of the 2nd Battalion, 7th Marines, was hit from three directions beginning at 2:30 a.m. The Marines held, in no small part because Pvt. Hector A. Cafferata Jr., a 19-year-old rifleman who grew up in Montville, New Jersey, refused to be pushed off Fox Hill. He waged a lone battle with his M-1 rifle and his grenades after all the other members of his fire team were hit. The action was fast and furious, but it seemed like slow motion to Cafferata and he fired at the Chinese and batted back grenades with a shovel while buying time for reinforcements to reach him. Later that morning, Cafferata saw a Chinese grenade land in a shallow trench filled with wounded Marines. Under fire, he grabbed the grenade to save his buddies, but he lost part of a finger and was wounded in the right arm when the grenade exploded. But Cafferata, wearing a scarf cut out of a blanket, fought on until he was struck by a sniper's bullet and forced to evacuate. For five hours, he had fought in the frozen wastes without having time to put the boots on his bare feet. Cafferata was awarded the Congressional Medal of Honor, one of 13 given in the reservoir campaign.

"It was waves of fear and fighting panic. You didn't have time to think. I don't think I gave any of it any conscious thought. You have friends there who are wounded and hurt. You decide you have to stick it out. The thought of leaving never occurred to me. Besides, you couldn't run very far without running into more Chinese," Cafferata said. It took nine days for him to reach a hospital, and he spent the next year and a half under medical care.

On Chosin's east banks, the three Army battalions also were trapped by the Chinese. The 3rd Battalion

Even the symbol of mercy is shot up but this ambulance is still rolling, evacuating casualties, somewhere in Korea.

Providing a delaying action, a detail of Marines waits at a curve in the road near Yudam as the 1st and 7th Regiments withdrew from the Chosin Reservoir under pressure from three Red divisions.

FRANK "PAPPY" NOEL

Fourteen months after being captured by the Chinese in North Korea, Associated Press photographer Frank Noel got a camera in his hand and went back to taking pictures—while a POW.

Noel and a small group of Marines were captured near Koto in northeast Korea on November 29, 1950. He had been attached to the 1st Marine Division and was with the 7th Marine Regiment when that unit first encountered Chinese Communists northwest of Hamhung earlier in November. He was the only news photographer there at the time. During the night of November 29, Noel accompanied a convoy scheduled to carry supplies and reinforcements into Koto for the hard-pressed Marines in that area. The column was ambushed and Noel was among those captured.

When Noel's name appeared on the prisoner list turned over to the United Nations during armistice talks in December 1951, AP colleagues began trying to persuade the communist correspondents at Panmunjon to take Noel a camera.

Finally, early in 1952, arrangements were made with the communist military authorities and AP photographer Robert Schutz slipped his camera to Chu Chi-ping of the Chinese newspaper Ta Kung Pao over a fence in the backyard of one of the buildings in the conference area.

Near the end of January, Schutz flew to Tokyo with Noel's pictures, taken at prison camp No. 2 at Pyoktong. The first photos showed Noel—nicknamed "Pappy"—was in good health and spirits. "Outside of needing a shave, he looks fine," said AP photo editor Max Desfor, who was a close friend of Noel's.

The photos, radioed to San Francisco from Tokyo, had to pass both Chinese Communist censors at Pyongyang and U.S. Army censors in Tokyo. Communist correspondents at Panmunjon said several of the photographers were withheld.

Noel, who was then 52, wrote to Robert Tuckman, the AP's correspondent at Panmunjon: "Got a late start and have only this one film pack. The first five were made in the hospital where the men have plenty of medical care and getting in good shape. There will be more of these hospital shots when I get a full day to work....The rest of the pack shows group shots, which I do not like to make, and the negatives to come will show small groups doing something, chopping wood, in the galley, playing cards and other feature getups.

"This deal is certainly a good one and I will try to produce enough good copy at this end to warrant the work you people have done there....

"I'm still pinching myself.

"The very best to you and Schutz. Would write more, but in a hurry.

"F.N."

"Pappy" had won a Pulitzer Prize for news photography in 1942 with a dramatic lifeboat picture of a Lascar Indian seaman begging for water. The shot was taken as Noel drifted in a lifeboat in the Indian Ocean after his ship had been torpedoed as he fled the surrender in Singapore.

Noel had a knack for being where the action was. He was in Southeast Asia on a round-the-world photo assignment when the Japanese attacked Pearl Harbor. He stayed to cover the Malayan jungle campaign, then covered the war in Burma and India. After World War II, he was assigned to the Mediterranean area where he spent four years watching the Trans-Jordan conflict from behind his camera.

He was staying at the King David Hotel in Jerusalem in 1948 when a bomb destroyed his equipment and personal effects—but he was at the front at the time, taking pictures.

When the Korean War erupted, he volunteered and was on the front line a month later.

Noel, a native of Dalhart, Texas, returned to New York after his release from the Korean prison. He was sent to Tampa in 1958 and finished his career in Tallahassee, retiring in 1965. He died a year later.

---

of the 31st Regiment was supposed to pass into the lead and press the attack ahead of the 1st Battalion of the 32nd Regiment, who were called the "Polar Bears" because they had fought in Siberia in World War II.

They were supported by the 57th Artillery. Waiting for them was a Chinese division. By nightfall, the Chinese had flanked the soldiers and completed a double envelopment. The surrounded soldiers were less prepared for the cold. Most GIs wore field jackets with pile liners over summer-weight cotton fatigues. Steel pots, which absorbed the cold, were discarded in favor of pile caps with ear flaps. Men moved their limbs constantly to keep from freezing. Engines were kept running and weapons were fired every half-hour to keep them working.

The X Corps was still unaware of the forces surrounding Chosin, or of the debacle befalling Eighth Army in the west. At noon on November 28, Gen. Almond helicoptered into the Army pocket. Accompanied by his aide, Lt. Alexander Haig, Almond unfolded a map on the frozen hood of a jeep and confronted men shaken by the battle the previous night. "The enemy who is delaying you for the moment is nothing more than the remnants of Chinese

Caught in a Red trap in northeast Korea, men of the 1st Marine Division try to warm themselves at an airstrip in the Chosin Reservoir area. Parachute packs in the foreground are from air-dropped supplies.

divisions fleeing north. We're still attacking and we're going all the way to the Yalu. Don't let a bunch of Chinese laundrymen stop you. Retake the high ground lost during the night. And prepare to attack north," Almond told the soldiers. The general also awarded decorations, pinning the Silver Star on Lt. Col. Don Carlos Faith, commander of the 1st Battalion of the 32nd Regiment, who had distinguished himself as an aide to Matthew Ridgway in the 82nd Airborne Division during World War II. Faith had led counter-attacks in the bone-chilling darkness against the Chinese. When Almond departed, Faith tossed his Silver Star into the snow in disgust because of the way the battle was being fought.

Later on November 28, it was apparent the Chinese were more than just remnants of fleeing divisions. Forces were besieged at Yudam-ni, the east side of the reservoir, Hagaru-ri and Koto-ri. The Chinese in-

tended to cut them off and destroy them piecemeal. Radio Peking was saying "the annihilation of the United States 1st Marine Division is only a matter of time." And the 2,500 men in the Army battalions were attacked from all sides. That afternoon, Gen. Almond was whisked to Tokyo for a council of war with Mac-Arthur and Eighth Army commander Walton Walker. MacArthur ordered Almond to withdraw X Corps back to the beachheads. Meanwhile, the Army was told to abandon its foothold 86 air miles to the north on the Yalu River.

The key to X Corps survival was the base at Hagaru-ri, which supported the Marines and the Army along separate forks. At 10:30 p.m. on November 28,

Right: They can still smile. Marines rest in the snow on their way out of the circling Chinese at the Chosin Reservoir.

the Chinese tried to overrun the village. Engineers working by floodlights to complete their airstrip were pressed into the fight. Some Chinese actually broke through a four-mile perimeter, but they took to looting instead of exploiting their advantage. The Marines, commanded by Lt. Col. Thomas Ridge, cleared them out in hand-to-hand fighting.

To save Hagaru-ri, Col. Lewis "Chesty" Puller of the 1st Marine Regiment organized a rescue effort to attack north from his base at Koto-ri. "We're surrounded. That simplifies our problem of getting to these people and killing them," Puller said. The relief team included 922 men, 29 tanks and 141 other vehicles burdened with supplies. The column included George Company of the 1st Marines, Baker Company of the Army's 31st Regiment and the 41st Independent Commando of the British Royal Marines. It was called Task Force Drysdale after the British commander, Lt. Col. Douglas Drysdale, and moved out on November 29. Tanks blasted Chinese positions along the way with their 90-millimeter cannons and machine guns. But about halfway between Koto-ri and Hagaru-ri, the Chinese set up an ambush in a mile-long valley marked with hills on the right and a frozen creek with open ground to the left. A mortar hit a truck in the center of the procession, splitting it into two sections. Drysdale had been told to proceed at all costs, so 17 tanks and most of the British and American marines drove on. Those in the rear—about 61 British commandos, most of the Army company and a group of U.S. Marines from a headquarters section—would have to fend for themselves in what became known as Hell Fire Valley.

Among those trapped in Hell Fire Valley was Associated Press photographer Frank "Pappy" Noel. At about 2 a.m., he and two other men volunteered to run the gauntlet to get help, but they were captured before they moved 100 yards. Others were forced to give up when their numbers dwindled to about 40 able-bodied fighters and no one had more than eight rounds of ammunition left. The Chinese had given an ultimatum at 4:30 a.m.—surrender in 10 minutes or be exterminated. Marine Sgt. Guillarmo Tovar tried to bargain with the Chinese to buy time. James Eagan, a wounded major, told Tovar: "You don't have the chance of a snowball in hell." The prisoners watched glumly as the Chinese raided U.S. trucks and ripped open Christmas packages containing ski socks, watches and other gifts from home. The marauding Chinese also swarmed over a PX truck, littering the frozen fields with wrappers from Toostie Rolls, Hershey bars and Dentyne gum.

The front of Task Force Drysdale journeyed through the shivery night. About 2,000 yards short of Hagaru-ri, within sight of Marine tents at the beleaguered base, the Chinese struck again. Col. Drysdale was wounded, and command passed to U.S. Marine Capt. Carl Sitter.

"Everyone off the trucks. Face out and shoot," Sitter barked. Under Sitter's command, a force attacked a Chinese regiment shooting up the column from their perches on a steep, ice-covered hill. Sitter and his men ejected the Chinese, then withstood a vicious counterattack. He rallied men at each gun position, refusing to budge even when the Chinese infiltrated his command post. In a hand-to-hand grenade fight, Sitter was wounded in the face, arms and chest. But Sitter, awarded the Congressional Medal of Honor, fought on until the high ground could be defended and the task force marched on. Of the 922 men who left Koto-ri, only one in three made it. About half of the vehicles were lost, but 17 tanks and dozens of supply trucks got through.

Meanwhile, on the Army side of Chosin, the Chinese struck hard on November 29 during a heavy morning snowstorm. The commanding officer of the 3rd Battalion, 31st Regiment, Col. Allan D. MacLean, was killed in action, leaving Col. Faith in charge of the marooned units, which were now known as Task Force Faith. Every Army weapon was being fired that morning as Faith led his men four miles south to consolidate positions into one pocket. During the day, airdrops of food and ammunition fell from two C-119 Flying Boxcars. But a relief column, including tanks, that had been sent north from Hagaru-ri was blunted and beaten back by the Chinese.

The X Corps situation was critical on the final day of November. With the offensive halted, Gen. Almond ordered a withdrawal to Hagaru-ri by the two Marine regiments and Task Force Faith.

By December 1, the 2,500-man Task Force Faith had suffered 600 casualties, and the Chinese had infiltrated their lines. Some soldiers were down to their final clip of ammunition. Howitzers were out of shells. Kitchen trucks were emptied to make room for the wounded; extra vehicles were set on fire and destroyed. Hagaru-ri was eight miles away. Col. Faith organized a procession of 60 vehicles, starting south from Sinhung-ni at noon on an agonizing trip. Leading the column was a full-tracked vehicle called an M-16, which was designed as an anti-aircraft weapon with dual 40-millimeter cannons. It was deadly efficient for sweeping enemy positions off ridges. Up to this point, air supremacy had kept the Chinese from annihilating the task force, but a terrible accident befell the GIs. A Marine Corsair dropped napalm on

After walking all day and night through Chinese lines and roadblocks, exhausted soldiers of the U.S. 2nd Division take sleep when and where they can get it. On the northwestern front.

a dozen shrieking GIs. "Men all around me were burned. They lay rolling in the snow. Men I knew, marched and fought with begged me to shoot them...I couldn't," said Pfc. James Ransome. Col. Faith restored order, but was told no reinforcements could reach him. A message received over his jeep radio from Gen. Smith said: "Secure your own exit to Hagaru-ri. Unable to assist you." Then things went from bad to worse. Just a few miles from where the column

had started, a bridge over a creek was blown. Fifteen vehicles forded the creek, but a Chinese ambush stopped the others. Brandishing his pistol, Col. Faith ordered the roadblock broken. When a South Korean soldier hiding under a truck chassis refused to join the assault, Faith shot him. "The son of a bitch is retreating. Shoot anyone who runs away," Faith was heard to say. The block was eliminated when an assault commanded by Capt. Erwin Bigger took a hill held by the Chinese. Bigger, wounded earlier by mortar fragments and hobbling on two canes, told his men: "If you are going to die, do it while on the attack."

But Faith's column encountered another roadblock at a hairpin turn. He personally led a charge to break through, but a grenade wounded him mortally just above the heart. The colonel was lifted onto a jeep and then transferred to a truck; he died at the head of his column. "When Faith was hit, the task force ceased to exist," said Maj. Robert Jones. One of the soldiers who found Faith was Louis Grappo, a 17-year-old private from Youngstown, Ohio. The youngest of 12 children, Grappo had his rosary inside his thick mittens.

"I'm a young kid. I don't even know what it is to have a girlfriend or go to a dance. If you will just let me live to experience life, I'll go to Mass and Communion every day for a year," Grappo prayed. Shortly thereafter, 13 pieces of Chinese shrapnel slammed into Grappo and knocked him out for 10 hours. When he came to, he crawled onto the frozen Chosin Reservoir in the direction of Hagaru-ri, where Marine sentries found him and took him to a hospital.

The remnants crept south. GIs encountered wounded soldiers along the road who had their arms outstretched for help, but there was no room for them all. A final roadblock was set up in Hudong-ni, and when the lead truck tried to run it, the driver was shot dead. The wounded spilled out onto the road. Two more trucks failed to get through, blocking the road completely. It was every man for himself. The able-bodied dragged as many wounded as they could across the frozen reservoir. The first survivors reached safety at 5:30 a.m. on December 2; others drifted in for the next three days. At the Marine perimeter, Lt. Col. Olin Beall of the 1st Motor Transport Battalion assembled a rescue team and headed out to pick up stragglers on make-shift sleds.

Among those left behind was Pvt. Ed Reeves, 18, of Joliet, Illinois. Mortar fragments crippled his legs the morning of November 28, and he and 25 seriously wounded comrades had been zipped into sleeping bags in the back of a deuce-and-a-half truck that had been disabled. Reeves witnessed a frightening scene. On December 1, Chinese soldiers came through and robbed helpless GIs of their rings and watches. Then they torched the trucks with Americans still inside. Reeves' truck was drained of its gas and wouldn't ignite, so a team of executioners climbed aboard to finish off the wounded. One started at the tailgate and moved toward the middle; a second Chinese concentrated on the other end. A shot was fired between the eyes of every American, who were unable to resist. Looking down the barrel of a Chinese rifle, Reeves hurriedly made amends with his Maker: "I talked to the Lord and asked for peace so I could die like a man. I sat there waiting to die. I found out you can still sweat when it's 35 degrees below zero." Reeves was blinded by the muzzle blast of a rifle, but somehow, the bullet fired from no more than three feet away produced just a scalp wound. Reeves was the only man in the truck who lived through the shootings, and he burrowed into his cover against the cold. Every time he tried to free himself from the truck, he fainted from the pain. He was trapped. Over the next three days, more Chinese looted the dead, stealing leather boots from GI corpses. Reeves was wearing shoe-pacs, which were not in demand, and he held himself stiff when the Chinese poked about. But on December 4, a Chinese soldier could tell by Reeves' body heat that he was still alive, and he was pitched from the truck onto the ground. Several Chinese soldiers beat him with their rifle butts and tossed him on a heap of dead bodies on the side of the road. "Jesus, here I come," Reeves uttered. But when his tormentors disappeared in the driving snow, Reeves snaked his way to a tree. In a desperate effort to stand up, he hugged the tree with his arms and pulled himself up three times. But each time he tried to walk on numb legs, he fell face first into the snow. "I realized I wasn't walking anywhere, so I told myself I had to crawl before I could walk," Reeves said. Using his elbows and knees to support him, Reeves crept toward the frozen reservoir and wondered why Chinese snipers didn't shoot. At first, he counted cadence learned in boot camp. Then he switched to melodies he learned in Sunday school: "Yes, Jesus loves me, the Bible tells me so..."

The morning of December 5, Pfc. Ralph Milton, a driver for Col. Beall and one of the "Ice Marines" who volunteered to search for stragglers, found Reeves near death. He was driven directly to the airstrip, where a C-47 whisked him to a hospital in Yongpo. Reeves was evacuated to Japan, where a doctor told attendants not to bother tending him because he had so little chance of making it. But after what he had been through, Reeves refused to quit. He was ultimately evacuated to the United States, but both feet and all the digits on his hands had to be amputated. Back home, Reeves married and raised seven children, who bore him 13 grandchildren. "I've been blessed. I came back. I raised by family in freedom. I guess the Lord didn't want me to die on that road," said Reeves, who was perhaps the last of the 350 GIs plucked off the ice by the Marines. In the wrecked trucks along the east shore road at Hudong, the Marines found 400 dead soldiers and not a single survivor.

Of the 2,500 men in Task Force Faith, only 1,050 made it back. Of the survivors, only 385 were able-bodied. Lt. Fred Brunt, who was in Beall's rescue party, said it was a pathetic sight. "Many were crying and hysterical. Some were sick and vomiting. Some had so many wounds you could hardly touch them. The Chinese would not shoot at the wounded on the ice, but they would shoot at us when we started toward them. We drew fire all the time and water would spurt three feet high when a bullet went through the ice. The men's hands were black with frostbite. Some had no shoes. The Chinese had taken them. Some of those able to walk were so dazed they didn't know where they were and just walked in circles. It makes you want to cry to see our people shot up like that,"

Brunt said. The battered battalions, however, did buy time for Hagaru-ri by tying up a Chinese division for five days.

Associated Press writer Charles Moore was among the war correspondents at Hagaru-ri. He interviewed survivors from their hospital cots, and filed this report:

NORTHEAST FRONT, Korea, Dec. 2 (AP)—Survivors of a Communist ambush said today that fanatical Chinese burned wounded American prisoners alive and danced around the flames "like wild Indians" while the GIs screamed in pain.

Other men of the U.S. 7th Infantry Division said the Chinese threw some wounded soldiers onto a highway and ran over them with halftracks, bayonetted others in the face and machine-gunned their flag of truce when they tried to surrender.

The 7th Division men made a bloody retreat down the east side of the Chosin Reservoir in northern Korea to Hagaru at the southern tip. From there, U.S.

Marines of the 1st Division head south over snow-crusted roads in convoy to break through the encircling Chinese. Their attack was successful when they met other Marines south of Koto-ri.

Marine and Air Force pilots in probably the greatest mercy flight in history flew 1,000 casualties to rear area hospitals.

One of the three survivors with whom I talked was Pfc. Benjamin Butler, 19, of Browns, Ill., of the 32nd Regiment. He said his group of trucks was attacked around midnight after it ran into a roadblock in the snow-covered hills.

"When some of our guys tried to surrender, the Chinese bayonetted them in the face," he said. "Others waved a flag trying to surrender and the Chinese opened up on them with submachine guns.

"After my ammunition was gone, I played dead in the truck. If a man was shot in the leg, they would shoot him again and again and kill him. They took most of the men's clothes and guns....

"They threw about 10 or more into a truck, some naked, some still alive, threw blankets and gasoline over them and set them afire. This bunch took off and we dragged some of them out of the fire."

Butler said while he was playing dead in a truck, a Chinese climbed in and stomped on his face—which showed bruises.

The other survivors with whom I talked were Pfc. Dayle Logan, 19, of Smithers, W.Va., and Pfc. Jackie Brooks, 18, of Richmond, Va., both of the 31st Regiment.

The soldiers, interviewed separately, said the Chinese also bayonetted their own wounded.

Brooks said he was riding as guard on a truck loaded with litter patients.

"We had fought through three roadblocks," he said. "Some trucks made it and some didn't. Just after midnight, the trucks ahead of us were shot up and blocked the road. The Chinks started down out of the hills blowing trumpets and whistles.

"Most of them had Thompson submachineguns. A few had .30 caliber carbines with bayonets. The guy in the next truck had a .50-caliber machine gun and I had an M-1 rifle. They killed the machine gunner with a grenade. I got down in the truck body and fired at them. I stayed there till almost dawn.

"They poured gasoline over the truckloads of wounded men and set them afire. I actually saw them do it to four trucks. There must have been about 40 men in each one. Some of them had already been killed by bullets.

"I could hear the men on the trucks screaming 'Help me.' I couldn't do anything. I was out of ammunition by then and there were Chinese between me and the nearest truck.

"They would pour gas on a truck and set it afire and run around it yelling like a bunch of wild Indians. I could see their faces in the light from the flames and they were all grinning and laughing.

Left: Smoke and flame rise from bombs and napalm as U.S. planes hit a Red concentration in the low hills and Marines prepare to move against the enemy.

"They turned over one truckload of wounded men and ran over several of them with halftracks."

A high-ranking intelligence officer, who talked to the survivors, called it "a story the American people ought to know."

The Marines broke out of Yudam-ni on December 1, in one of the trickiest military maneuvers possible—a withdrawal under fire. Gen. Smith's plan for the 1st Marine Division was to pull back like a contracting telescope all the way to the Sea of Japan—78 miles away from the farthest outposts. Gen. Almond of X Corps told the Marines: "Don't worry about your equipment. Once you get back, we'll replace it all." But Smith vowed to bring back every jeep, truck, tank and tracked vehicle he had. "This is the equipment we fight with," Smith told his Army commander. The Marines also lived up to tradition; they insisted on bringing back their wounded and their dead, which were stacked like cordwood and lashed onto vehicles.

The leading edge of the column back to Hagaru-ri was the 3rd Battalion, 5th Marines, commanded by Col. Robert Taplett. Two-and-a-half months earlier, the battalion was the first ashore at Wolmi-do during the Inchon invasion. When Taplett got his new assignment, he sought the Catholic sacrament of confession with Chaplain Bernie Hickey. "For your penance, when the going gets tough on that hill, you make the sign of the cross and say, 'Not my will but Thy will be done.' And you'll be successful," the priest told him. The Chinese held long stretches of the main supply route, and they stuck to their tactics of surrounding the Marines. That meant the leathernecks had to fight for every foot of ground, and some compared the ferocity of the fighting to Iwo Jima. But the Chinese deployment worked to the Marines' advantage. "If the Chinese had concentrated their troops at the point of exit, we could never have gotten out of the trap. By trying to keep us constantly encircled, they dispersed their strength," said Col. Ray Murray of the 5th Marines. Bone-chilling temperatures were a separate enemy from the Chinese, and a new invention appeared on the battlefield. It was the warming tent, a wrap of olive drab canvas that housed space heaters. And every few hours, men could come in from the front lines and restore feeling to their numbed bodies.

Four rifle companies of the 7th Marines swooped up the hills off the road and dispersed the Chinese from the heights. Into a biting wind, the riflemen headed for Toktong Pass to relieve Fox Company still holding Fox Hill in a death grip. The four companies assigned to relieve the embattled defenders on Fox Hill at the Toktong Pass were under the leadership of

Two armored artillery pieces of the 3rd Army Division cover the retreat of Marines in their breakout from the Chosin Reservoir.

the bright, tough battalion commander Lt. Col. Raymond G. Davis, who later rose to rank of four-star general and served as commandant of the Marine Corps. For the cross-country assault, each man had to pack four meals, an extra canteen of water, extra ammunition and a mortar shell. An individual load was 120 pounds of gear, a weighty haul under the best of conditions but a backbreaking amount for these gloomy hills. All they had to do was traverse imposing terrain at night, supplied with only the stuff they could carry, to relieve their embattled remnants and hold a road open so two regiments could escape a trap. At 7 p.m. on November 30, with the tempera-

ture at minus-24, the Marines moved out. To guide them, Davis plotted an azimuth on his compass, which he checked periodically. "It was numbing cold. There were some old pits the Chinese had dug, and to be sure we were going in the right direction, I would get down in them...and recheck my orientation with a compass. I remember twice crawling down, my poncho over my head, with a flashlight, getting my map oriented to check out the direction. I would fix my hand for a marker, turn the light out, and lift off the poncho and get out to check the direction, and I

Right: Retreat from Chosin Reservoir

Nov. 27, 8:10am: Marines attempt to take the high ground at Yudam-ni. By Nov. 28 Yudam-ni, Hagaru-ri and Koto-ri are beseiged by the Chinese.

Nov. 30: X Corps order a withdrawal to Hagaru-ri. By Dec. 1 the Marines break out of Yudam-ni and plan to pull out to the Sea of Japan (78 miles away).

Nov. 27 1st Bat. of 32nd Reg. is surrounded.

Dec. 1st: Task Force "Faith" (3rd Bat. of 31st Reg.) suffers 600 casualties and starts a withdrawal to Hagaru-ri.

Dec. 2, 5:30 a.m.: First survivors of Task Force "Faith" reach safety by crossing Chosin Reservoir. Others drift in for next 2 days. Out of 2,500 men only 1,050 made it back.

December 4: The last of X Corp's rear guard reach Hagaru-ri.

December 6: Marines begin attack south.

Dec. 7th: By midnight last of rear guard reach Koto-ri A mass grave is dug for 117 dead Americans and Britons.

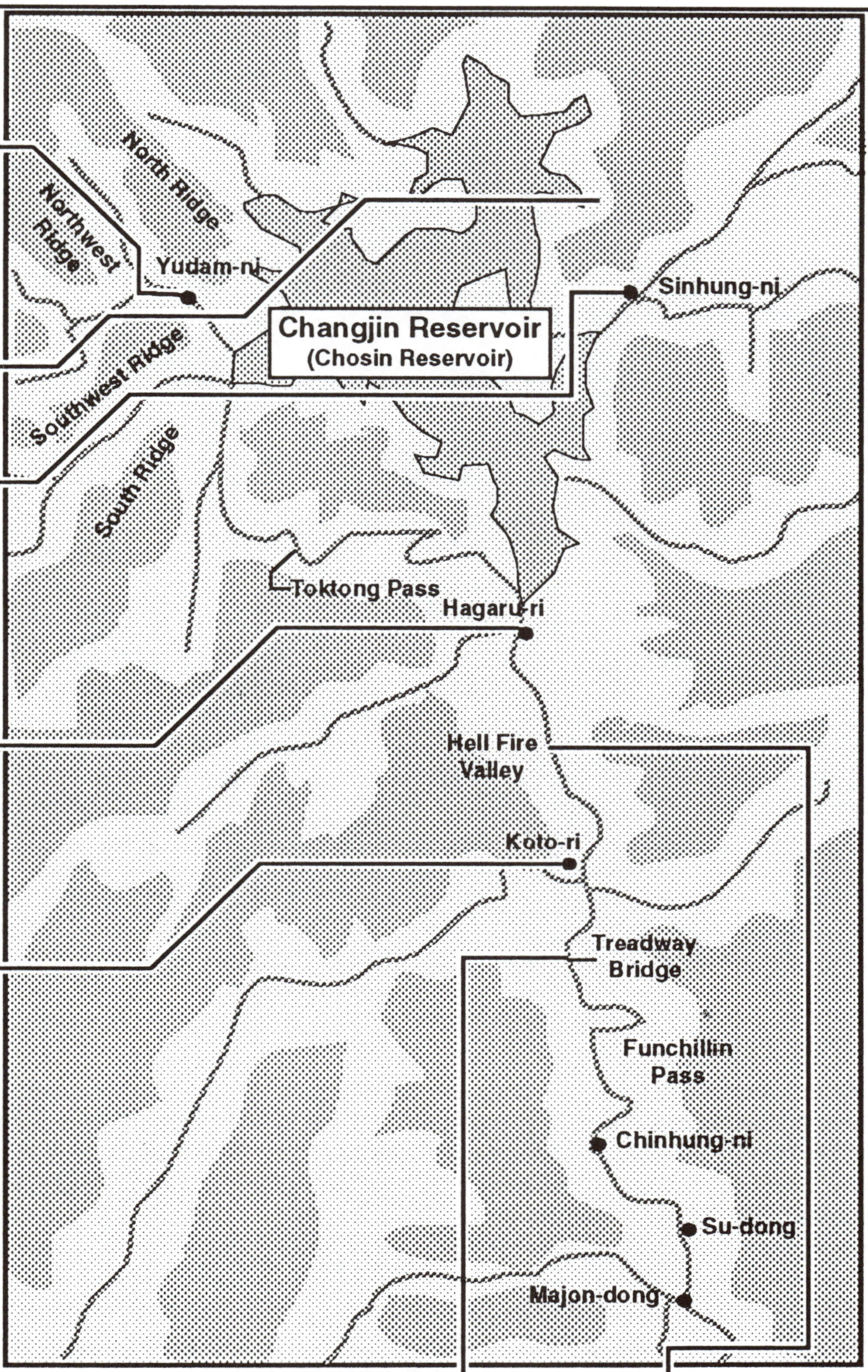

North Ridge

Northwest Ridge

Yudam-ni

Southwest Ridge

South Ridge

Sinhung-ni

Changjin Reservoir (Chosin Reservoir)

Toktong Pass

Hagaru-ri

Hell Fire Valley

Koto-ri

Treadway Bridge

Funchillin Pass

Chinhung-ni

Su-dong

Majon-dong

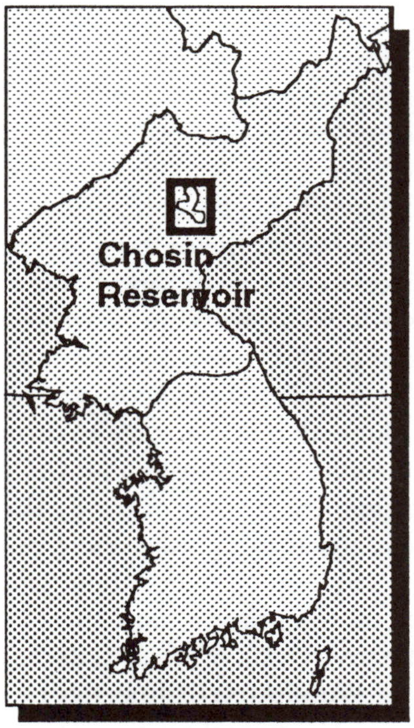

Chosin Reservoir

Treadway Bridge

A section of an existing apron bridge on the road to Chinhung-ni is blown up by the Chinese. Army Engineers construct eight sections of a treadway bridge which are dropped by planes attached to the world's largest parachutes. Six sections make it and are enough to do the job.

Hell Fire Valley

Nov 29: Task Force "Drysdale" moves from Koto-ri to Hagaru-ri. After an ambush 61 British commandos, most of an Army company and Marines from a headquaters div. are stranded in Hell Fire Valley. By 4:30 a.m. they surrender.

A patrol of the Army's 3rd Division sent to rescue a convoy under fire is pinned down itself by Chinese in northeast Korea.

wouldn't remember what had happened down there under that poncho. I'd get up and just stand there in a daze. Two or three people standing around would have a few words to say, and by that time I had forgotten what it was I was trying to do. I'd have to go down and do this thing all over again. Everybody had to repeat back to you two or three times to be sure of what was supposed to happen. We were just absolutely numb in the cold," said Davis, who was awarded the Medal of Honor for his actions. Marines slicked hair oil, called Wild Root cream oil, on their cold steel weapons. As a field expedient, when the actions on the Browning automatic rifles froze shut, the men in their fighting holes would urinate on the metal. But even that would freeze hours into the night.

Of the 240 men in Fox Company, 26 were killed and 89 were wounded keeping the Chinese at bay. Taplett's battalion reached the Toktong Pass on December 3. Six inches of new snow provided an eerie

serenity while the Marines smashed a Chinese roadblock. All during the march, Marine Corsairs from aircraft carriers in the Sea of Japan prowled the skies and attacked Chinese strongpoints. It took 79 hours to cover the 14 bloodstained miles to Hagaru-ri, but the last of the rear guard entered the outpost at 2 p.m. on December 4. Reduced to rations of candy bars and biscuits, men had the look of walking scarecrows; mufflers wrapped around their raw faces left only the tiniest slits to see through. But the four companies of the 7th Marines who slogged cross country to protect the column added some verve to the moment. Calling themselves the Ridgerunners of Toktong, these bearded and dauntless fighters dressed their ranks smartly and marched into the village, their heavy boots beating cadence on the granite-hard turf. "The garrison defending the town took off their hats," said Pfc. Edward Phillips of Woodbury, Connecticut.

The Marines trucked 1,500 casualties into Hagaru-

A Chinese roadblock bottles up Marines on an icy trail after the Chinese drove across the Yalu River.

ri. The wounded stacked up outside unheated medical tents; they were laid on straw and covered with tarpaulin. At 30 degrees below zero, blood froze on wounds before it could coagulate. Plasma was useless because it froze in its tubes. Corpsmen placed ampules of morphine in their mouths to keep them thawed. What care they could give was crude. Medics could not apply bandages if they worked with gloves; they sometimes dipped their fingers into the blood of patients to keep them warm. There were so many frostbite cases that they weren't considered battlefield injuries. "The only way you could tell the dead from the living was whether their eyes moved. They were all frozen stiff as boards," said Navy Capt. Eugene Hering, the division surgeon. In five days, twin-engine C-47s evacuated 4,312 wounded via the primitive 3,200-foot airstrip.

The Air Force offered to evacuate Gen. Smith's entire command, with the proviso that the Marines abandon their vehicles and heavy equipment. Smith elected to fight his way out of the trap. "We're going to break out over the road. We'll need every able-bodied man for the fight. We intend to leave behind no equipment we can salvage," Smith said.

By now, war correspondents gathered to chronicle the saga. Smith admonished them for using the word *retreat* and carved his way into Marine Corps legend. "We are not retreating. We are merely attacking in another direction," Smith said.

Ray Murray of the 5th Marines had a similar message for his exhausted officers. "We're coming out of this as Marines, not as stragglers. We're going to bring out our wounded and equipment. We're coming out, I tell you, as Marines, or not at all. This is no retreat," Murray said.

Gen. Almond arrived to present Silver Stars to Smith, Murray, Homer Litzenberg of the 7th Marines and Col. Beall, the man who had led the effort to

A Marine Corsair fighter (center) zooms skyward after dropping napalm (right) on an enemy position.

rescue the remnants of Task Force Faith. Smith noted that the X Corps commander had tears in his eyes. "I don't know what he was weeping about. Whether from the cold or emotion, or what," the Marine general said.

An awesome array of air power was assembled to cover the breakout from Hagaru-ri to Koto-ri. Every available land-based fighter and bomber in Korea and Japan was on call. The U.S. Navy had seven aircraft carriers off the coast in the Sea of Japan—*Leyte, Valley Forge, Philippine Sea, Princeton, Sicili, Baedong Strait* and *Bataan*. The flattops worked in miserable weather, launching planes off icy decks into vicious winds.

After two days of striking tents and packing gear, the attack south began at 6:30 a.m. on a frosty December 6—the day after Pyongyang was abandoned in

Back from patrol, Marines set up shelters near Koto-ri on the road back from the Chosin Reservoir.

the west. The 2nd Battalion of the 7th Marines was in the lead, buttressed by the 385 GIs from Task Force Faith. A tank-led vanguard rumbled along the lone road, while infantry climbed the hills and ridges on either side and a close-in company provided security in the rear. The formation was a moving hedgehog with guns firing in every direction. Almost immediately, the Chinese opened up with mortars and machine guns. By 10 o'clock that night, the column had traversed 8,000 yards and crept into Hell Fire Valley, where the remains of Task Force Drysdale were junked. The Chinese had prepared an ambush that stalled movement for two hours; a tank cleared the way by blasting the final machine gun nest. Air cover was so precise that planes buzzed overhead through the night; even in the dark, night-fighting Corsairs dropped deadly loads just 30 yards in front of the Marines. During one Chinese attack at daybreak on December 7, howitzers were unlimbered to fire direct at swarms ranging from 500 yards to 40 yards. Of 500 Chinese attackers, only 50 survived. As terrible as the cold was for the Americans, the Chinese suffered even more in their canvas sneakers. Many froze to death in their foxholes; others, nearly comatose, wandered into American lines with their black, frostbitten hands frozen to their rifles.

By 10 a.m. on December 7, no Marines were left in Hagaru-ri except for demolition teams and the rear guard. By midnight, the last of them had covered the 12 miles to Koto-ri perimeter. The entire operation took 38 tortuous hours, but 9,000 Marines, 800 soldiers, 125 British Commandos and 40 South Korean police had escorted 1,000 vehicles another step toward survival. Inside the Koto-ri perimeter were 2,500 members of the 1st Marine Regiment and 1,500 GIs from the Army's 7th Division, giving Gen. Smith a total force of 14,000 for the final leg of the trip.

One night, while checking his men on the perimeter, Col. Chesty Puller came across Sgt. Bob Cornley, who had served with Puller in the steamy jungles of Guadalcanal. From out of nowhere, the colonel produced a drink of Old Grand Dad whiskey. "It was like something from heaven, not just a drink of tanglefoot. You can't know what that did for a freezing man who'd been up there six hours without relief, watching, watching. He knew when a little nip could save a fellow from going mad or becoming a casualty," Cornley said.

Once again, the Air Force worked miracles to evacuate the wounded. One C-47 managed to land in a snowstorm on a 1,750-foot airstrip to haul 19 men out; others were loaded onto smaller liaison planes and old torpedo bombers pressed into service as fly-ing ambulances. If the Chinese holding the snow-shrouded peaks had artillery, the base might have been obliterated. But their horse-drawn cannons were back at the Yalu River.

Reluctantly, a mass grave was blasted out of the rock-hard ground with explosions. The frozen corpses of 117 Americans and Britons were buried. The 23rd Psalm, "Yea, though I walk through the valley of the shadow of death..." was heard above the howling gusts. The location was marked and mapped in case United Nations forces ever returned.

Spirits were heartened as firepower was concentrated, but there was no time to rest. The base at Chinhung-ri was 10 miles to the south, and the first Marines exited Koto-ri on the morning of December 8. The 3rd Battalion of the 7th Marines led the way, but ran into a Chinese roadblock just 2,000 yards from the starting blocks. Regimental commander Homer Litzenberg suggested that a third company be used to take a hill. "All three companies are up there—50 from George, 50 from How, 30 from Item. That's it," said Maj. Warren Morris. The battalion had been reduced to less than the normal compliment of a single rifle company. Still, the block was removed and the procession fought its way south.

The morning of December 9 dawned clear and bright—but still brutally cold. David Douglas Duncan, a former Marine and a photographer with *Life* magazine, came across a leatherneck attempting to eat a can of beans for breakfast. The C-ration was crystallized ice, and this husk of a man picked and picked to prod one bean onto his spoon. "If I were God and could give you anything you wanted, what would you ask for?" Duncan inquired. The beleaguered Marine went back to his meager meal, then answered: "Gimme tomorrow." All that mattered was one more day, one more night, one more step down the road.

In addition to hills filled with Chinese, two major obstacles had to be overcome on the final leg back. Three-and-a-half miles south of Koto-ri was an apron bridge spanning a 1,500-foot deep gorge where the Japanese had built a hydroelectric system carrying water to turbines in the valley below. The Chinese had blown a 16-foot gap in the bridge. And since there was no way to bypass it, the Chinese figured the trapped Marines would be forced to abandon their equipment. But engineers came up with a solution that had never been done before. Using parachutes,

Right: Trudging through deep snow, Marines carry a wounded comrade to safety near Koto-ri, North Korea, part of the battle to Hungnam.

Puerto Rican soldiers of the 65th Regiment, Third Infantry, set up a machine gun and firing line after withdrawing from Oro-ri, which is burning in the background. The soldiers blew up the bridge (right) after using it to cross the river.

they would drop a new bridge from C-119 Flying Boxcars. A December 6 test drop in Japan was a failure, so experts ordered larger parachutes. There was no time to test them again. Eight sections of a treadway bridge—each six feet long and weighing 2,500 pounds—were attached to the largest parachutes in the world and dropped from 800 feet. One section

landed in Chinese hands and one was mangled when it hit the ground, but the remaining six were enough to do the job. A treadway of two steel beams supported the treads of a tracked vehicle, such as a tank or self-propelled gun. The beams had a 50-ton capacity; the wood placed between the treads had a 20-ton capacity. When the beams were set, the bridge came

Marine Pfc. Clarence Godeard of Osage, Oklahoma, has bound his feet in canvas against the cold. He was one of the thousands who fought their way out of a Chinese trap at the Chosin Reservoir.

up five feet short. Chinese prisoners were used to fill the gap with cross ties and debris. By noon on December 7, repair work started on the chasm and was completed in two days. The procession from Koto-ri arrived at 3:30 p.m. on December 9, but disaster threatened to undo all the hard work. The first vehicle—a tractor towing an earth-mover—broke through the bridge's plywood center and blocked the way. An expert driver, Tech. Sgt. Wilfred Prosser, safely backed it off. Now came the tricky solution. If the two treadways of the new bridge were spaced apart at their maximum width of 136 inches, Marine tanks could clear it with two inches to spare. The inboard edges of the treadways were 45 inches apart, which provided jeeps with one-half inch of clearance. Guided by road guards holding flashlights, the first jeep crossed in the dark. A bumper-to-bumper parade of trucks, tanks, and half-tracks inched ahead.

The second problem was a hairpin turn called the Funchilin Pass south of the bridge. A key height had to be cleared to protect the withdrawal; otherwise, the Chinese could fire at will at the convoys. The security job fell to Able Company of the 1st Marines. During a below-zero blizzard, the unit moved north from Chinhung-ni with 223 men; it was reduced to 111 able-bodied men by the time the Chinese were evicted from the Big Hill on December 9. They counted 530 dead Chinese on the mountain. The final knob was taken with mortars and the help of four Corsairs.

Of course, there's always the unexpected. About 2,000 yards north of the bridge, the brakes locked on a tank in the rear vanguard, trapping eight other tanks with it. A 28-man reconnaissance platoon commanded by Lt. Ernest Hargett protected the tanks as a mob of refugees straggled behind. From the crowd, five Chinese emerged to surrender, but the lead man stepped aside and his four comrades fired burp guns. Har-

Demolition teams take out the Songchon River bridge at Hamhung as U.N. troops pull out of the northeastern Korean industrial city.

The rear guard, the men of 65th Regiment, 3rd Division use ox-carts to carry equipment as they move into Hungnam from the hills. The smoke is from a village they left behind, burning everything that might be useful to the enemy.

A vanguard of Marines 20 miles north of Hamhung rolls over the plains. Behind them are the mountains fought through for 12 days in their retreat from the Chosin Reservoir.

gett's carbine had frozen, so he swung the rifle like a club. Cpl. George Amyotte opened up with his Browning automatic rifle, but the last tank and its crew were slain before the attackers were killed. A grenade exploded on Amyotte's back, but he was spared by a new invention of war—a vest of body armor made from fiberglass. Finally, a crew freed the disabled tank and two were able to move forward; the rest were lost or abandoned. When the last tank crossed the bridge and all Americans were thought to be across, explo-

Above: The X Corps pulls out of Hamhung, moving to the harbor for evacuation, as Sgt. 1/C John Moore of Eufaula, Alabama, Cpl. Billy J. Dupriest of Dallas, and Pfc. John A. Sapp Jr. of Reynolds, North Carolina, lower flags of the U.S., U.N., and South Korea.

Below: Landing craft nose ashore to help with the Hungnam evacuation.

Right: A victory ship waits to onload military equipment in the foreground at Hungnam.

sives reduced the makeshift span to rubble. There was one man left. During the final firefight, Pfc. Robert DeMott was blown over the side of the road by a satchel charge. When he regained consciousness, he mixed in with the refugees and started walking. The hydroelectric plant had a walkway for pedestrians, and DeMott—the last American—shuffled out. There had been 1,000 casualties on the final leg of the breakout. When the procession got through the Funchilin Pass, Gordon Greene counted only 18 men left in his 64-man platoon that had been guarding the road. "I feel that I've gone through hell and come out alive," Greene said. By 11:30 p.m. on December 11, the last vehicles had reached Chinhung-ri, where the Army's 3rd Division guarded an assembly point for the ride to Hungnam and the sea. Marines and soldiers snuggled onto any available space of tanks and trucks, giving them the appearance of ants on a sugarcube.

Above: A tank is swung aboard a ship as evacuation of Hungnam harbor gets underway.

Below: North Korean women stevedores march to work to help load up freighters for the evacuation of Hungnam.

Col. Puller yelled at every unit that crossed the bridge: "Don't forget that you're 1st Marines. Not all the communists in hell can overrun you."

Associated Press writer Jack MacBeth was part of the final march from Koto-ri. He filed this report:

WITH U.S. MARINES, Korea (AP)—American Marines walked out of 13 days of freezing hell today, full of fight after a gory nightmare of death in Korea's icy mountains.

The U.S. 1st Marine Division was rolling slowly into the northeastern Korea plains of Hamhung. The men's eyes and bearded faces, their tattered parkas and the strangely careless way they carried their rifles, showed the strain.

These thousands of leathernecks did it on guts. They turned their encirclement into one of the fightingest retreats in military history. It was the longest pullback in Marine records—50 tortuous miles.

They broke out of a death trap sprung by many thousands of Red Chinese and Koreans that converted what looked like certain disaster into a moral triumph if not a military victory.

I watched the retreat.

The story began in the flea-bitten village of Yudam, on the western edge of the Chosin Reservoir.

Three Red Chinese divisions and one Chinese regiment attacked two Marine regiments in a surprise offensive the night of Nov. 28.

The pressure was overwhelming. The Marines struck right back.

When orders were given to pull back, the leather-

necks responded—with an offensive.

For five hectic, heroic days, they matched guts and wits against Chinese mass tactics. Neither was enough to win. They had to pull out.

Five days after leaving Yudam, the Marines reached Hagaru, at the south end of the reservoir. Then they joined another small group that was encircled by strong enemy forces.

At daybreak, Dec. 6, the Hagaru Marines jumped off southward toward Koto.

For 24 hours, they fought one of the bloodiest battles of the Korean war.

I was in Koto when they came in. It was a gruesome sight—wounded men with their blood frozen to their skins; their clothes stiff with ice; grotesque dead men lying across trailers and stretchers; live men stumbling along, grimacing from frostbite, using their rifles as crutches.

The dead count is high. Two days ago, I watched nearly 200 bodies nosed into a single grave by a bulldozer. There was no time for more elaborate arrangements.

For the record, the U.S. 1st Marine Division, one of the country's finest, has suffered heavily. The communist enemy knows this.

The leathernecks inflicted casualties on the enemy many times those suffered. The weather also took a heavy toll on the Chinese.

Tension greeted the order for all the Marines to break from Koto.

One senior officer wept.

A grizzled Marine blurted, "These kids are too good to have this happen to them."

Saturday at sunrise, patrols struck out from Koto.

Intelligence reports had said the enemy was in this area in strength. There were fears another bloodbath was in store similar to that on the Hagaru-Koto road earlier.

But the patrols reached their objectives on schedule. One suffered moderate casualties, the other made it almost without incident. Immediately after these groups had left, the vehicular columns began to move. Equipment considered more of a burden than its actual value was destroyed.

By noon, the column was stretched about two miles south of Koto.

Dismal little Koto lies on a plateau 3,500 feet above sea level. For two miles south, the narrow road, if anything, went up. Then it twisted down a narrow gorge 12 miles to the valley below. It was covered with ice. The temperature was 25 degrees below zero.

For four hours, the column stood motionless. A bridge had been blown by the Reds.

Before the engineers could work on it, a company of Marines had to drive off a pocket of Chinese guarding it. This was done.

Then the column started to roll, but road conditions made progress slow. By nightfall Saturday, some 100 vehicles had moved across the new bridge.

The entire operation depended on the effectiveness of this bridge. There was no possibility of a bypass. One side was a rugged cliff, on the other a chasm.

Their backs to the sea, the crew of a quadruple .50 caliber unit scans the sky over Hungnam as the evacuation fleet stands offshore.

Throughout the night, there was sniping from the hills overlooking the winding road.

Shortly after midnight, the column came to a halt. It didn't move appreciably for four hours. Two miles south of the bridge, at a hairpin turn, two trucks skidded and blocked the road. About 100 husky Marines shoved them out of the way.

There was only starlight and brief flashes of brilliance as shells hit the towering hills around us.

Four Marines on the truck I was riding huddled in blankets. All chewed gum and spoke occasionally in soft tones. They knew they dared not sleep. A machinegun was mounted on the back of the truck, but was not needed.

These kids mainly had two thoughts uppermost in their minds: their families and their determination to whip the enemy.

"I'm still carrying a small hunk of steel in my ankle," said one. "When I get home, that will make me think of this damned place."

The column, stretching bumper to bumper all the way up the road, moved in fits and starts.

Just before daylight, the mountain grade became less severe and the turns less harrowing. We were nearing the bottom.

For some reason, I thought at this point of the

The evacuation fleet being loaded at Hungnam harbor during the evacuation of the beachhead.

Barrels of petroleum are loaded aboard ship to deny them to the advancing Chinese.

dramatic 1st Cavalry Division sweep which I had accompanied across country toward Seoul in victory-flush September. The contrasts of this now-successful retreat quickly dispelled such pleasant reminiscences.

One of the Marines on the truck had a Korean pup. The dog had been whining through most of the night. As the full light of day appeared, the pup got up, stretched a bit and wagged its tail. The pup's cheerfulness appeared to have been caught from his leatherneck companions for whom nearly two weeks of concentrated hell had just ended. The Marines rubbed their sleepless red eyes and grinned.

When the ordeal of Chosin was behind them, the Marines sang an irreverent and prescient parody of the old British marching tune "Bless 'Em All." The survivors substituted a four-letter word for bless:

Bless 'em all, bless 'em all,
The Commies, the U.S. and all;
Those slant-eyed Chink soldiers struck Hagaru-ri

"And now know the meaning of U.S.M.C.
But we're saying goodbye to them all,
We're Harry's police force on call.
"So put back your pack on,
The next stop is Saigon,
Cheer up, me lads, bless 'em all.

Of the 25,000 troops engaged in the Chosin Reservoir campaign, 6,000 were killed, wounded or captured. At least 6,000 others suffered from frostbite. During the 13-day battle, the 1st Marine Division had 718 dead, 192 missing and 3,508 wounded, not counting their thousands of frostbite cases. By comparison, in the bloodiest Marine battle in World War II, the 1st Marine Division lost 985 dead and 2,183 wounded at Tarawa in November of 1943. After Chosin, President Truman awarded a Presidential Unit Citation that read: "The 1st Marine Division Reinforced emerged from its ordeal as a fighting unit with its wounded,

Americans wade out to landing craft, one followed by his dog at Hungnam beach. In two weeks, 105,000 troops, 100,000 civilians, 17,500 vehicles and 350,000 tons of supplies were shipped out.

with its guns and equipment and with its prisoners, decisively defeating seven enemy divisions, together with elements of three others."

History records it as a defeat because X Corps was forced from the battlefield. "It had some of the aspects of Bataan, some of Anzio, some of Dunkirk, some of Valley Forge, some of the Retreat of the 10,000 as described in Xenophon's Anabasis....It was defeat—the worst the United States ever suffered," *Time* magazine said. Thirty-three years later, Marine veterans formed a last-man organization called the Chosin Few. Its charter reads: "Whatever we were in that frozen long-ago and whatever we are now, we are bound as one for life in an exclusive fraternity of honor. The only way into our ranks is to have paid the dues of duty, sacrifice and valor by being there. The cost of joining, in short, is beyond all earthly

wealth." And don't tell a Marine about defeat. "Everyone who got out saw it as a victory because we weren't supposed to get out," said Jack Hessman, a Navy corpsman and one of the founders of the Chosin Few.

Chinese losses were much more severe. According to Marine records, there were 25,000 Chinese killed and 12,500 wounded. The Army inflicted 5,000 more casualties. Another 30,000 Chinese were frostbitten, putting the total casualties for battle and weather at 60 percent of the 120,000 men engaged. When liaison officer Col. Wong Lichan drove from Kanggye through the battle area to Chinghung-ni, he was puzzled by snowmen dotting the bleak landscape. Who would build snowmen in pairs and clusters in such a forbidding place? Then he realized they were his own soldiers, thousands of them. Entire platoons per-

A landing craft jammed with U.N. troops heads for ships waiting offshore.

ished in place. Lifeless soldiers sheathed in show squatted with rifles on their shoulders, and kitbags on their backs, on this ghostly freezing ground.

At Hungnam, with the Navy conducting a Dunkirk-style operation, the Marines were loaded onto ships and sailed away by December 15. The last of the Army troops were pulled off on December 24. In all, the Navy removed 105,000 troops and 91,000 suffering refugees, most of whom expected to be killed by Chinese or North Korea troops if they stayed

behind. Ships also carted off 350,000 tons of stores and 17,500 vehicles. Still, mountains of stockpiles and ammunition left on shore—including 400 tons of frozen dynamite thought to be too unstable to move and 500 1,000-pound bombs—were blown up by demolition teams. The explosions shook the earth and sea. "God help the taxpayers," said one officer aboard the last ships to leave on Christmas Eve. The shoreline was a smoking ruin. So was the "Home-by-Christmas" offensive.

Above: The last of the evacuees, troops of the 3rd Division wave and cheer on the deck of a landing craft as it pulls away from Hungnam beach, Christmas Eve 1950.

Right: Exploding ammunition and port facilities form a blast cloud as Navy demolition teams are the last to leave Hungnam.

Lt. Col. James Polk, one of MacArthur's intelligence officers, wrote his wife: "Well, when a gambler pulls one off he is hailed as a genius, and when he fails, he is a bum. This time (MacArthur) failed and he has to take the consequences of failure as I see it."

7

Ridgway Takes Charge

The deepest days of December 1950 were a turning point in the Korean War. A new ground commander was needed to replace Eighth Army's Walton Walker, who, like his mentor George Patton, was killed in a vehicle accident. Walker had presented a Silver Star to his son, Lt. Sam Walker, and was on his way to give an ROK Presidential Unit Citation to a British brigade. The general was killed when his jeep collided with a weapons carrier. (President Syngman Rhee ordered the South Korean truck driver put to death, but his sentence was commuted to three years in prison.) The 61-year-old Walker, who defended the Pusan perimeter by moving his combat units like the queen on a chessboard, was posthumously promoted to a four-star general.

Above: Lt. Gen. Matthew B. Ridgway, Eighth Army commander, inspects front line positions with Maj. James H. Lee of Dallas, Texas.

New Year's Eve Korean style. Mortars, machine guns, and recoilless weapons turn the sky into a fireworks display.

The new commander was a man for the moment— Lt. Gen. Matthew B. Ridgway, 55, the Army's deputy chief of staff who had commanded airborne troops at Normandy and in the Battle of the Bulge. One of the nation's finest combat officers in World War II, Ridgway was sipping a cocktail at the home of Washington friends when he got the call from J. Lawton Collins of the Joint Chiefs of Staff. "Matt, I'm sorry to tell you that Johnny Walker has been killed in a jeep accident in Korea. I want you to get your things together and get out there as soon as you can," Collins told him. Ridgway allowed his wife, Penny, to enjoy the evening, and didn't tell her until the next morning. Then Ridgway flew off to war. He landed in Tokyo at 11:30 p.m. on Christmas Day and met with Douglas MacArthur, who was Ridgway's superintendent at West Point. From the start, he thought aggressively.

"General, if I get over there and find the situation warrants, do I have your permission to attack?" Ridgway asked.

"Do what you think best, Matt. The Eighth Army is yours," MacArthur said.

The next day, Ridgway got his first look at Korea from a plane window. "The sight of this terrain was of little comfort to a soldier commanding a mechanized army. The granite peaks rose to 6,000 feet, the ridges were knife edged, the slopes steep, and the narrow valleys twisted and turned like snakes. The roads were trails, and the lower hills were covered with scrub oaks and stunted pines, fine cover for a single soldier who knew how to conceal himself. It was guerrilla country, an ideal battleground for the walking Chinese rifleman, but a miserable place for our road-bound troops who rode on wheels," Ridgway noted.

One of his first orders of business was to meet

President Rhee in Taegu. Tears formed in the president's eyes when Ridgway told him: "I'm glad to see you Mr. President, glad to be here, and I mean to stay."

In the field, Ridgway shivered in Pentagon-weight uniforms that were no match for the Korean cold. His first task was to win over his own forces—365,000 troops from various countries fighting under the United Nations banner. He visited with corps and division commanders, and he also listened to the gripes and bitches of his infantry. His first impressions were not good.

"There was too much of a looking-over-your-shoulder attitude, a lack of that special verve, that extra alertness and vigor that seemed to exude from an army that is sure of itself and bent on winning. This was a bewildered army, not sure of itself or its leaders,

Left: An exhausted U.N. soldier sleeps on the edge of a snow-covered road, his automatic rifle strapped to his back. Somewhere north of Seoul, January 1951.

Below: Evacuating Seoul, five American GIs carry a wounded comrade across Seoul Municipal Airport as buildings are set afire by engineers.

A tank trailing a long line of U.S. infantry crosses the Han River over a pontoon bridge in the retreat from Seoul. Later the bridge is blown.

not sure what they were doing there, wondering when they would hear the whistle of that homebound transport. There was obviously much to be done to restore this army to a fighting mood," Ridgway said. "I told the field commanders that their infantry ancestors would roll over in their graves if they could see how road-bound this army was, how often it forgot to seize the high ground along its route, how reluctant it was to get off its bloody wheels and put shoe leather to the earth, to get into the hills and among the scrub and meet the enemy where he lived."

Ridgway looked like a commander who meant business. He taped a hand grenade to the right strap

of his web gear, which was as distinctive as Patton's pistols. Because Ridgway also wore a first-aid kit strapped to his left strap, GIs nicknamed him "Iron Tits." Drawing from a morale boost he learned at the Battle of the Bulge, Ridgway carried extra winter gloves in his jeep to distribute to infantrymen. He tended to small details like getting stationery for a soldier who had no paper to write home. And he visited the Mobile Army Surgical Hospitals to comfort the wounded. "One replacement who has been wounded and comes back to his own unit, back with his own buddies—he's worth four of five of the men who have come 9,000 miles," Ridgway said. "To me,

Looking for information on enemy strength and positions, a patrol threads its way over snow-covered hills north of Seoul.

a basic element in troop leadership is the responsibility of the commander to be where the crisis of action is going to happen. He does not belong back at the command post." Once, when a heavily laden radioman marching to the front became stuck in the muck, Ridgway stooped down to tie the private's loose bootlaces. "Thanks, pal," the private said. Then he was startled to see the three stars on the general's shoulders. Higher ranks got the message too. Division commanders were told in no uncertain terms to learn the territory around their positions, whether it could support tanks or needed aggressive foot patrols. When an assistant chief of staff presented plans to withdraw Eighth Army to the old Pusan perimeter, Ridgway dismissed him on the spot.

The political realities of fighting a limited war

PENG TEH-HUAI

Peng Teh-huai, commander of the Chinese Peoples Volunteers, was a career soldier and long-time communist who had been a top lieutenant of Mao Tse-tung since the 1920s.

Known for his courage and shrewd tactics, Peng had led peasant uprisings against Chinese warlords, waged guerrilla struggles against the invading Japanese and defeated Chinese Nationals before entering the Korean War as the second-ranking general in the Communist Chinese army.

It was his unwavering devotion to the peoples' struggle as much as his military strategy that made him such a formidable fighter. Born into a peasant family in 1898, Peng was raised by a tyrannical grandmother after his mother died. Accused of a "lack of filial peity," he ran away from home at the age of 9. Peng reportedly angered his grandmother by kicking over her can of opium.

Peng worked as a cowherd, coal miner, shoemaker's apprentice, sodium miner and dike builder before he joined the army in 1918. He had led a band of hungry peasants in storming and sacking the house of a wealthy rice hoarder during a famine.

A graduate of the Hunan Military School, Peng was commissioned as an officer and commanded a regiment. Then in 1927, this burly captain broke ranks when Chiang Kai-shek tried to purge communist elements from the Nationalist Party, or Kuomintang.

Peng denounced the Kuomintang and joined the Communist Party, becoming one of the founders of the People's Liberation Army under Mao Tse-tung, who like Peng was born in Hunan Province. Peng's guerrilla band operated out of a traditional bandit hideout where the doctrine of people's war was born. Soldiers carried spears, swords and homemade grenades. Artillery was non-existent. But the army learned to fight by capitalizing on sheer force of numbers.

Peng led the vanguard of the Long March, the 6,000-mile communist retreat from central China to a northwest sanctuary in 1934-35. The trek to the impoverished cave city of Yenan became the Chinese communists's measure of a man's stoutness, and Peng—twice wounded in the march—was a hero. When the Japanese invaded China in 1937, the warring Communist and Nationalist factions temporarily set aside their own differences to fight a common foe. Peng was a deputy commander of the Eighth Route Army, which sent 100 regiments in guerrilla battles against Japan.

Following Japan's defeat in 1945, Peng was the communist spokesman on military matters when George C. Marshall visited in a vain attempt to seek a truce between China's warring factions.

And when the civil war raged anew in July of 1946, Peng was in command again. He scored a decisive victory over Chiang's U.S.-equipped forces in a battle south of Yenan in March 1948. His army fought first with equipment captured from the Japanese, then foraged for weapons from the beaten Nationalists.

With the communists in control of the mainland and Chiang's Nationals dispatched to Taiwan, Peng held political and party posts such as vice chairman, under Mao, of the People's Revolutionary Military Council and membership on the Central Government Council. He was in command of the First Field Army in northwest China when North Korea invaded the South. A man of medium height and a stocky build, Peng had a rough wit and preferred the spartan life of his soldiers. He was a big proponent of physical fitness and did not smoke or drink.

The major strength of the Chinese was an inexhaustible supply of infantry. But as a student of the an-

posed unique challenges for the army. Washington and London were coming to a consensus about stabilizing the lines along the 38th parallel and pursuing a settlement. There were still fears the Soviets hoped to get the Americans bogged down in Korea while they opened war in Europe. Nobody wanted World War III, and Europe, not Asia, was America's top priority. The Joint Chiefs of Staff told MacArthur to fight within the boundaries of Korea with the forces he had; no major re-inforcements were coming. "We believe that Korea is not the place to fight a major war. Further, we believe that we should not commit your remaining available ground forces to action against Chinese Communist forces in Korea in face of the increased threat of general war," the Joint Chiefs said in a December 29 cable.

In Tokyo, MacArthur grappled with the concept of limited war. He believed the cable suggested defeatism and seemed to indicate a loss of "the will to win." He responded with suggestions of his own: a blockade of China, increased bombing to destroy North Korean industry and the use of Nationalist Chinese forces from Taiwan to fight on the Chinese mainland. MacArthur openly wondered why the Chinese should have sanctuaries on its own territory, and he questioned the wisdom of expending American lives to achieve nothing more at the end than what existed at the beginning. Omar Bradley figured that MacArthur's belligerence stemmed from the battlefield defeats. "The only possible means left to MacArthur

cient strategist Sun-Tzu, who wrote "The Art of War," Peng noted: "Manpower alone will not win a war in Korea. Korea will be a battle of supply." Like his American counterparts, he knew that the farther an army got from its supply points in a peninsular war, the tougher it would be to deliver the "beans and bullets" of logistics. Almost three weeks after the Inchon invasion, Peng was summoned to a council of war held by the Central Committee. Peng slept on a rug instead of a luxurious spring bed while China's leaders debated getting involved in Korea.

Mao argued that 80 percent of Chinese industry was located in Manchuria, and he could not tolerate U.S. forces on the Chinese border. And Peng agreed with Mao's philosophy: "When a neighbor is in mortal danger, it is hard just to stand by and watch." Peng's thinking as the United Nations crossed the 38th parallel was: "Sooner or later the tiger devours the man; the timing only depends on the tiger's hunger." He believed China must resist and defend every inch of ground. "I came to the conclusion that sending aid and troops to North Korea was the correct, necessary and farsighted course of action, and that the situation was so serious we could not hesitate any longer," Peng wrote in memoirs published under his name in 1984. He

told the Central Committee: "If the fatherland suffers great destruction, it only means that our victory will be delayed by several years, as it was in the war of liberation."

The Chinese never declared war and insisted on calling its soldiers "volunteers" to prevent broadening the war to the mainland. In a triumph of ancient Chinese cunning over modern technology, Peng succeeded in moving a cotton-clad army undetected into North Korea. His army swept the United Nations forces from the banks of the Yalu River, but it failed to drive the U.N. forces into the sea. Later, when the United Nations counterattacked and beat the Chinese back across the 38th parallel, Peng organized the honeycomb of tunnels and defense in depth that discouraged renewed offensives. Far from home, Peng's soldiers dwelled in caves without the niceties of regular mail from home or plentiful rations. Peng represented China at the Panmunjom talks and signed the armistice for Mao. He was awarded medals and cheered as a hero by North Korea's Supreme People's Council.

But later years were not so kind to this war veteran. In 1954, Marshal Peng became China's minister of national defense and a member of the Communist Party's ruling Politburo. But in 1959, he quarreled bitterly with Mao over policies of the Great Leap Forward, an economic

plan that was doomed to fail. Mao's plan emphasized ideological purity over professional expertise, both in the military and in the economy. Mao wanted to industrialize peasant society and to form a vast network of rural communes. In a letter to the Central Committee, Peng called the plan unworkable. Peng also argued for modernization of the Chinese army based on the Soviet model, which conflicted with Mao's view of a people's army. Peng believed Mao was weakening the army and leading the country to disaster by not accepting Soviet aid.

After meeting secretly with Soviet leader Nikita Khrushchev, Peng was dismissed in a purge and his name was erased from Chinese history. During the Great Proletarian Cultural Revolution of 1966, Maoists accused their opponents of being supports of Peng. Sent to a labor camp and confined to an old village in Peking's western suburbs, Peng built sewers, collected manure and comforted the sick during his exile. He was tortured by Red Guards and died in disgrace November 29, 1974. However, in the odd quirks of revisionism, Peng was officially rehabilitated in 1978, two years after Mao died. Articles praising him appeared in Chinese newspapers in 1988, and four movies about his life and army career have been made in China.

Gen. Peng Teh-huai (left) during the Korean War. A veteran of the Long March and the Chinese Civil War, he used his extensive combat experience as one of China's leading commanders during the Korean War.

to regain his lost pride was now to inflict an overwhelming defeat on those Red Chinese generals who had made a fool of him," Bradley wrote.

The Chinese, meanwhile, had plans of their own. Flushed with success, the army—called the Chinese Communist Forces by the United Nations—entertained thoughts of a follow-up attack that would drive Eighth Army into the sea. Their commanders made the fateful decision to cross the 38th parallel, and the

The last tanks cross the Han River before the bridge is blown.

consequences were similar to what happened on the other side in October. "The imperialists will run like sheep. Our problem is not Seoul. It is Pusan. Not taking it—just walking there!" Gen. Peng Teh-huai said at a staff meeting just before the third phase of the Chinese offensive. Ridgway's first appraisal of the number of forces against him was a circle drawn on the map with the number 174,000 written in it; the Chinese actually had more than double that, includ-

ing the rehabilitated North Korean Peoples Army.

The Chinese attacked at 4:40 p.m. on December 31. Foot soldiers slopped lard on their legs and feet before

Right: Refugees heading for South Korea choke a narrow pass. An estimated half-million are herded into southwestern Korea to clear the Pohang-Pusan area for battle.

A train overflowing with refugees waits for a British Centurian tank to cross the tracks, all fleeing the Chinese army.

crossing the icy Imjin River. Holding the line on the left were the U.S. 25th Division, ROK 1st Division and British 29th Brigade of I Corps; in the center was the U.S. 1st Cavalry Division and 24th Division, the ROK 6th Division, the British Commonwealth Brigade and Greek and Philippine battalions of IX Corps. ROK units held the right flank, with X Corps rehabilitating in the south.

Across a 40-mile front, nine Chinese divisions bore down on Seoul. The brown-clad hordes were supported by artillery for the first time. Once again, the Chinese struck ROK forces first. Ridgway had ordered

a cohesive withdrawal to make the Chinese pay for every yard. What he witnessed were panicked ROK units streaming south.

"I'd never had such an experience before, and I pray to God I never witness such a spectacle again. They were coming down the road in trucks, the men standing, packed so close together in those big carriers that another small boy could not have found space among them. They had abandoned their heavy artillery, their machine guns—all their crew-served weapons. Only a few had kept their rifles. Their only thought was to get away, to put miles between them

After Seoul is abandoned, U.N. troops watch a pontoon bridge across the Han River burn to impede the advance of the Chinese. It only slowed them down.

and the fearful enemy that was at their heels," Ridgway said. He ordered American MPs to set up roadblocks to stop the flight, but he noted: "I might as well have tried to stop the flow of the Han...We were obviously a long way from building the will to fight that we needed."

Ridgway knew the ROKs must have rigorous training and resolute leaders. And he confronted President Rhee, saying the South Korean army would receive no more equipment or reserves until the incompetents were weeded out. "We aren't going to get anywhere with your army until we get some leadership," Ridgway told him.

"Do not be discouraged. They will fight again," Rhee promised. But it was too late to save Seoul. With the Chinese threatening to flank Eighth Army from the northeast, Rigdway ordered a general withdrawal of Seoul to begin on January 3, 1951. The city

had little military value—it was more advantageous to fight the communists on better ground to the south—but it had psychological weight. All over Korea, children were crying again. Associated Press correspondent Hal Boyle found an abandoned, forlorn child on the steps of city hall. "We just can't leave him here," Boyle told his media colleagues. The waif was bundled in heavy quilt and taken back to the Chosun Hotel for at least one night of warmth and safety. In another room of the same hotel, Ridgway left behind a pair of ripped pajamas with this message: "To the commanding general Chinese Communist Forces with the compliments of the commanding general Eighth Army." Once again, the bridges leading south across the Han River were bumper-to-bumper with military traffic. The Air Force again covered the withdrawal, averaging more than 500 sorties a day for the first five days of January. At dawn on January 5, the

A U.S. Air Force C-19, combat cargo plane, drops supplies to U.N. troops in the Wonju area.

red-starred flag of North Korea flew over Seoul. The capital had changed hands for the third time in less than six months. Stockpiles of supplies and ammunition were burned. Kimpo's airfield was abandoned, but not before 500,000 gallons of fuel and 23,000 gallons of napalm were destroyed.

What was branded into Ridgway's conscience was the refugees—who had fled south at the beginning of war, moved back with the U.N. success and escaped south again. Bewildered peasants hauled all their worldly possessions in brightly colored bundles or nudged their two-wheeled carts. On the last train south to Taegu, peasants clung to ladders, undersides, any available perch. "Off to the right and left of the

bridges was being enacted one of the great human tragedies of our times. In a zero wind that seared the face like a blowtorch, hundreds of thousands of Koreans were running, stumbling, falling, as they fled across the ice...Some pushed little two-wheeled carts piled high with goods and little children. Others prodded burdened oxen. Now and then an ox would go down, all four legs asprawl, and the river of humanity would break through and flow around him, for in this terrible flight no man stopped to help his neighbor...Without a sound, except the dry whisper of their slippers on the snow, and the deep pant of their hard-drawn breath, they moved in utter silence," Ridgway wrote.

Sticking to the roads, Eighth Army fell back 20 miles a day. The Chinese had oxen and ponies instead of trucks. They couldn't keep up with the withdrawal. In an attempt to stiffen South Korean units, the U.S. 2nd Division—battered in the last offensive—was dispatched to shore up the right shoulder of the right flank at Wonju, a critical rail and road center in central Korea. If the Chinese took Wonju, they felt they could march all the way to Pusan. They had sheer weight of numbers, but great clouds of artillery shells cascaded on them from 2nd Division positions south of Wonju. The town fell January 8, but the Chinese had

Setting up a mortar for action in Wonju are (sitting left) Pfc. John S. Hagen of Delavin, Wisconsin, and Cpl. James E. Helvey of Detroit. Passing ammunition to Hagen is Cpl. Frank G. Bickel (standing right) of Pittsburgh, Pennsylvania. Watching are Pvt. James J. Cowell (left) of Chicago and Sgt. Henry Sprenger of Fergus Falls, Minnesota.

Left: Temperatures as low as 21 degrees below zero don't stop these allied troops on their way to attack an enemy-held hill on the central Korean front.

fought themselves to a standstill. Their infantry waded through waste-deep snow in fields strewn with mines and booby traps. They stripped dead Americans of their boots and rations because their own supply lines were stretched to the limit. Logistics again was the Achilles heel of a communist advance.

The high tide was 45 miles south of Seoul at Pyongtaek. The Chinese had gone through Osan and its blazing airfield, and past the point where Task Force Smith put up the first American defense of Korea back in July 1950. On the map, the Chinese offensive gained 50 to 60 miles, but they had suffered 38,000 casualties.

"There is a marked absence of vaunted American resourcefulness," Ridgway had messaged Washington. "My one overriding problem, dominating all oth-

Heavily armed infantrymen on attack of an enemy hill on the Wonju front.

F-84 jets get a boost from JATO rockets as they lift off an airfield somewhere in Korea, bound for a strike against the Chinese at the port of Inchon.

ers, is to achieve the spiritual awakening of the latent capabilities of this command."

In these dismal days, the Joint Chiefs of Staff ruled out MacArthur's suggestions of extending the war to Chinese soil. Priority was given to saving the troops in the field, even if it meant having to abandon the peninsula. "Should it become evident that evacuation is essential to avoid severe losses of men and materiel, you will at that time withdraw from Korea to Japan," the Joint Chiefs cabled MacArthur.

It was a time of soul searching, and MacArthur messaged back for clarification of what the mission was now. "The troops are tired from a long and difficult campaign, embittered by the shameful propaganda which has falsely condemned their courage and fighting qualities in misunderstood retrograde maneuver, and their morale will become a serious threat to their battle efficiency unless the political basis upon which they are asked to trade life for time is clearly delineated, fully understood, and so impelling that the hazards of battle are cheerfully accepted," MacArthur said. "Is it the present objective of the United States political policy to maintain a military position in Korea—indefinitely, for a limited time, or to minimize losses by evacuation as soon as it can be accomplished? As I have pointed out before, under the extraordinary limitations and conditions

imposed upon the command in Korea, its military position is untenable, but it can hold for any length of time up to its complete destruction if overriding political considerations so dictate."

With Truman's approval, the Joint Chiefs replied that U.N. forces were to hold out and make the Chinese prove they could push them out. In effect, the ball was back in MacArthur's court. "It is important also to United States prestige worldwide, to the future of UN and NATO organizations, and to efforts to organize anti-communist resistance in Asia that Korea not be evacuated unless actually forced by military considerations, and that maximum practicable punishment be inflicted on communist aggressors," the Joint Chiefs said.

The mood at home reflected the feelings of the top brass. In January of 1951, a poll showed that 49 percent of Americans felt sending troops to Korea was a mistake, and 66 percent said the United States should abandon the peninsula.

Eighth Army had fallen back 275 miles in six weeks, and troops tried to regroup. Staff Sgt. W.B. Woodruff Jr. had joined Love Company of 25th Division's 35th Regiment on December 8 and had done nothing but withdraw. "I had seen no enemy, fired no round, and the company had sustained no casualty. I felt disgusted, ashamed and frustrated. Talk that Eighth Army was about to evacuate Korea was common; there was lots of speculation as to the port from which we would depart. My morale was at bottom," Woodruff said.

In a letter home to his mother in late January, Capt. Norman Allen, commander of Item Company in the 5th Cavalry Regiment, expressed what many soldiers were feeling. They were fighting for their lives, not some grand ideal. "Trying to convince us that we aren't just so much sacrificial cattle will be difficult to do. Let no one question our fighting heart, for there is no doubt if we go down it will not be without a nasty fight first. But if anyone is attempting to be idealistic, well—don't try our reason. It is nothing more than survival, sheer, base, common survival. This place holds no value now, military, political or idealistic. The only thing of value it holds for the men here is a 6x6x6 plot of burial ground and what future is that to look forward to?" wrote Allen. He was later wounded and 42 mortar fragments were removed from his legs, back and groin.

Ridgway moved to instill purpose into his troops. He composed a January 21 statement—entitled "Why Are We Here? What Are We Fighting For?"—that was to be read to every person assigned or attached to Eighth Army. "We are here because of the decisions

A heavy snowstorm cloaks an allied prowl force approaching Wonju. Tanks and white-clad infantry took the battered road and rail hub without opposition.

Above left: Infantry of the U.S. 24th Division move into rugged Korean hills on patrol.

Below left: Another patrol in strength probes north toward the enemy, but in the approaches to Seoul they didn't contact any heavy concentrations.

of the properly constituted authorities of our respective governments...The issue now joined right here in Korea is whether communism or individual freedom shall prevail; whether the fight of fear-driven people we have witnessed here shall be checked, or shall at some future time, however distant, engulf our own loved ones in all its misery and despair. You will have my utmost. I shall expect yours."

Now the ground war reversed once more. Ridgway had made a difference, but there were practical reasons for the turnaround. Eighth Army had a narrower front to defend. The terrain favored the defenders because Korea's mountain spine sloped to the east, opening up flat farmlands better suited to tanks and artillery. With X Corps integrated into Eighth Army, Ridgway had the use of three additional combat divisions. This was a war machine that started hitting on all cylinders. Its supply lines were shorter, and troops were getting everything they needed. And the Chinese punch was gone. They were lightly equipped, far from home and poorly supplied. There was a rhythm to the Chinese attacks; they lost steam after the first few days because troops exhausted the supplies they carried and there was no way to replenish stocks. If troops fought in disciplined fashion until superior firepower could be brought to bear, the Chinese would be caught in a war of attrition they would be unable to sustain. In effect, Eighth Army had put up a wall and let the communists wear themselves out on it. In the trenches, the technique became known as the meat grinder.

Little had been known about Chinese strength and their intentions, so Ridgway ordered a reconnaissance in force. It discovered a soft front, because the Chinese preferred to withdraw to replenish supplies rather than stand in place and be vulnerable to air attacks. Launched on January 15, it was called Operation Wolfhound, after the name of John Michaelis' 27th Regiment. The operation involved seven infantry

The China Photo Service released this picture with the caption saying it is "an American plane shot down by the Korean People's Army."

Page 176: American GIs man a high wall surrounding the ancient city of Suwon after taking it from Chinese forces. Sgt. Charles F. Robbs, Jr., of Chattanooga, Tennessee, (closest to camera), was one of the first into the town.

Page 177: Marines line a ridge in firefight with communist guerrillas. By the end of January allied forces were reported to have inflicted 50 percent casualties on five Korean divisions.

Below: A collapsed bridge traps a T-34 Red tank as allied troops move on Seoul.

Young Chinese captives beg for their lives under the mistaken belief they were about to be shot on the western front, 1951.

battalions, three artillery battalions and 150 tanks. The force went through Osan and then to Suwon before finding any meaningful resistance. "Ridgway took that defeated army and turned it around. He was a breath of fresh air, a showman, what the army desperately needed," Michaelis said. To get a first-hand appraisal of Eighth Army morale, the Joint Chiefs had dispatched Lawton Collins to the field. Collins, who had fought alongside Ridgway at the World War II Battle of the Bulge, reported back: "Eighth Army in good shape and improving under Ridgway's leadership. Morale very satisfactory considering conditions." Back in Washington, Omar Bradley cheered the good news. "As the word spread through the upper levels of government that day, you could almost hear sighs of relief," Bradley said. MacArthur's voice was also part of the chorus. At a January 20 news conference in Taegu, the commander told reporters: "No one is going to drive us into the sea. This command intends to maintain a military position in Korea just as long as the statesmen of the UN decide we should do so."

Ridgway seized the moment with a series of coordinated, methodical counterattacks. But there would be no more ventures into the unknown. Supported by artillery, air strikes and tank support, a unit would move up. Then units on either flank stepped up to sweep away guerrillas or stragglers, who were pounced upon as soon as they were flushed out. The shoulder-to-shoulder advances also prevented the Chinese from using their double envelopments. This was basic soldiering, relying on the time-honored Army maxim: Find 'em, fix 'em, fight 'em, finish 'em.

But before Ridgway ordered his troops north, he did his own personal reconnaissance to make sure he wasn't sending them into a death trap. Flying over the terrain, Ridgway noted: "Hardly a moving creature did we spot, not a campfire smoke, no wheel tracks, not even trampled snow to indicate the presence of a large number of troops." Finally, at the head of a desolate valley, the snow showed a line of cart tracks heading into a village. "It was clear that here, in this village, the enemy was taking shelter against the bitter cold by night, moving out before sun-up to hide in the woods; for with our bomber aircraft hunting targets like hungry hawks hunting mice, a village

Americans retake Inchon and sweep on north toward the 38th parallel. February 1951.

Bombs from the lead plane in a B-29 formation head toward targets in the hills below. It is the 150th combat mission for the Air Force's 19th Bomber Group.

was no safe place by day."

At last, Ridgway got his chance to counterattack. Operation Thunderbolt was launched January 25 by I and IX Corps to push the Chinese back to the Han River. It was deadly effective. Chinese dead littered the snow-covered hills on a 20-mile wide swath. Fighting was heavy around Suwon, but Inchon fell without much of a struggle. The U.S. 25th Division retook Kimpo airfield, which again put American planes near the front of battle. One day after his 71st birthday on January 26, MacArthur returned to Suwon where he had witnessed the war first-hand way back in June. "This is exactly where I came in seven months ago to start this crusade. The stake we fight for now, however, is more than Korea—it is a free Asia," the general said.

Next came Operation Roundup, which Ridgway designed as a drive up the center of the peninsula.

ROK troops on the eastern front take cover against small arms fire as they take yet another town on the way to the 38th parallel, February 1951.

The ROK 5th and 8th Divisions, the U.S. 2nd and 7th Divisions, and the 187th Airborne Regimental Combat Team were deployed. The Chinese pulled back from Wonju. And on the night of January 29, the 2nd Division's 23rd Regiment and a French battalion were assigned to the task of taking two railroad tunnels 20 miles northwest of Wonju near Chipyong-ni. They were to occupy the high ground so the road to Suwon could be defended. The fighting was fierce, and on the morning of February 1, waves of Chinese hit the French. The French commander was Lt. Col. Ralph Montclar, who had been wounded 13 times in two previous wars and who had given up his four-star rank to lead the battalion in combat. During the crucial point in the fighting, when the Chinese seemed on the verge of victory, the French fixed bayonets and shouted *"Camerone"*—the battle cry of the French Foreign Legion as they defended a Mexican village in a previous century. There, the Legionnaires had stood to the last man, and the French were prepared to do

it again. Their bayonet charge turned the tide.

The 23rd Regiment under Col. Paul Freeman also found itself in jeopardy. By mid-afternoon on February 1, two of his battalions appeared as if they would be crushed under the weight of a Chinese attack. Plans were made for a last stand, then the weather cleared to allow air strikes. "The crisis had arrived. Then, just like a Hollywood battle, the sun broke through," Freeman said. Air power turned the tide. Opposing infantry were so close to each other, fighter planes circled several times to pick out who was who. Then, like birds of prey, the jets swooped down with their 500-pound bombs and chattering machine guns. The Chinese were mowed down "like prairie grass in a wind storm," Freeman said. When the Chinese began to flee, they were pursued by U.S. tanks and quad-50s—

Right: Allied troops slog through the mud on the western front, heading for Seoul and the Red's Han River defense line.

which were known as meat choppers because of the killing power of their four .50-caliber machine guns. GIs and their French comrades charged out of their holes in hot pursuit. The 23rd Regiment had 105 casualties, and the French had 125. Chinese losses were staggering. About 1,300 Chinese dead were counted on the hills. Another 3,600 were wounded or captured. It was called the Wonju turkey shoot.

The Chinese struck back on February 11, sending three divisions in an assault against the ROK 8th Division near Hoengsong, 10 miles north of Wonju. The South Korean division lost 7,000 men killed, wounded or captured, plus most of its equipment. The war had become a real slugging match.

Further to the west, about six miles from Wonju, the 23rd Regiment and the French made another stand at Chipyong-ni when three Chinese armies attacked on February 14. If the Chinese got through, they could sweep behind and cut off X Corps positions. They came in droves against Freeman's rectangular defense. But artillery and mortars had already sighted every piece of key terrain, and the Chinese charged into a meat grinder. Still, Freeman was hit by shrapnel in the left leg and his regiment was surrounded. Help was on the way—the British Commonwealth Brigade was fighting from the east and the 5th Cavalry Regiment was advancing from the west with an armored column. Headquarters offered to send a plane to evacuate Freeman, but he refused. "I brought them in here. And I'll take them out," the colonel said. Fighting raged through the night. The Chinese took a hill occupied by G Company from which it could fire into regimental headquarters. Company commander Lt. Thomas Heath rallied a makeshift force of artillerymen in an attempt to retake the position. "Get up on that hill. You'll die down here anyway. You might as well go up on the hill and die there," Heath said during the ebb and flow of the hilltop struggle. The key position was retaken just as the 5th Cavalry's lead tanks rumbled into view. The beaten Chinese suffered 5,000 dead. Along a 15-mile corridor were sprawled 5,000 Chinese bodies, covered with

Map on the ground before him, Gen. MacArthur and his staff survey the field of fighting on his tenth visit to the front.

Yanks of the 1st Cavalry Division assail Red positions with the help of 24th Division tanks which pummel the hill in their path.

inches of fresh snow. Cpl. Victor Fox of Item Company, 5th Cavalry Regiment, described "a human carnage right out of hell. All along the flanks of the steep, winding road, I saw the bodies of hundreds of Chinese piled in grisly heaps. Everywhere I looked were these mounds of frozen Chinese bodies lying every which way in their mustard-colored quilt uniforms. Artillery and tank fire must have blasted the Chinese at point-blank range."

Eighth Army was moving forward again. The advancing troops found signs that the Chinese were being hurt—abandoned gear, bloody bandages and stacks of unburied bodies. And the shift in momentum was felt in the political arena as well as on the battlefield. A cease-fire proposal surfaced in the United Nations. Although the United States believed it to be unsatisfactory, Secretary of State Dean Acheson played his political cards deftly. The Americans announced they supported the plan, figuring correctly that the Chinese would reject it. So when the communists turned it down as wholly unacceptable, the United Nations passed a resolution in early February that labeled the Chinese as aggressors.

If the atomic bomb wasn't going to be used in Korea, MacArthur conceived a plan to use nuclear poison to stem the flow of supplies and reinforcements from China. "I would sever Korea from Manchuria by laying a field of radioactive wastes—the by-products of atomic manufacture—across all the major lines of enemy supply. Then I would make simultaneous amphibious and airborne landings at the upper end of both coasts of North Korea, and close a gigantic trap. The Chinese would soon starve or surrender," MacArthur proposed. The Joint Chiefs said it was out of the question.

But Ridgway proceeded with his careful plans. He drew up Operation Killer, an eight-day action that began on February 21. Some in Washington felt the name was too graphic, but Ridgway reminded them that war is about killing and dying, and if more people remembered that, maybe decisions about sending men and women off to war would be more carefully

The United Nations at work as Pfc. Emerson Dean of Salina, Kansas (center), mans a machine gun near Yong-dungpo, flanked by British brothers, Trooper William Kirten and Cpl. Dennis Kirten of Birmingham, England. Their eyes search for movement in Red positions across the Han River in enemy-held Seoul.

considered. Killer was designed to destroy as many communists as possible. It wasn't as productive as hoped, because the Chinese withdrew before IX and X Corps advanced. And the weather was atrocious. "The days we spent as part of Operation Killer were like a bad dream. We advanced slowly, ridge by ridge.

Using heavy mortars to keep the Reds off balance, allied troops keep up the pressure in Korea.

Patrol, assault, patrol again, assault again—and again, and again. The weather was miserable, and we were often soaked to the skin by cold drizzle or sleet," said Pfc. Jerry Emer of Item Company. But Ridgway said of the operation: "We are not interested in real estate. We are interested only in inflicting maximum casualties on the enemy with minimum losses to ourselves. To do this we must wage a war of maneuver, slashing

Right: Fighting the slipstream of their C-47 which blows propaganda leaflets back into the plane, Cpl. Robert D. Petosky of Jeannette, Pennsylvania, and Army Psychological Warfare technician Pfc. Ralph J. Balash of Pittsburgh try to round up the strays. Some 180,000,000 of the surrender leaflets were dropped between 1951 and 1952.

Below: The snow turned to mud, Pvt. Gerald Singer of Wilkes-Barre, Pennsylvania (left), and Cpl. Thomas Matthews of St. Clair Shores, Michigan, slog through their own reflections on the western front.

Bayonets fixed, GIs advance against what they are told is an important hill position with close support from artillery and allied planes.

at the enemy when he withdraws and fighting delaying tactics when he attacks."

Killer also had peculiar political overtones. Ridgway had briefed war correspondents about Killer before MacArthur flew up to Wonju. But when MacArthur learned of the details, he held a news conference of his own in which he seemed to claim it as his own idea. "I am entirely satisfied with the situation at the front where the enemy has suffered a tactical reverse of immeasurable proportions. His losses have been among the bloodiest of modern times...Our strategic plan—notwithstanding the enemy's great numerical superiority—is indeed working well and I have just directed a resumption of the initiative by our forces," MacArthur said. Ridgway noted later that his commander's words were an "unwelcome reminder of a MacArthur that I had known

but had almost forgotten."

The gloom and doom of December had been replaced with a renewed fighting spirit. Morale improved because of a new program called Rest and Recuperation—in which troops were granted five-day leaves from the front lines and allowed to take in the bathhouses and bars of Tokyo. It was a brief but welcome relief from the peril and exhaustion of battlefield duty, and the fraternization between Americans and their Japanese hosts went a long way to healing leftover wounds between the two countries from World War II. Following Killer came Operation Ripper, another Ridgway plan, that kicked off on March 7. This time, he deftly asked MacArthur to delay his visit to the front. MacArthur's presence on the eve of other offensives had tipped off the Chinese that an attack was coming. But when he did speak out, Mac-

The remains of a Red ambush, wrecked vehicles and a dead GI in the foreground, come under scrutiny of fellow Yanks in a gully near Hoengsong on the central front.

Arthur stated that unless he was authorized to attack Chinese bases in Manchuria, a deadlock would develop on the battlefield. "Assuming no diminution of the enemy's flow of ground forces and materiel to the Korean battle area, a continuation of the existing limitations upon our freedom of counteroffensive action, and no major additions to our organizational strength, the battle lines cannot fail in time to reach a point of theoretical military stalemate," MacArthur said. Troops called it MacArthur's "die for a tie speech"— they felt they were fighting an unwinnable war. Leaders in Washington had also acknowledged the realities of Korea, but unlike MacArthur, they were willing to accept a stalemated settlement.

Under Ripper, IX and X Corps advanced along a 50-mile front in central Korea back to the 38th parallel.

The objective was to capture the transportation center at Chunchon and make it difficult for the Chinese to retreat. Roads had turned to muddy paste in the spring thaw. And the U.S. 25th Division faced the natural barrier of the Han River, which had to be crossed in boats before all of its bridges had been demolished. Men huddled as low as possible during the perilous trip across the swollen river. World War II veterans advised the younger troops to keep moving when they reached the far side; to freeze in place on a river bank invited death. Weapons were oiled and polished. Prayers were said. The lead elements

Right: Potato masher grenades mark an abandoned Red foxhole. Marine Pfc. Bob Scott of Rock Island, Illinois, makes sure its former resident is gone.

were the 27th and 35th Regiments, and the crossing came with no small amount of anxiety. "I thought back to Mark Twain's story about the miscreant who, having been tarred and feathered, and in the process of being ridden out of town on a rail, mused to himself that if it were not for the honor of the thing, he would just as soon be somewhere else," said Staff Sgt. W.B. Woodruff. But preceding the boats was the blam! blam! blam! of a mighty artillery curtain, and GIs made nervous jokes about the Chinese having hot metal for breakfast. "I had seen firepower demonstrations involving multibattalion concentrations, but nothing prepared me for this. The earth shook, and a deafening roar went on and on. Across the entire visible expanses of these mountains, shells burst in absolute profusion, each burst first flaring orange, then turning to black smoke against the whiteness of the snow. I watched, nearly hypnotized," Woodruff recalled later.

The ROK 1st Division, meanwhile, fought past Seoul in the west. With Eighth Army units on both flanks of Seoul, the Chinese were in a poor position to defend it. For the fourth—and last—time in nine months of war, Seoul changed hands on March 14. The city was a shambles, but the Chinese virtually abandoned it without a repeat of the house-to-house fighting following the Inchon invasion. There was no elaborate liberation ceremony either. "Even under our existing conditions of restraint, it should be clearly evident to the communist foe now committed against us that they cannot hope to impose their will on Korea by force," MacArthur told the media.

To keep the pressure on the Chinese, another paratroop operation was planned a week after Seoul was liberated. The 187th Airborne was originally ordered to drop at Chunchon, but it was diverted to Munsan-ni on the Imjin River about 20 miles northwest of Seoul. Again, it failed to trap many Chinese. By the end of March, however, Eighth Army was back to the 38th parallel. President Truman had already been questioned about where the man-made line would be crossed again. "That is a tactical matter for the field commander. A commander in chief 7,000 miles away does not interfere with field operations. We are working to free the Republic of Korea and set it up as the United Nations wants it. That doesn't have anything to do with the 38th parallel," Truman told reporters. Ridgway elected to cross it, but with prudence.

Still, Eighth Army expected a spring offensive from

Aussies help an injured Yank when he is unable to keep up with 11 other wounded Americans, freed by the Reds and left to stumble into the Aussie camp.

the Chinese in the Iron Triangle around Chorwon, Kumwha and Pyongyang. This was high, rugged country easier to access from the north. There were no roads leading into it from the south, which limited the approaches of a mechanized army. Ridgway established a series of phase lines—Idaho, Kansas, Utah and Wyoming—that could absorb Chinese punches. And if the Eighth Army had to fall back, it would have prepared positions as a defense in depth. Operation Ripper had already moved Ridgway's advance to the Idaho Line; Operation Rugged stepped up to the Kansas Line—strung along the commanding ground above the 38th parallel. The line included the Hawchon Reservoir, which provided Seoul's water supply. Finally, Ridgway moved his forces up to the Utah line. After four days of nasty fighting beginning April 5, U.N. troops were now just south of Chorwon.

But events on a higher level overshadowed the battleground.

Previous page, top: 3rd Division GIs move warily through a vacated enemy post on the south bank of the Han River.

Previous page, bottom: Battle-weary Marines plod past wreckage on the march north of Hoengsong.

Above: Artillerymen of the 1st Cavalry ram home the big stuff on a cannon somewhere on the west central front, March 1951.

Near right: A stranded jeep, loaded with 1st Cavalry GIs, gets tow from a passing tank.

Far right: Right on target, two Air Force B-26s drop napalm on two Korean supply trains which obliged by arriving side by side at Munchon, north of Wonsan on Korea's east coast.

8

MacArthur Is Sacked

The return to the 38th parallel gave President Truman an opportunity to end the Korean War. In late March, he was prepared to discuss conditions for a settlement in the United Nations. But before he did, he directed the Joint Chiefs of Staff to seek out Douglas MacArthur's views on the war so Washington could play its strongest possible hand. What followed was a series of events that abruptly ended MacArthur's military career. "Strong United Nations feeling persists that further diplomatic efforts towards settlement should be made before any advance with forces north of the 38th parallel. Time may be required to determine diplomatic reaction and permit new negotiations that may develop.

Left: North of the 38th parallel, GIs move up a lonely trail on the western front. Chinese troops hold the hills and there are reports of an enemy build-up.

Above: Generals MacArthur and Ridgway confer about progress in the 1st ROK Corps area at Kangnung before a jeep trip to Yang Yang, 15 miles north of the 38th parallel.

A 1st Cavalry tank looking for a shallow crossing misjudges the rain-swollen Pukhan River. A disgruntled crewman waits for the tank retriever which will pull it ashore.

Recognizing that the 38th parallel has no military significance, State has asked Joint Chiefs of Staff what authority you should have to permit sufficient freedom of action for the next few weeks to provide security for United Nations forces and maintain contact with the enemy. Your recommendations required," the Joint Chiefs messaged MacArthur.

The general responded with this March 21 cable:

"Recommend that no further military restrictions be imposed upon the United Nations Command in Korea. The inhibitions which already exist should not be increased. The military advantage arising from restrictions upon the scope of our air and naval operations coupled with the disparity between the size of our command and the enemy ground potential renders it completely impracticable to attempt to clear North Korea or to make an appreciable effort to that

U.N. assault force crosses the Hwachon Reservoir in North Korea to attack communist forces on the other side.

end." But no one was asking him to clear North Korea at this point.

With the situation at a delicate stage, Truman had ordered that no one release policy statements unless they were cleared by the State Department. Yet MacArthur issued a statement in Tokyo on March 24 that Truman believed undermined his peace initiative. It said the communists had been evicted again from South Korea, and China lacked the industrial might to wage modern war.

"Even under inhibitions which now restrict the activity of the United Nations forces and the corresponding military advantages which accrue to Red China, it has shown its complete inability to accomplish by force of arms the conquest of Korea....The enemy therefore must now be painfully aware that decision of the United Nations to depart from its tolerant effort to contain the war to the area of Korea through expansion of our military operations to his coastal areas and interior bases would doom Red China to the risk of imminent military collapse....Within my area of authority as military commander, however, it should be needless to say I stand ready at any time to confer in the field with the commander in chief of the enemy forces in an earnest effort to find any military means whereby the realizations of the political objectives of the United Nations in Korea, to which no nation may justly take exception, might be accomplished without further bloodshed," MacArthur said.

MacArthur called it a "routine communique" in the "local voice of the theater commander." But Washington interpreted MacArthur's words as an attempt to formulate U.S. policy by going over Truman's head. "It was in open defiance of my orders as President and commander in chief," Truman wrote later. "By this act, MacArthur left me no choice. I could no longer tolerate his insubordination." When Dean Acheson read MacArthur's statement, he said: "Whom the gods destroy, they first make mad."

At about the same time, Representative Joseph Martin, the House Republican leader, had written MacArthur to agree with the general's opinion that Chinese Nationalists should be dispatched from Taiwan to wage war with the communists. MacArthur's response was read by Martin in Congress on April 5. It read in part: "It seems strangely difficult for some to realize that here in Asia is where the Communist conspirators have elected to make their play for global conquest, and that we have joined the issue thus raised on the battlefield; that here we fight Europe's war with arms while the diplomats there still fight it with words; that if we lose this war to communism in Asia that the fall of Europe is inevitable; win it and Europe most probably would avoid war and yet preserve freedom. As you have pointed out, we must win. There is no substitute for victory...." Truman called a meeting of his top advisors the next day. He

A 3rd Infantry Division GI dashes to join his comrades seeking cover from small arms fire somewhere in Korea, April 1951.

U.S. Marines ignore the invitation on the side of the hut as they move carefully through an abandoned North Korean village.

had already made up his mind to dismiss Mac-Arthur—"This looks like the last straw. I've come to the conclusion that our Big General in the Far East must be recalled," he wrote in his diary—but he was seeking a consensus. "If you relieve MacArthur, you will have the biggest fight of your administration," Acheson had warned Truman. But the Joint Chiefs gave their consent following an April 8 meeting. Secretary of Defense George Marshall also agreed. Unanimity was required because of MacArthur's immense personal appeal. The son of a Congressional

Medal of Honor recipient from the Civil War, MacArthur graduated from West Point in 1903 and commanded the 42nd (Rainbow) Division in World War I. Later, he became the youngest man to become superintendent of the U.S. Military Academy and U.S. Army chief of staff. A former military advisor and field marshal in the Philippines, MacArthur was summoned from retirement to lead allied forces in the Southwest Pacific during World War II. Like his father, MacArthur was awarded the Medal of Honor—for his defense of the Philippines. Promoted to a five-star

U.N. infantrymen with rocket launchers and automatic weapons guard a pontoon bridge over the Pukhan River as trucks and tanks cross to safety. A new Red offensive failed to cut the road to Seoul.

Below: A Red counterattack forces U.N. infantry to pull back to new positions on the western front.

general of the Army in 1944, MacArthur presided over the Japanese surrender on the deck of the USS *Missouri* in Tokyo Bay on September 2, 1945. Now, after the success of Inchon and the sting of defeat in North Korea, he was being fired by his boss. The top brass

had decided to replace him with Matthew Ridgway, and to promote Lt. Gen. James Van Fleet to take over Eighth Army. Truman signed the orders on April 10. Secretary of the Army Frank Pace, who was already in the Far East, was supposed to deliver the message to MacArthur's home on April 12, but communications broke down. Washington decided to send the dismissal order by cable. Truman followed it with his own message: "Full and vigorous debate on matters of national policy is a vital element in the constitutional system of our free democracy. It is fundamental, however, that military commanders must be governed by the polices and directives issued to them in the manner provided for by our laws and Constitution. In time of crisis, this consideration is particularly compelling. General MacArthur's place in history as one of our greatest commanders is fully established. The nation owes him a debt of gratitude for the distinguished and exceptional service which he has rendered his country in posts of great responsibility. For that reason I repeat my regret at the necessity for the action I feel compelled to take in his case." But the cable didn't arrive in time. Word came that the *Chicago Tribune* had learned of MacArthur's dismissal and was about to break the news. Truman called a hastily arranged news conference at the unusual hour of 1 a.m. on April 11. His statement read: "With deep regret I have concluded that General of the Army Douglas MacArthur is unable to give his whole-hearted support to the policies of the United States government and of the United Nations in matters pertaining to his official duties. In view of the specific responsibilities imposed upon me by the Constitution

of the United States and the added responsibilities entrusted to me by the United Nations, I have decided that I must make a change of command in the Far East." News bulletins arrived in Tokyo ahead of the official cable. An aide to the general, Col. Sidney Huff, heard the news on a commercial station. He summoned Mrs. MacArthur from a luncheon, and she passed the news to her husband. "Jeannie, we're going home at last," MacArthur told his wife. He finished lunch as if nothing had happened, but the firing and the way it was handled clearly hurt the pride of the 52-year career officer. In his autobiography *Remembrances*, MacArthur noted: "No office boy, no charwoman, no servant of any sort would have been dismissed with such callous disregard for the ordinary decencies." When MacArthur departed Tokyo for the last time, 2 million Japanese lined the way to the airport. However imperiously and autocratically, MacArthur had supervised Japan's reconstruction and democratization following its ruinous path in World War II. Japan's 2 leading newspapers said of its former conqueror: "We feel as if we had lost a kind and loving father." A crowd of 500,000 people greeted MacArthur in San Francisco when he arrived April 17.

The public was clearly on MacArthur's side because it did not understand the reasons for the firing. Truman received a torrent of angry mail, but when

Gen. MacArthur tells a Joint Session of Congress the U.S. cannot appease communism in Asia "without simultaneously undermining our efforts to halt it in Europe."

The front line stiffens and infantrymen of the 187th Regiment hold their ground firing at an enemy 50 yards away and 30 feet above them.

he went on national radio to talk of his actions, the President said: "In the simplest terms, what we are doing in Korea is this: we are trying to prevent a third world war."

MacArthur was invited to Washington to address a joint session of Congress. In a 37-minute televised address, he told a listening nation: "It has been said that I was in effect a war monger. Nothing could be further from the truth. I know war as few other men now living know it, and nothing to me is more revolting....But once war is forced upon us, there is no other alternative than to apply every available means to bring it to a swift end. War's very object is victory—not prolonged indecision. In war, indeed, there can be no substitute for victory. There are some who, for varying reasons, would appease Red China. They are blind to history's clear lesson, for history teaches, with unmistakable emphasis, that appeasement but begets new and bloodier war....The world has turned over many times since I took the oath on the Plains at West Point, and the hopes and dreams have long since

Below: A ticker-tape storm comes down on Gen. MacArthur as he salutes a color guard of the 1st Army, April 20, New York City.

Mortar fire pins down troops of the 25th Division near the Hantan River on the central front.

vanished. But I still remember the refrain of one of the most popular barrack ballads of that day which proclaimed most proudly that 'Old soldiers never die, they just fade away.' And like the old soldier of that ballad, I now close my military career and just fade away—an old soldier who has tried to do his duty as God gave him the light to see that duty. Goodbye." MacArthur left for New York City, where a seven-hour parade honored the war hero. A record 3,249 tons of ticker tape, shredded newspaper and confetti rained down from the concrete canyons—twice the amount that fell on aviator Charles Lindbergh. Then MacArthur was back in Washington for hearings by the Senate Armed Services and Foreign Relations Committees. From May 3 to June 27, the panel heard 14 witnesses give 2 million words of answers on the conduct of the Korean War and Far East policy. Rather than clarify issues, however, the hearings left things clouded. Gen. Omar Bradley offered one of the most quoted phrases of the Korean War, saying about extending the war to China: "Frankly, in the opinion of the Joint Chiefs of Staff, this strategy would involve us in the wrong war, at the wrong place, at the wrong time, and with the wrong enemy."

And Secretary of Defense Marshall noted that the military agreed with Truman's decision to dismiss MacArthur. "It became apparent that General MacArthur had grown so far out of sympathy with the established policies of the United States that there was grave doubt as to whether he could any longer be permitted to exercise the authority in making decisions that normal command functions would assign to a theater commander. In this situation, there was no other recourse but to relieve him," Marshall said.

MacArthur continued to speak out, but he was in fact fading from the public arena. "I only wanted to end the war, not spread it. I had not started it, and many times had stated, 'Anyone in favor of sending American ground troops to fight on Chinese soil should have his head examined,'" he argued. The retired general said the great tragedy of Korea was trying to fight with "our arms in a straitjacket." Even

Above left: For the third time in less than a year refugees flee the changing battle lines, carrying what few belongings they have.

Below left: Members of the First Commonwealth Division on parade. Left to right, Cpl. W. Gains of Dublin, Ireland; Cpl. R. MacEwan of Glasgow, Scotland; L/Cpl. P. Cranitch of Toowoomba, Queensland, Australia; S/Sgt. A. M. Foisy of Ottawa, Canada, and ambulance driver Amrit Lal of India.

as late as December 2, 1952, he told the Congress of American Industry in a speech: "Never before has this nation been engaged in mortal combat with a hostile power without military objective, without policy other than restrictions governing operations, or indeed without even formally recognizing a state of war."

William Manchester, MacArthur's biographer, wrote that the frustrations of Korea had worn on the general. "Brave, brilliant, majestic, he was a colossus bestriding Korea until the nemesis of his hubris overtook him. He simply could not bear to end his career in checkmate," Manchester said. With Ridgway moving to Tokyo to replace MacArthur, James Van Fleet arrived in Korea on April 16, 1951, to take over the Eighth Army. A 1915 graduate of West Point, Van Fleet commanded a machine gun battalion in World War I. He led an Army corps in France and Germany in World War II and had led a military advisory group in Greece to help stop the communist takeover of that country. Van Fleet had whipped the ragtag Greek army into shape, beating the communists in a mountainous, peninsular campaign. It was hoped he could continue Ridgway's work in Korea.

Asked what the goal was in Korea, Van Fleet said: "I don't know, the answer must come from high authority."

How would he know if the goal was achieved if he didn't know what it was, reporters asked him.

"Somebody higher up will have to tell us," he said. But the troops in the ranks, the ones slogging through the mud and over the forbiddin terrain, recognized the equilibrium the opposing sides were reaching. The mission, it seemed, was to "die for a tie."

The army in the field was unlike any other seen in history. It was the first time the United Nations had assembled a force, and 16 nations sent ground troops that were attached to the Eighth United States Army in Korea (EUSAK). A more recent example is the 27-member coalition assembled to evict the Iraqi army from Kuwait during Operation Desert Storm, which was a United Nations action under the command of the U.S. military.

In Korea, about 40,000 non-U.S. troops were in the field. About half of them were British or from Australia, New Zealand and Canada. Within the Eighth Army, 13 different languages were spoken, not counting dialects and derivatives, which taxed the housekeeping chores of command and control. Diet was a unique problem because American eating habits conflicted with other cultures. To feed the Greek battalion, U.S. quartermasters had to deliver extra olive oil. And during Easter, Eighth Army filled a special request of

A GI mans his machine gun in front of the Korean Capitol in Seoul as the battered building still under repair is threatened for the third time. A South Korean brings more sandbags.

15 live lambs that were to be religiously slaughtered and roasted. The virgin lambs were airlifted from Japan with a supply of hay and an accompanying shepherd—a major in the U.S. Army's veterinary corps. In addition, Greeks would not eat corn. Turkish soldiers for religious reasons would not eat pork, and they had an aversion for corn and spices and condiments. The Turks received an extra bread ration and loved American canned spinach. Filipinos got extra rice. Thai soldiers got three times the normal amount of spices and condiments, but would not touch beets, cake mix, dry cereals, citrus fruit or sweet pickles. The French baked their own bread and imported cases and cases of wine to go with their meals. The Greeks favored cognac while the British insisted on having hard liquor and beer.

Clothing was another matter. The Turks had wide feet, which did not fit easily into American combat boots. Thailand soldiers found U.S. footwear too big for their size 5 feet, so special orders were placed for

Taking a stand, these Marines await an expected Red Chinese attack. At left is Pfc. Richard Pantoliano of Brooklyn, New York, with rifle. At foreground right is Pfc. Robert Curtis of Torrance, California.

A Marine flame thrower wipes out an enemy pillbox on the central front while white phosphorus mortar shells shroud the attack.

smaller boots. Logisticians coped with "a thousand petty headaches," Ridgway wrote. "The Dutch wanted milk where the French wanted wine. The Moslems wanted no pork and the Hindus no beef. The Orientals wanted more rice and the Europeans more bread. Shoes had to be extra wide to fit the Turks. They had to be extra narrow and short to fit the men from Thailand and the Philippines....Only the Canadians and Scandinavians adjusted easily to United States rations and clothes."

But Ridgway had also said of Eighth Army: "I believe it is quite possible that because of this action history may someday record that the crest of the communist wave of cold-blooded aggression was broken against the arms and the will to fight of the United Nations battle team in Korea; and that this menacing flood, reaching its high water mark on the Korea front, thereafter began its recession in Asia."

On the battlefield, the Chinese had pulled back to replenish their supplies and their depleted ranks. But by now, the Eighth Army intelligence officers knew the Chinese were like a snake coiling back just before it strikes. By April 19, all units of I and IX Corps were along the Utah Line, and in central Korea, the communists set fires in the forests to shroud their movements from the air. In the west, the U.S. 24th and 25th Divisions had made the deepest penetrations into the communist front, advancing to the Wyoming Line.

The Chinese launched their spring offensive by the light of an April 22 moon. The fifth phase of their involvement in Korea involved 350,000 men. Radio

Right: Marines of the 1st Division dart through smoke in what is described as close contact with enemy troops somewhere on the Korean front. Fire burns brush behind them.

B-26s plaster enemy buildings with napalm. The liquid flames enter one side of a building and come out the other. Pukchang, North Korea, May 1951.

Pyongyang said its objective was the destruction of the United Nations command, and it boasted success would be rapid. It was wrong on both counts. The main assault, just as it was in the beginning of the war, was aimed at Seoul. The Chinese crossed the Imjin River in several places against ROK 1st and U.S. 3rd Divisions. The exposed U.S. 24th and 25th Divisions were hit with furious force. Although they absorbed the attack, the two divisions had to fall back to more defensible positions along the 38th parallel.

Meanwhile, to the east, the ROK 6th Division fell back 10 miles the first day, and even more on the second. The mountains restricted use of tanks and artillery, and it prevented lateral movement of reserve forces. "The rout and dissolution of the regiments was entirely uncalled for and disgraceful in all aspects," said Maj. Gen. William Hoge, the new IX Corps commander. The ROK retreat again left American units exposed, and X Corps commander Ned Almond gave an angry order to Col. William McCaffrey, com-

U.N. soldiers fire at a fleeing enemy, seen running down a ridge on the central front, southwest of Chunchon.

mander of the 31st Infantry of the 25th Division. "Make them return to their position. Shoot them if you have to," Almond told McCaffrey, the youngest man to lead a regiment in Korea. Nobody shot the fleeing South Koreans, but a 10-mile hole had been opened in the central front.

The 1st Marine Division was rushed into the breach at a spot called Horseshoe Ridge. Leathernecks had two hours of tactical warning that an attack was coming, and they prepared for the Chinese bugles and whistles. The clamor was enough to test the stoutest of defenders. "The hair on my neck stood up. Trying for some humor, I told my foxhole buddy, 'They sure could use some music lessons.' All of a sudden it got quiet. You could hear the guys bracing themselves, you know, getting ready. I thought, who's gonna live and who's gonna die?" said Pfc. Floyd Baxter, a member of Weapons Company.

The Marines had to give substantial ground. But they absorbed the attack and inflicted high casualties.

"They came on in wave after wave, hundreds of them. They were singing, humming, and chanting, 'Awake, Marine....' In the first rush they knocked out both our machine guns and wounded about 10 men, putting a big hole in our fire—and those grenades, hundreds of grenades. There was nothing to do but withdraw to a better position, which I did. We pulled back about 50 yards and set up a new line. All this was in pitch-black night with Chinese cymbals crashing, horns blowing, and their god-awful yells," said 2nd Lt. Joseph Reisler of Charlie Company. About 25 miles to the west on the I Corps front, the British 29th Brigade fought one of the storied actions of the Korean War. Three infantry battalions and a Belgian battalion—about 6,000 men—were dug in on the heights of the south bank of the Imjin River, protecting an invasion route to Seoul. Three Chinese divisions attacked across a seven-mile wide front, cutting off the battalions in a bid to destroy them piecemeal. The burp guns and bugle calls shattered the night silence on

MEDIA

The Korean War was a watershed for the media. It was the last conflict that was the domain of print journalists and still photographers. Television was in its infancy, and the images of Korea came on black and white film that had to be developed and flown back to the states—a process that took days under the best of conditions. There was no satellite transmission of electronic images. Instead of television sets bleeding into living rooms on the nightly news, film images were packaged into newsreels.

When North Korea invaded, there were five wire service reporters in Seoul. At the time of the first American ground battle, 70 reporters were in South Korea. And by the end of September of 1950, 238 American and foreign reporters were accredited to Far East Command. The highest number of reporters during any point in the war was 270. By contrast, there were 419 news media representatives accredited to Military Assistance Command Vietnam in 1966.

The only censorship at the beginning of the war was voluntary. General of the Army Douglas MacArthur, who as a young major had been the Army's first censor in World War I, thought censorship was abhorrent. Given free rein, war correspondents came up with several scoops. The surprise invasion at Inchon, for example, was all the more remarkable because correspondents in Tokyo had dubbed it Operation Common Knowledge. Stories about it were in the newspapers while ships were at sea.

But censorship became a reality with the death of Eighth Army commander Walton "Johnnie" Walker on December 23. For security reasons, 11 hours after Walker died, the copy of all correspondents went under military surveillance. According to the Army, 90 percent of the press correspondents in Korea said they wanted censorship, and a good many campaigned to get it. The competition for breaking stories was so heated, many writers thought security was being breached as a result.

The Eighth Army policy was: "We will proceed in the belief that the folks at home would rather get news a few hours late of a son who is living than news of a battle before it begins and then of a son who is dead."

On December 29, 1950, new Eighth Army commander Matthew Ridgway told the media bluntly he would strictly enforce censorship and he expected reporters to abide by the rules "as members of the team." But the media and the military make strained bedfellows. Reporters live by immediacy and independence; the military demands discipline and insists on delays if it believes the lives of its members may be jeopardized. On the one hand, correspondents and photographers participated in amphibious landings, parachute jumps, combat patrols and day-to-day soldiering. On the other hand, reports of retreats or sensitive issues at the negotiating table were often stamped "delayed."

"What is at stake in a war zone combat crisis is the freedom or very life of a man, a platoon, a battalion, a division, an army or even an entire nation....Under such circumstances, with the enemy pounding at the main gate, one does not shout to him that the bricklayers have left a hole in the city wall on the other side of town," said Lt. Col. Melvin B. Voorhees, public information officer and chief censor for Eighth Army.

In the skirmishes between the media and the military, the censorship rules from World II were resurrected and enforced. During the early months of censorship, stories were screened at Eighth Army headquarters. Then beginning in March of 1951, stories were also reviewed by military censors in Tokyo. Three months later, Tokyo headquarters assumed all responsibility for reviewing copy and pictures.

One example of censorship came at a February 19, 1951, news conference held by Gen. Ridgway. "In two or three days we shall attack....If they'll leave that North Korean corps down our right flank another couple of days, we'll cut it off and destroy it," Ridgway announced. But censors deleted his remarks because it might jeopardize future operations.

But enforcing censorship wasn't always easy. Operation Killer was launched under a news blackout. But MacArthur broke the blackout

April 22. And for 60 crucial hours, despite being doomed to death or captivity, the resolute Britains made a desperate stand. The nuances of language hampered delivery of air and artillery support. When it became apparent the Chinese were attacking in strength, Brig. Tom Brodie radioed I Corps that his situation was "a bit sticky." No one understood that Brodie meant things were critical. If it had been an American officer, he would have screamed, "We're being overrun by Chinamen. Pour everything you got into here." As it was, the British fought until they ran out of food, ammunition and radio batteries. One battalion of the Gloucestershire Regiment was atop Hill 235, or Gloucester Hill, completely surrounded by communist hordes. The stark orders from headquarters called for "every man to make his own way back." The Gloucesters stunned the Chinese by charging north into the teeth of the attack. Most of them in Japan by announcing to the world that Eighth Army was about to strike. Friction developed over matters of interpretation. In the spring of 1951, Eighth Army forbade correspondents from referring to the 38th parallel in print. The military later lifted the ban but ordered its public information officers not to mention the demarcation line.

One writer even penned lyrics about censorship sung to the music of *The Battle Lymn of the Republic*:

Mine Eyes Have Seen the Censor with My Copy on His Knee;
He is cutting out the passages that mean the most to me.
"This sentence hurts morale as it's defined in Section 3;
glory, to the censor; glory, glory to the censor;
Glory, glory, to the censor; This passage must come out!"

But in a more serious vein, relations between the media and military were frayed during the sensitive and extended period of negotiations. When news was hard to come by from American delegates, Western journalists began to turn to writers from communist publications—specifically Australian Wilfred Burchett and Alan Winnington of the *London Daily Worker*.

Ridgway became so concerned about "fraternizing and trafficking" with the enemy, that he issued this scolding memorandum to correspondents.

"It has come to the attention of General Headquarters, UNC, that the provisions made by the United Nations Command which permit fullest possible news coverage of the Military Armistice Negotiations are being abused by certain UNC corre-

spondents for the purpose of fraternization and trafficking with the enemy. Such practices could have serious adverse effects on the conduct of the current negotiations and might well imperil the security of UNC forces.

Military personnel were strictly prohibited from such practices.

"The UNC has viewed with growing apprehension the practices of certain UNC correspondents of excessive consorting including drinking alcoholic beverages with communist 'journalists'—this as differentiated from required professional contacts. Unguarded conversations during such unnecessary social sessions might well jeopardize the security of military forces. It is a basic policy to afford all UNC correspondents complete access to and freedom of movement through UNC positions and installations. Any portion of such a wealth of military knowledge, were it to be divulged inadvertently to the enemy, could endanger the lives of many of our men.

"Certain UNC correspondents have entered into surreptitious and personal arrangements with the enemy to deliver modern camera equipment into the POW camps where our soldiers are being held, to receive photographs taken in communist prison camps and to receive recordings for radio broadcast of UNC prisoner-of-war interviews made in communist prison camps.

"General Headquarters is well aware and appreciative of the fact that many correspondents accredited to the UNC view with deep concern the problems of ethics and public responsibility involved in these dealings and contacts with the enemy. Their views are fully shared by this Headquarters.

It has therefore become necessary to request all UNC correspondents entering the Panmunjom neutral area for the purpose of covering the armistice talks to conduct themselves in such a manner so as to avoid any suggestion that military security is being placed in possible jeopardy or that traffic is being held with the enemy. This request is intended in no way to impugn the loyalty or integrity of any UNC correspondent or news-gathering organization. Any such implication would be without foundation and in complete contradiction to the spirit in which precautionary measures are being taken.

Still, discord between the media and military never reached the level it did during the entanglements of Vietnam, which led to the concept of pool coverage in Grenada, Panama and the Persian Gulf.

Peter Braestrup, a combat Marine officer in Korea and *Washington Post* bureau chief in Saigon during the Vietnam War, said of Korea: "The inconclusive war became unpopular at home...but neither James Van Fleet nor other U.S. commanders in Korea later blamed this evolution on the security lapses, mood swings, exaggerations or forebodings of the press."

Ten American correspondents died in Korea, most of them in the chaos of the early part of the war. Among them was Associated Press writer William R. Moore, killed in the fighting around Taejon in the first month of the fighting. Associated Press photographer Frank Noel was taken prisoner near the Chosin Reservoir and spent two-and-one-half years in a POW camp.

were taken prisoner. Only 39 men made it back to U.N. lines. The unit took 1,000 casualties and lost most of its equipment, but they inflicted 10,000 casualties on the Chinese and delayed the assault on Seoul. "Only the Gloucesters could have done it," Brodie wrote in his radio log. Van Fleet called it "the most outstanding example of unit bravery in modern warfare." The Chinese advanced 25 miles toward Seoul, cutting the Seoul-Chunchon highway. They ulti-

mately made it to just four miles outside the city, but Van Fleet insisted that it be held. Asked if Seoul would be abandoned again, Van Fleet bellowed: "No!" Ridgway issued a public statement: "It appears to me at this time that this attack is another major effort by our communist enemy to drive United Nations forces from Korea, or destroy them, regardless of the further destruction of his own troops, and the continued criminal devastation of Korea. The battle is joined. It

A tank of the 6th Armored Battalion churns up dust as it passes American troops withdrawing on front of a new Red offensive.

may well prove decisive." The Chinese offensive, weakened with resupply and ammunition problems, ran out of steam on April 29. That day, planes caught 6,000 Chinese in small boats trying to ferry across the Han River. "It was here that our command of the air worked most tellingly. Our pilots swooped down

upon the attackers while they were still waterborne and decimated them," Ridgway reported. Eighth Army formed a front that was not part of the established phase lines, so it naturally became known as the No-Name Line, which ran from north of Seoul and angled northwestward. By the end of April, Van

Gen. Ridgway at an advance base somewhere in Korea huddles with top field commanders as the Chinese offensive continues. Left to right, Lt. Gen. Edward Almond, commander X Corps; Ridgway; Lt. Gen. James A. Van Fleet, commander Eighth Army; Maj. Gen. G.C. Thomas, commander 1st Marine Division.

Fleet's forces held a strong, continuous front across Korea.

Engineers quickly muscled up the No-Name Line. Trenches were dug, interlocking gun placements set, wire entanglements strung, mine fields placed and booby traps set. Patrols ranged seven miles above the front as the Chinese coiled for yet another strike. Eighth Army knew it was coming when resistance stiffened May 10, but it didn't expect it to come so far

to the east.

The sixth phase Chinese offensive exploded the night of May 15-16, when 21 Chinese and nine North Korean divisions charged across a 32-mile wide front in the rain. The ROK 5th and 7th Divisions felt the full weight of the attack, holding for a time before they broke and fell back. Air strikes slammed the Chinese just 100 yards in front of the main line of resistance. In the 24-hour period of May 17, artillery

An integral part of open warfare, a tank provides cover for infantry and the infantry sees what the tankers can't see.

spit 38,000 rounds to slow the Chinese.

When the retreating ROKs opened a cavernous gap in the No-Name Line, the U.S. 2nd Division was shifted to the east and found itself holding a critical shoulder for the third time in the war. "The Chinese are flowing like water around my right flank...I think we are in a very serious situation," Ned Almond of X Corps said in a situation report. The 187th Airborne was called up from reserve, and the U.S. 3rd Division was also shifted east. Supported by French and Dutch battalions, the 2nd Division inflicted 35,000 casualties before it pulled back to a more defensible position. Its May 18 expenditure of artillery rounds was 41,000.

With the collapse of the ROK divisions, the Chinese gained 20 miles. But by May 20, the 2nd Division and its reinforcements proved it could hold. Now came an opportunity to saw off the Chinese who had found

themselves out on a limb.

Ridgway and Van Fleet planned a counterattack. The I, IX and X Corps advanced while the ROK I Corps moved up in the west; the ravaged ROK II Corps was disbanded. By the end of the month, Eighth Army had again cleared the invaders from South Korea. With Eighth Army well above the 38th parallel for the third time in the war, Ridgway messaged the Joint Chiefs on May 30: "The enemy has suffered a severe major defeat. Estimates of enemy killed in action submitted by the field commanders come to total so high that I cannot accept it. Nevertheless, there has been inflicted a major personnel loss far exceeding, in my opinion, the loss suffered by the enemy in the April 21 offensive....I therefore believe that for the next 60 days the United States government should be able to count with reasonable assurance upon a mili-

U.N. troops fire barrages of rockets into the hills south of Chunchon. After 3 1/2 hours, the attacking Chinese withdraw with heavy casualties.

tary situation in Korea offering optimum advantages in support of its diplomatic negotiations." The body count of communist dead was 17,000, plus 10,000 captured. The retreating Chinese had also left behind costly stores of mortars, ammunition and automatic weapons—and piles of dead rotting in the spring sun.

Eighth Army didn't stop. Under Operation Piledriver, I and IX Corps jumped off on June 1 to reach the Wyoming Line just south of the southern foundations of the Iron Triangle at Chorwon and Kumwha while the Marines moved on the Punchbowl, a circular volcanic depression with knife-like ridges that was three miles wide at bottom and six miles wide at top. By June 11, Chorwon and Kumwha were in Eighth Army control. The northern point of Pyonggang was secured two days later, but the Chinese held the northern heights in such strength it had to be abandoned. Now it was the Chinese turn to dig their own no-name line. They burrowed deep into the hills, reinforcing

their underground rooms with earth berms and tree trunks. The Chinese established a defense in depth that could be cracked only with extreme losses of men. And only a direct hit with a 155-millimeter howitzer had a chance of damaging the bunkers.

The Chinese plans of driving the Americans into the sea had ended in defeat. Now they were fighting a war of endurance. The days of rolling up and down the peninsula were over; positional war—so brutally waged 40 years earlier in World War I—had come to Korea.

The Joint Chiefs told Ridgway he could continue air and naval operations in Korea, but he was prohibited from attacking Soviet territory, Manchuria and hydroelectric plants along the Yalu River. Even if Chinese broke through his lines, he could not retaliate against the Chinese mainland. His job was "to inflict maximum personnel and materiel losses on the forces of North Korea and Communist China operating

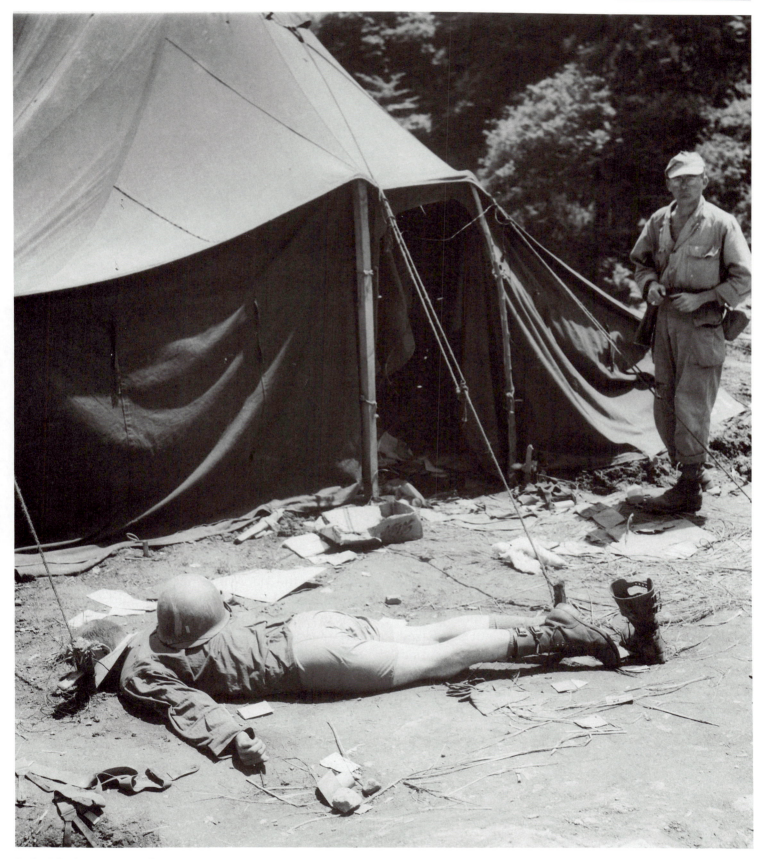

Left: Marines press forward to mop up after a flame thrower wipes out an enemy pillbox.

Above: A GI stands guard over the body of an American lieutenant. He lies as he fell in front of a U.S. Battalion Command Post when it was overrun by the Chinese, only to be retaken later by the Americans.

In the wake of the battle the Chinese leave their dead behind, and U.N. forces collect them at Chunchon. The uniform of the dead soldier in the foreground still smolders.

within the geographical boundaries of Korea and the waters adjacent thereto." The principal goal now was to "create conditions favorable to a settlement of the Korean conflict." On June 2, Van Fleet told war correspondents that the Chinese would not be chased. In a statement, he said: "The Eighth Army's pursuit phase has now ended with the clearing, again, of enemy units from South Korea." The air campaign had not only supported ground fighting, but bombers had hit just about every target available in North Korea. At the MacArthur hearings in Washington, Air Force general Emmett O'Donnell said: "I would say that the entire, almost the entire Korean peninsula is just a terrible mess. Everything is destroyed. There is nothing standing worthy of the name."

A year after this bloody business had started, it was time to talk peace.

9

Talking Peace, Waging War

Wars are easier to get into than out of. The combatants in Korea proved that by taking more than two years from the start of truce talks to the signing of an armistice. In the interim, they pounded each other with guns and bombs, maiming and killing while talking peace.

With an uneasy equilibrium on the battlefield, Secretary-General Trygve Lie told the United Nations on June 1 that a cease-fire along the 38th parallel would fulfill the main purposes of the war—that of repelling armed aggression.

A U.N. tank pauses to return harassing fire from Red soldiers in a hill to the right where a shell burst erupts.

U.N. tanks and hitchhiking troops cross the Choyang River in hot pursuit of the Red Chinese. Trucks go back to the other shore to pick up more GIs.

Also in early June, George Kennan, the career statesman who proposed the policy of containment in dealing with communists, met informally in New York with Jakob Malik, the U.S.S.R.'s ambassador to the United Nations. The peace feelers were out, and Malik implied conditions were right to end the fighting. And on June 23, Malik publicly stated his views on a U.N.-sponsored radio program. "The Soviet peoples believe the most acute problem of the present day—the problem of armed conflict in Korea—could be settled....The Soviet peoples believe that as a first step, discussions should be started between the belligerents for a cease-fire and armistice providing for

the mutual withdrawal of forces from the 38th parallel. Can such a step be taken? I think it can, provided there is a sincere desire to put an end to the bloody fighting in Korea," Malik said in his broadcast. In a statement approved by President Truman, Far East commander Matthew Ridgway broadcast a June 30 message aimed at China and North Korea. "As commander in chief of the United Nations Command, I have been instructed to communicate to you the following: I am informed that you may wish a meeting to discuss an armistice providing for the cessation of hostilities and all acts of armed force in Korea, with adequate guarantees for the maintenance of such ar-

Cleaning up, two wary infantrymen enter another straw-thatched village south of Chorwon.

mistice. Upon the receipt of word from you that such a meeting is desired I shall be prepared to name my representative. I would also at that time suggest a date at which he could meet with your representative. I propose that such a meeting could take place aboard a Danish hospital ship in Wonsan harbor," Ridgway said. The statement was aired because the countries had no formal channels to talk directly.

Radio Peking responded with a reply from North Korean leader Kim Il Sung and Chinese commander Peng Teh-huai. "We are authorized to tell you that we agree to suspend military activities and to hold peace negotiations, and that our delegates will meet with yours. We suggest, in regard to the place for holding

talks, that such talks be held at Kaesong, on the 38th parallel. If you agree to this, our delegates will be prepared to meet your delegates between July 10 and July 15, 1951," it said.

But Ridgway didn't want to suspend military operations. There was fear of a new Chinese offensive in July and suspicions that the Chinese would use a lull in fighting to rehabilitate their battered army. "Their intent is clear that military action shall be suspended from beginning of armistice negotiations. Such action might gravely prejudice safety and security of United Nations forces. I consider this wholly unacceptable, and unless otherwise instructed, I shall categorically reject it," Ridgway cabled the Joint Chiefs. Washington agreed that the military effort should not be relaxed. Ridgway was instructed to reply to the Chinese: "I am prepared for my representatives to meet yours at Kaesong on July 10 or at an earlier date if your representatives complete their preparations before that date. Since agreement on armistice terms has to precede cessation of hostilities, delay in initiating the meetings and in reaching agreement will prolong the fighting and increase the losses."

A war of words was about to start.

One stumbling block was South Korean President Syngman Rhee, who stubbornly clung to his dream of unifying the peninsula by the sword and expelling the Chinese communists. "The Americans want an armistice. One million Chinese troops on the peninsula and they want an armistice. It's ridiculous. Our goal is unification. If we seek an armistice now, we accede to national division. I categorically oppose a truce," Rhee told government officials. Nevertheless, he instructed Paik Sun Yup, who would rise to the rank of four-star general and become the ROK army's first chief of staff, to attend the armistice talks.

A preliminary meeting to begin peace talks was set for July 8 in Kaesong, an ancient Korean capital that had been in South Korean hands before the war but was now in communist territory. Kaesong was known as the Closed Door Village. U.N. negotiators arrived aboard big green helicopters. The communists arrived in Russian or captured American jeeps. In a former teahouse at the foot of Pine Tree Peak, the two sides in this undeclared war met and decided the talks should start July 10.

In truth, Kaesong was a poor choice for peace talks because it was an armed camp, and the communists

Left: The Canadians join the fray. Infantry of the 25th Brigade take positions near the 38th parallel.

didn't hesitate in displaying force. And the wary opponents approached the talks with different objectives. For starters, the Americans insisted that the fighting should stop on the existing main line of resistance, roughly the Kansas Line, with an armistice commission to monitor troops and weapons. The Chinese adamantly wanted a demarcation line at the 38th parallel, with all foreign troops to withdraw from the peninsula. Secretary of State Dean Acheson indicated during the MacArthur hearings that a settlement along the parallel would be satisfactory, and the Americans had endorsed the January proposal—rejected by China—of a cease-fire along the man-made line. Backing down to the original boundary between the two Koreas, however, would have meant a loss of territory for the United Nations to a point where they had not built fortifications. And the United States feared that if it withdrew its forces, China would be in a better position to mass reinforcements in Manchuria.

The first armistice meeting was held July 10. The chief negotiator for the United Nations Command was U.S. Vice Admiral C. Turner Joy, commander of Navy forces in the Far East who spoke with calm, quiet dignity. "Success or failure of the negotiations begun here today depends directly upon the good faith of the delegations here present," Joy said in his opening statement at the old teahouse. His counterpart was Nam Il, a tall, youthful general who was chief of staff for the North Korean Peoples Army and vice premier of North Korea. But the proceedings bogged down immediately on what the agenda should be. Joy had placed a United Nations flag on the table; Nam Il countered after lunch by placing a larger North Korean banner on their side. Gaining the upper hand—or saving face—seemed paramount to substance. The Chinese sat in high upholstered chairs; the U.N. negotiators got smaller wooden seats.

That first day, the United Nations forces had 19 killed, 60 wounded and five missing. The toll would climb and climb and climb on each succeeding day over the next two years. Someone calculated that two combatants fell every minute the talks went on. Every death, every wound, every day spent away from home was all the more galling because both sides desired to end the fighting.

Another point of contention was media coverage. At first, only communist reporters were allowed in Kaesong. Western correspondents provoked such an outcry that Ridgway had to pacify them, and the communists allowed them into Kaesong on July 16. But news was hard to come by, due to the pace of the talks and Eighth Army's desire to put a clamp on

Gen. Ridgway poses with President Syngman Rhee and top commanders at Pusan, South Korea. Left to right, Gen. John B. Coulter, deputy commander Eighth Army; Lt. Gen. James Van Fleet, commander Eighth Army; Rhee; Ridgway; John J. Muccio, U.S. ambassador to South Korea.

developments in this delicate time. "Arranging for an armistice during the progress of actual fighting is one of the most delicate negotiations in human affairs and must necessarily be conducted in strictest secrecy.

Left: A GI, ready for anything, moves through Chorwon itself as the allied offensive continues.

Moreover, ultimate success must depend in some measure upon the willingness of the public to await concrete results and especially to refrain from violent reaction to incomplete or unfounded reports and rumors," said Maj. Gen. Floyd Parks, Eighth Army's chief information officer. Still, nobody expected to be there long. In a poll among war correspondents, most

Allied soldiers hold their ears and duck as they fire their 75mm recoilless rifle at enemy positions.

figured it would take two weeks to hash out an agreement, and the most pessimistic guess was six weeks. In reality, it took 24 bloody months in which participants on both sides were shelled, ambushed, snipered, booby-trapped, sickened or captured. Although no substantial territory changed hands in the next two years, the battles for numbered hilltops made Korea a bleeding wound.

To mollify Rhee, Ridgway summoned the president to Eighth Army headquarters on July 16 to explain the concept of a demilitarized zone and to break the word there would be no more offensives. The next day, Rhee wrote Ridgway: "The substance of the position of my government is that we cannot maintain our nation in half our country. A divided Korea is a ruined Korea, unstable economically, politically and

Below: Reaching beyond the front lines, a B-29 heads for targets deep in North Korea, while the mountainous terrain unfolds beneath it.

Litterbearers lead the way as men of the 24th Infantry Division cross a foot-bridge over a swollen stream and vehicles on the right ferry equipment and more men.

militarily....In every Korean heart and in every Korean mind the fact is clear that our nation would be plunged into irrevocable disaster by any acceptance of a continued dividing line....It is the Communist Empire which is rotten with internal weakness. Negotiations continued with this conviction should lead to success. In this spirit there is no need to settle short of the goal of re-unification and free elections." Joseph Muccio, the U.S. ambassador to South Korea, cabled Washington: "President Rhee, on blindly emotional ground, is attempting to sabotage armistice."

The pace of the talks was exasperating. The two sides didn't agree on an agenda until July 26. Its major points were: adopting the agenda; fixing a military demarcation line between both sides so as to establish a demilitarized zone as the basic condition for cessa-

tion of hostilities in Korea; making concrete arrangements for the realization of cease-fire and armistice in Korea, including the composition, authority and functions of a supervisory organ for carrying the terms of cease-fire and armistice; determining arrangements relating to prisoners of war; and making recommendations to the governments of the countries concerned on both sides. "To sit down with these men and deal with them as representatives of an enlightened and civilized people is to deride one's own dignity and to invite the disaster their treachery will inevitably bring upon us," Ridgway cabled the Joint Chiefs on August 6. Ridgway wanted to tell the delegates to "employ such language and methods as these treacherous savages cannot fail to understand, and understanding, respect." But the Joint Chiefs calmed

On reconnaissance, Lt. (jg) John S. Gregory, Naval Reserve, out of Linden, Wisconsin, flies his Grumman F9F Panther jet from the carrier *Boxer* over the Chosin Reservoir in North Korea.

him down and the talks went on and on and on.

The seminal moment of the early talks came on August 10, when Nam Il insisted on stopping the war at the 38th parallel and asked if the United Nations had given up its insistence about the present battle line. "We will not discuss further the 38th parallel as a military demarcation line," Joy said. "Don't try to recover at this table what you lost on the battlefield." A frozen silence followed, and the two sides sat across from each other without uttering a word for 2 hours

An F-80 Shooting Star dives through the smoke from bombs from other planes toward a target in North Korea. Commanders have called for even closer support from the air.

and 11 minutes before adjourning.

Future days brought more diatribes. Joy spoke of the "haughty stubbornness, the arbitrary inflexibility and unreasoning stubbornness" of the Chinese position. "By your obdurate and unreasonable refusal to negotiate you have brought these meetings to a standstill. You have slammed every door leading to possible progress....You refuse to negotiate except on your own terms, thus seeking to falsely portray yourself as a victor dictating to the vanquished," Joy said. Nam Il retorted: "Your statement does not frighten us and cannot change our stand." The talks adjourned for several weeks on August 23 when the communists charged that a U.N. aircraft had strafed Kaesong, a charge that U.N. commanders said was a fabrication. When talks resumed, they were moved to Panmunjom, a tiny village of mud huts that was six miles east of Kaesong and about midway between the front

Right: Two GIs in bullet proof vests, and one without, move up a steep slope. In foreground are Chinese felled in earlier action.

lines. The change of location did nothing to speed the process, however. In a closely guarded secret that wasn't made public until after the armistice was signed, a mobile force of U.S. Marines stood by just outside the neutral zone throughout the negotiations, ready to dash in and rescue U.N. delegates in the event of communist treachery. Organized in October of 1951, the 300-man rescue force was equipped with flame-throwing tanks and armored personnel carriers. A designated platoon—known as the "snatch platoon"—was supposed to fight its way in and out to free delegates if they were abducted. Other members of the force were supposed to set up blocking posi-

Marines of the 1st Division hold a memorial service for fallen comrades as the fighting comes to a standstill while U.N. and Chinese cease-fire negotiators talk at Kaesong, July 1951.

tions. The force was never needed, but its existence underscored the distrust between the two sides.

The pace of the talks was worrisome to ground commander James Van Fleet, and he worked his troops to keep them from losing their fighting trim. "A sitdown army is subject to collapse at the first sign of an enemy effort....As commander of the Eighth Army, I couldn't allow my forces to become soft and dormant," Van Fleet said.

Less than two weeks after the talks started in July, Van Fleet planned operations to straighten and shorten his line, plus deny some high ground for North Korean guns massed around the north, west and east rims of the Punchbowl crater. At the end of July, the U.S. 2nd Division took a foothold on the western edge of the Punchbowl. Summer rains slowed its progress. Several miles to the southeast, the ROKs attacked a J-shaped ridge that the North Koreans had fortified. It took nine days of bloody fighting to clear the North Koreans from their bunkers, and it was a harbinger of the tough fighting to come for hilltops.

With Ned Almond having gone back to the United States, the new X Corps commander, Maj. Gen. Clovis E. Byers Jr., directed an operation to seize the Punchbowl and a ridge system to its west. On Army maps, the ridge was topped off by Hill 983. War correspondents named it Bloody Ridge. At the Punchbowl, the 1st Marine Division took the northeast rim and the 5th ROK Division assaulted the northwest heights. The U.S. 2nd Division was supposed to take Bloody Ridge, with the ROK 7th Division protecting its flank by occupying the western hills.

A direct assault by the 9th Regiment produced heavy casualties but failed to dislodge the North Koreans atop Bloody Ridge. Then came a double envelopment by the entire division, with the 23rd and 38th Regiments sweeping the sides and the 9th Regiment charging straight up the slope. The resolution came the night of September 4-5, when the North Koreans abandoned the ridge and left 500 dead behind. In three horrible weeks, the Americans and ROKs suffered 2,700 casualties while the communists had 15,000 killed or wounded. Commanders were shaken by the toll needed to assault hilltops fortified by dug-in and determined defenders. A pattern was also set for future combat. Korean hills had the look of wastelands because artillery blasts sheered off tree limbs and trunks, erased all vegetation and exposed the rocky spines of the ridgelines.

Now that Bloody Ridge was occupied, commanders decided to clear the ridge system to the north, where North Koreans had fallen back and burrowed bunkers, trenches and gun positions. There were three major features atop the ridge—Hills 894, 931 and 851—that ran south to north like the backbone of a fish, with numerous ribs running off on either side. The entire system was called Heartbreak Ridge.

The U.S. 2nd Division again got the assignment. The 23rd Regiment was to assault Heartbreak to take 931 and cut the ridge in half. Then one battalion was to turn north to 851 and another battalion south to 894. The attack began with a 30-minute artillery salvo on September 13, but the assault battalion was pinned down and had to dig in. The next day, the 9th Regiment joined the assault, supported by tanks and artillery in a drive up the southwest fingers. GIs got to within 650 yards of the southern crest, then seized 894 the next day. They hunkered down immediately and faced repeated North Korean counterattacks over the next several days.

The 23rd Regiment was still under fire in the center. On September 16, Col. James Y. Adams attacked with three battalions abreast, but they failed to advance. Communist guns and winding paths leading up the ridge severely hampered transportation; it could take 10 hours to carry a wounded man down the sides and almost as long to haul ammunition and food to the top. The 1st Battalion reached Hill 931 on September 23, but when its ammunition ran out, it was forced off by a communist counterattack. The French battalion also climbed the crest and moved north, but the North Koreans chased them off too. Finally, after two weeks of bitter fighting, commanders called off the assault and worked on new plans. Engineers cleared mines and repaired roads for a tank assault up the rocky slopes. Fighter-bombers softened communist positions. Then at the climactic moment on the afternoon of October 5, artillery poured down on three North Korean regiments and Marine Corsairs delivered napalm, rockets and machine gun fire. By noon of October 6, Hill 931 was taken and the only remaining enemy bulwark was Hill 851. At daybreak of October 13, the French stormed the pinnacle and secured possession of Heartbreak. The place earned its name—the 2nd Division had 3,700 casualties in 30 days of combat. Communist losses were estimated at 25,000.

In describing the fighting for Bloody and Heartbreak Ridges, the 2nd Division historian wrote: "Sweating, heart-pounding heavy-footed soldiers dragged their throbbing legs up those tortured, vertical hills. Those who succeeded in grasping their way close to the bunkers were greeted by the crump and shower of black smoke, dirt and sharp steel as grenades were tossed down on them. Dirty, unshaven, miserable, they backed down, tried again, circled,

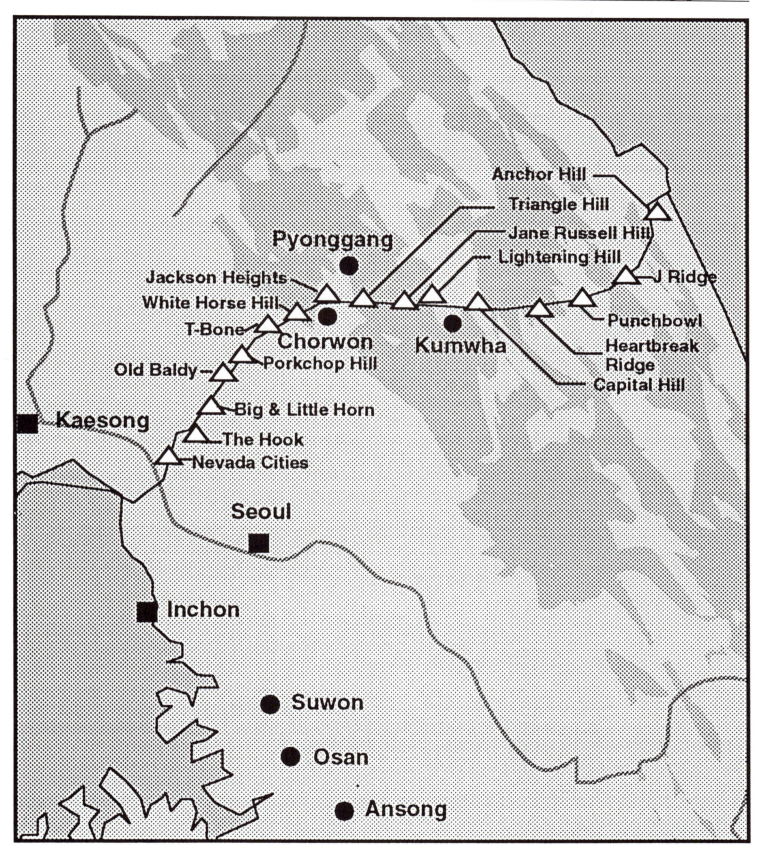

Korean Front, 1951-1953

climbed, slid, suffered, ran, rolled, crouched and grabbed upward only to meet again the murderous fire, the blast of mortar and whine of bullets and jagged fragments. Minutes seemed like hours, hours like days, and days like one long, terrible, dusty, blood-swirled nightmare."

Van Fleet explained his strategy of the summer campaigns. "My basic mission during the past four months has been to destroy the enemy, so that the men of the Eighth Army will not be destroyed....In prodding the enemy in the deep belly of the peninsula we have taken many casualties....It is mandatory that we control the high ground features, so that we can look down the throat of the enemy and thereby better perform our task of destruction....As we open our autumn campaign, the enemy potential along the front has been sharply reduced by our hill-hopping tactics. The communist forces in Korea are not liquidated, but they are badly crippled," he wrote in a command report. But while a sag in the Eighth Army lines had been eliminated, countless hills loomed to the north, each one a potential citadel of communist firepower. The cost of attacking them became prohibitive.

The lesson was driven home again in Operation Commando on Eighth Army's left flank. The aim was to keep Chinese artillery fire off a railroad line leading from Seoul to the southern bases of the Iron Triangle. Those tracks carried the bulk of supplies to the U.N. front lines. Five reinforced divisions participated— the 1st ROK, the newly created British Commonwealth and the U.S. 1st Cavalry, 3rd and 25th Divisions. The 1st Cav in the center ran smack into an entrenched Chinese field army that was determined not to yield a yard of ground. Much of the combat centered around a hill the GIs called Old Baldy, one of the most contested pieces of Korean real estate. It got its name because its crest was completely denuded of trees. It took 17 ghastly days to move six miles, during which the 1st Cav's four artillery battalions fired 380,856 rounds. The division's historian wrote: "The effort required in driving an entire Chinese army from an excellent defensive line was so great as to almost defy description....Survivors of companies joined with remaining fragments of other companies to return and assault again the positions that had previously all but wiped them out."

The 1st Cav had 2,900 casualties in the fight. In a fight for a nook called the Bloody Angle, the 3rd Division took 500 casualties. I Corps was ordered to dig in on its new line. "Future operations would be confined to those necessary to maintain existing positions," the British historian noted. At an October 16 news conference, Ridgway said the battlefield situation "could readily be construed as a military stalemate. It all depends on how you look at it." A U.S. public opinion poll that fall described Korea as "an utterly useless war." In November, the 1st Cavalry Division was withdrawn back to Japan and replaced in the line by the 45th Division (Oklahoma National Guard). The 1st Cav had expected to be in Korea for six weeks; it had endured 16 nightmarish months.

After tallying the toll of Operation Commando, Gen. Ridgway instructed Eighth Army to assume an "active defense." Troops should be prepared to exploit targets of opportunity, but offensive actions were limited to the capture of outposts not more than 5,000 yards ahead of the front lines. Any attack larger than battalion-size required the consent of the U.N. commander. Defensive positions were organized and constructed with coils of barbed wire, stacks of sandbags, artillery-absorbing overhead cover, cots strung with rope, peep holes for gun placements and rows of trenches. This was no push-button war in the nuclear age. Korea was a throwback to trench warfare at Verdun and Flanders, where World War I infantrymen gazed across the main line of resistance.

The Chinese had also switched tactics, building a system of interlocking and formidable positions that would require a terrific price in firepower and blood to crack. The war of maneuver characterized at Pusan, Inchon, Seoul, Pyongyang and Chosin was over. But stalemate didn't mean an end to the bloodletting. The two sides punched and counterpunched at outposts such as the Nevada cities hills of Carson, Reno, Elko and Vegas. There was Berlin and East Berlin, Bunker Hill and Boulder City. In addition to Jane Russell Hill, other crests were called Hedy Lamarr, Alice, Esther, Dagmar and Hannah. Along the line were The Hook, The Rock, The Yoke, Spud, Outpost Harry, Big and Little Nori, Little Gibraltar, Porkchop, T-Bone, Eerie, Jackson Heights, White Horse, Arsenal, Arrowhead, Boomerang, Capital, Alligator, Alligator Jaws and the Anchor. The name for everything north of the line was "Goonieland."

Meanwhile, the war brought social change to an army that since the Civil War had segregated its black soldiers into separate regiments. It happened before the U.S. Supreme Court's 1954 order eliminating segregation in public schools, and it came at a time when blacks could work in a white restaurant but couldn't eat there. Up to this point, the Army believed that integration would hurt morale and harm fighting efficiency, despite President Truman's 1948 order directing "equality of treatment" in the armed forces. The manpower demands of the war hastened the end of formal segregation. In July of 1951 at Fort Jackson, South Carolina, draftees were assigned platoons on the order they arrived, not the color of skin. Men began living and working in close quarters with people they would never have associated with in civilian life. "The attitude of Southern soldiers was that this was the Army way; they accepted it the same way they accepted getting up at 5:30 in the morning," said

Brig. Gen. Frank McConnell, Fort Jackson's commander. Units in Korea were in dire need of replacements that fall, and on October 1, by order of Matthew Ridgway, the 24th Infantry Regiment (Negro) of the 25th Division was desegregated. Long before the Civil Rights Act, the Army had begun eliminating its practice of separating soldiers by race.

Peace talks resumed October 25 in Panmunjom, where a large brown tent had been erected with flooring, heating and lighting for the conferees. A breakthrough came November 7 when the communists proposed that the existing front lines serve as the demarcation line, with both sides to withdraw two kilometers to form a demilitarized buffer zone. Ridgway opposed it, insisting that the demarcation line be set at the time of the armistice. That way, if Eighth Army gained territory, it would not be given back. And the existing line would give the communists Kaesong, which Ridgway argued could have easily been taken if the armistice talks had not started. But Washington ordered Ridgway to accept the loss of Kaesong, much to the dismay of the negotiators. Ridgway told them: "I dislike these orders just as much as you do, but we are military people. We have stated as clearly as we know how our position. We have now been instructed to do something we believe to be wrong. But you are military people and you will carry out your orders." By November 23, orderlies had traced the battle line on official maps, and it was established four days later. Except for a small segment in western Korea, it generally ran six to 12 miles north of the 38th parallel at a slight northeast angle. It had taken 65 meetings spread over four months at two different sites to clear the first hurdle.

The next question was how to make sure an armistice was enforced. In early December, the communists conceded that neutral nations could carry out inspections to ensure compliance. But the item bogged down in a dispute over repairing North Korean airfields from which the communists could launch air strikes. It became such a stumbling block that the issue was set aside.

Now the issue came down to the exchange of prisoners as troops bundled up against a second Korean winter. Debate on POWs dragged the war on for 19 bloody months. The Americans took the position that any POW who did not want to return to communism would not be forced to go back. Essentially, the Americans were giving freedom of choice to their prisoners, many of whom were Chinese Nationalists impressed into the communist army or South Koreans that had been made to fight against the United Nations. "Just as I had always insisted that we could not abandon the South Koreans who had stood by us and freedom, so I now refused to agree to any solution that provided for the return against their will of prisoners of war to communist domination," Truman wrote. He also issued a statement that read: "We will not buy an armistice by turning over human beings for slaughter and slavery." But the Chinese were equally insistent that all prisoners be returned whether they wanted to or not. Lists of prisoners weren't exchanged until December 18, but the accounting only served to widen the dispute. The communists said they had 11,559 POWs, of which 3,198 were American. The Americans were shocked at the low number. Their own lists had 11,500 Americans and 88,000 South Koreans in captivity. On the other side, the United Nations said it had 132,474 POWs, including 95,531 North Koreans, 20,700 Chinese and 16,243 former ROKs who had been impressed into Kim Il Sung's army. The irony of the negotiations was that the warring sides suffered more casualties in the remaining war than there were POWs in camps.

As the year ended, Van Fleet prodded his corps commanders to set ambushes and capture prisoners. Although the battlefield appeared calm, Van Fleet wanted "to keep the Army sharp through smell of gunpowder and the enemy." On New Year's Day, 1952, Adm. C. Turner Joy made a special broadcast to the American people. "In six months, we have made some progress toward an honorable, equitable and stable armistice. That progress has been painfully slow to us here at the armistice camp, as it has to the men in the foxhole, to the men in the prisoner-of-war camps, and to you at home. But in dealing with the communists, there is no other way," he said. In his diary, Joy noted that there was no end in sight. "With each passing day, there is less and less reason to think the communists want a stable armistice. Certainly no one can accuse them of being in a hurry to demonstrate good faith," Joy wrote.

Harry Truman was also frustrated. On January 24, 1952, the President wrote in his diary: "Dealing with communist governments is like an honest man trying to deal with a numbers racket king or the head of a dope ring. It seems to me that the proper approach now would be an ultimatum with a 10-day expiration limit, informing Moscow that we intend to blockade the China coast from the Korean border to Indochina, and that we intend to destroy every military base in Manchuria, including submarine bases, by means now in our control, and if there is further interference, we shall eliminate any ports or cities necessary to accomplish our peaceful purposes....This means all out war." But it never happened.

THE ARMED FORCES DESEGREGATE: REFORM FOLLOWS FUNCTION

The beginning of the Korean War meant the end of liberal reform. That was the lament of progressives like Sen. Hubert Humphrey of Minnesota, who said that as a result of the war, "every liberal movement has been stopped cold."

But the war gave a push to one liberal cause that even a presidential order had failed to advance: desegregation of the armed services, particularly the Army. Short of manpower, flooded with black draftees, and hindered by having to run two services—one white, one black—the Army came to regard integration as being in its own interest.

The end of World War II had found the military almost as segregated as it was at the end of the Civil War. Black soldiers served in black units, often performing demeaning or demoralizing roles: cooking, cleaning, carrying, carting. President Truman's sensitivity to discrimination in the military was heightened by a series of attacks on black veterans who returned home after V-J day. But not until July 26, 1948, with the black vote in the fall election hanging in the balance, did he issue Executive Order 9981, directing "equality of treatment and opportunity for all persons in the armed services."

Truman's order said nothing about desegregation, and it allowed the military wriggle room. After stipulating that the new policy "shall be put into effect as rapidly as possible," the order added these words: "having due regard to the time required to effectuate any necessary changes without impairing efficiency or morale."

Over the next two years there was some progress: the Air Force announced plans to end most forms of discrimination; the Navy promised to seek more blacks; the Marines eliminated segregated basic training. But the Army—the largest service and the one with the most blacks—balked.

Finally, in 1950, Secretary of the Army Gordon Gray issued a directive that generally reiterated Truman's order. But E.W. Kenworthy, executive secretary of a presidential committee charged with helping to implement desegregation, concluded that "the Army intends to do as little as possible toward implementing the policy which it adopted and published."

Then came Korea.

Brig. Gen. Frank McConnell was commandant of the infantry training base at Fort Jackson, South Carolina—a typical, segregated installation. But in the early days of the war about 1,000 draftees, many of them black, poured in each day. Treating whites and blacks separately was slowing the whole training process.

When McConnell summoned his staff and proposed ignoring the color line, one aide suggested that he might be "going off the deep end." So McConnell pulled out Secretary Gray's directive. "It was all the authority I needed," he later recalled. "I said that if we didn't ask permission, they can't stop us." He ordered that the next 55 draftees who arrived be put in the same platoon; it was the beginning of the end of segregation at Fort Jackson.

Those who predicted trouble were disappointed. "I would see recruits, Negro and white, walking down the street off-duty, all grouped together," McConnell remembered. "The attitude of the Southern soldiers was that this was the Army way; they accepted it the same way they accepted getting up at 5:30 in the morning."

Journalist Lee Nichols visited a barracks and found blacks from Mississippi and Arkansas and

In the early days of the war, the only ways for U.S. troops to leave Korea alive were to be wounded, be injured in an accident or get sick. Then the military began to rotate home individuals instead of replacing whole units. Troops were selected on the basis of combat time, wounds received and length of service. The first to return to the United States were GIs of the 24th Division, the survivors of Task Force Smith and the first ground battles of July of 1950. Later in 1951, a point system was established with 36 points needed for a trip home. Each month at the front was worth four points, so a minimum nine-month tour of duty was necessary. Service elsewhere in Korea was worth two points a month. In the winter of 1951-52,

about 20,000 soldiers and Marines were rotated home each month, cut loose from combat to return to a world where few beyond family and loved ones acknowledged their service.

To break the deadlock in negotiations, Joy presented a package proposal on April 28. The U.N. Command agreed to accept reconstruction of North Korean airfields provided the communists agreed to no forced repatriation of POWs. The Chinese rejected it, even though Joy called it the "final and irrevocable" offer. On May 6, Ridgway said the responsibility for peace now rested on communism's shoulders.

At this point, a war within a war broke out in the U.N. prison camps. The flashpoint was Koje Island, whites from Georgia and South Carolina sitting next to each other on their bunks, "busily cleaning their rifles...with no apparent antipathy." Soon the color line was disappearing at all Army training bases.

Meanwhile, as North Korean forces pushed the South Koreans and their American allies back into a corner of the peninsula, the same kind of necessity was dictating an end to segregation on the battlefield.

During World War II, some all-black platoons had been incorporated into all-white infantry units. But now, black soldiers were sent into all-white units as low as company level, where they fought shoulder-to-shoulder with whites.

The impetus for change came not from the generals in Washington, but from the commanders in Korea. Col. John G. Hill commanded the 9th Infantry Regiment, one of the first American units to land on the peninsula. Hill's all-black 3rd battalion had 10 percent more men than needed, while his two white battalions were shorthanded to begin with and even more so after a few battles.

Circumstances, Hill later wrote, dictated his next move: "We had no replacements....We would have been doing ourselves a disservice to permit (black) soldiers to lie around in rear units at the expense of the still further weakening of our (white) rifle companies."

So he began integrating his units, and soon noticed a change. Black soldiers who had been unreliable in combat became dependable, and more blacks began volunteering for dangerous missions.

Other commanders followed suit. Most found that once integrated, blacks fought as well as whites, and that whites accepted the change. By 1951, according to historian Eric F. Goldman, the color line among the armed forces in Korea "was scarcely visible."

The black press focused on Capt. Daniel "Chappie" James, an Air Force pilot who gained prominence flying dangerous, unarmed reconnaissance flights over North Korea. Articles usually stressed that the camera in the back seat of his jet was operated by a white airman. James later became the service's first black general.

Integration also received an unintended boost from the performance of the 24th Infantry Division, the Army's oldest and largest black unit. According to an official Army history written in 1961, many troops of the 24th succumbed to "mass hysteria" early in the war and fled at the first sign of the enemy. Troops repeatedly defied superiors' orders to fight, and the unit suffered from inordinately high rates of straggling, desertion and self-inflicted wounds.

Many of veterans of the 24th have argued that the Army in general fought poorly at first in Korea; that the 24th was poorly trained and poorly led by its white officers; and that the 24th won the first American victory of the war, at Yechon. In the summer of 1951, observing that "Negro troops are more efficient when integrated with white troops," the Army announced plans to disband the division and transfer its soldiers to integrated units. Most went happily.

"This outfit never did function the way it should have," said Cpl. George Johnson, a jeep driver from New York City. "The least little thing we did wrong, they scored us for it. Lots of outfits have had to leave a hill, but when we left a hill they said, 'Yellow.' We got a good group of men here, but...you can't segregate folks and have it just the same."

Although integration at first was limited to the Eighth Army in Korea, eventually Army Chief of Staff Gen. J. Lawton Collins wrote all overseas commanders a confidential letter calling for gradual integration. In 1954 the Army pronounced itself officially integrated—no unit was more than half black.

It had been a case of reform following function. "We didn't do it to improve the social situation," Collins' deputy, Gen. Anthony McAuliffe, later explained. "It was merely a matter of getting the best out of the military personnel that was available to us."

a fortress off the southern tip of Korea where 100,000 communists were held in compounds ringed with barbed wire. Some prisoners had renounced communism and intended to defect after the war; the communists organized ranks to keep comrades in line. In this nasty place, gangs on either side could sentence a man to death or beatings. During a rock fight on December 18, 1951, 14 prisoners died and 24 were wounded. Then in another uprising on February 18, 1952, 77 prisoners were killed and 140 wounded while one American guard and 38 United Nations troops were injured. A new commandant, Brig. Gen. Francis Dodd, took over Koje on February 20. After months of screening prisoners, the U.N. delegates told the

communists that only 70,000 of the 132,000 POWs were willing to return home.

Another irony emerged over camp conditions. The United Nations camps were open to inspection by the International Red Cross. But the communists refused outside inspectors while charges surfaced about torture, beatings, brainwashing, filthy conditions and ill treatment in the camps. Documentation was another matter, however. Bob Eunson, head of the Tokyo Bureau for The Associated Press, was ultimately able to get a camera and a generous supply of film to Frank "Pappy" Noel, the photographer who had been captured as part of Task Force Drysdale. Instead of atrocities, many of his pictures in a communist camp

The communists recognized the propaganda value of the pictures taken by Pappy Noel. Here he captures on film POWs playing ball on a snow-covered field near the Yalu River.

showed U.S. prisoners playing volleyball, basketball and football at the same time Koje Island was in the headlines.

The simmering trouble at Koje reached a full boil just as the United Nations was changing commanders. Ridgway was off to Paris to replace Dwight Eisenhower as commander of the North Atlantic Treaty Organization, and his replacement was Gen. Mark Clark, who had commanded U.S. forces in Italy during World War II. Just as Clark was arriving, the prisoners kidnapped Gen. Dodd on Koje at 2 p.m. on May 7. The prisoners raised a sign: "We capture Dodd. As long as our demand will be solved, his safety is secured. If there happen brutal act such as shooting, his life is danger."

The prisoners provided Dodd with a telephone and passed along medication for his ulcers. Dodd gave orders to guards not to use force against the prisoners while ROK navy boats ringed the mutinous island and a battalion of the U.S. 9th Infantry Regiment was sent from the mainland to beef up security. Ridgway broke the news to Clark as the two generals flew to Korea from Japan for an inspection tour. "We've got a little situation over in Korea where it's reported some prisoners have taken in one of the camp commanders, General Dodd, and are holding him as a hostage. We'll have to get into that situation when we arrive at Eighth Army headquarters and find out what the score is," Ridgway said. On the ground, the outgoing commander ordered Van Fleet "to establish or-

Pappy Noel's pictures are of great solace to families back home. Here are four of his subjects at POW camp No. 5 at Pyokdong: Left to right, Pvt. William Hall of Indianapolis, Indiana, Pfc. Charles Cook of Trenton, New Jersey, Cpl. Abraham Kerns of Wichita, Kansas, and Cpl. William Cox of Gary, Indiana.

der in the camp immediately and maintain it thereafter, using whatever force was required, even tanks." An armored battalion from the 3rd Division was dispatched, and five of the 20 tanks were equipped with flame throwers.

At Koje, a new camp commander was named—Brig. Gen. Charles Colson, chief of staff of I Corps. Colson demanded that Dodd be freed by 10 a.m. on

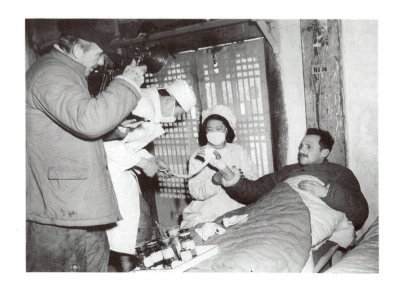

Right: Associated Press photographer Frank (Pappy) Noel was captured with a small group of Marines in Koto, Korea, November 1950. But captivity became an opportunity. He was smuggled an AP camera and film, and soon pictures were getting out of American POWs. Here he gets his first picture, a communist doctor and nurse tending to Pfc. Theodore Pallas of San Francisco.

One American and 69 Korean internees were killed in a communist riot at the sprawling Koje Island stockade where 160,000 prisoners — Chinese and Korean POWs and North Korean civilians — are housed.

May 10. But inside the compound, the prisoners tried Dodd on 19 counts of death or injury to inmates. There was an exchange of statements, and Colson—with Dodd's help on the telephone—issued a reply that said in part "I do admit there has been instances of bloodshed where many POW have been killed and wounded by UN Forces. I can assure in the future that POW can expect humane treatment in this camp according to the principles of International Law." Dodd was released without bloodshed at 9:30 p.m., but it was the prisoners who had won a propaganda victory. Later, at a news conference in Seoul, Dodd said "the demands made by the POWs were inconsequential and the concessions granted by the camp authorities were of minor importance." In Tokyo, Clark called Colson's statement "unadulterated blackmail" and later said it had "no validity whatsoever." Dodd and Colson both lost their stars and were

busted to colonel.

Koje's new commander was Brig. Gen. Haydon "Bull" Boatner, assistant commander of the 2nd Division. His orders from Gen. Clark read: "You are to regain control of the rebellious prisoners on Koje and maintain control thereafter."

After inspecting the camp, Boatner reported the place needed immediate attention. "Within the compounds, the inmates were regularly holding mass demonstrations—marching and waving communist flags, singing and shouting in unison. Inside were statues of Stalin and Kim Il Sung, along with tall flagpoles with communist flags flying. The POWs would crowd against the perimeter fences and curse our Korean guards outside. In each compound, the prisoners had an observation post on a barracks rooftop from which semaphore messages were sent and received. Physically, the enclosures and com-

Gen. Ridgway in rear with Lt. Col. Thomas E. Douglas of Little Rock, Arkansas, escort Army Secretary Frank Pace. The jeep flies the Arkansas state flag (not visible) in honor of the secretary who is also from Little Rock.

More trouble at the Koje Island prison camp. This time 31 prisoners are killed and 139 wounded. Another GI died. No more kid glove treatment. June 1952.

pounds were in shambles. The prisoner fences were of twisted barbed wire strung on rotten sapling poles, and the corner perimeter guard towers had been built inside the perimeter fences. It was what any reasonable soldier would call an unholy mess," he said.

At Panmunjom, the communists made the most of the uprising. Nam Il said haughtily: "The final unalterable and irrevocable facts are the determined resistance of our captured personnel against your inhuman treatment and the righteous struggle of our captured personnel against your forced screening; they are proof that your side will never be able to succeed in your attempt to retain our captured personnel as your cannon fodder." A final resolution came when the prisoners at Koje were transferred to

smaller, more manageable camps. When POWs resisted, paratroopers of the 187th Airborne Regiment helped maintain order. Wearing gas masks and riot gear, the paratroopers carried bayonet-tipped rifles. On June 10, without firing a shot, they herded rebellious prisoners into groups. The toll was 41 prisoners dead and hundreds wounded, with one paratrooper dead and 14 guards injured. In the empty compounds were 3,000 spears, 1,000 gasoline grenades, 4,500 knives and barbed-wire flails.

In the Soviet Union, *Pravda* said: "We have learned that 'civilized' Americans can be yet even more inhuman, yet more infamous than the bloody Hitlerites. Dachau was a death camp. Maidanek was a death factory. Koje is a whole island of death."

The propaganda war also raged on another front. When an epidemic of typhoid and plague sickened thousands of communists, Chinese Premier Chou En-

Left: Two Marines probe for mines while their buddies stay alert for snipers. The mine squad wears armored vests.

The USS *Saint Paul* fires one last nine-gun salvo from its eight-inch guns and steams for the open sea out of Changjin Harbor after an inshore firing run.

lai accused the United States of engaging in germ warfare to destroy communist armies. In March of 1952, Chou claimed that at least 448 air sorties had spread large quantities of germ-carrying insects over northeast China as part of "the criminal and vicious device of mass slaughter of peaceful people." Chou urged the United Nations to investigate. The United States, which denied the charges, suggested an investigation by the International Red Cross or the World Health Organization. But in mid-1952, the Soviet Union used its U.N. veto to block an investigation by the Red Cross into allegations of germ warfare.

The Chinese kept the issue alive by releasing "confessions" of downed airmen. One came from Lt. Keith Enoch and Lt. John Quinn, whose B-26 was shot down January 13, 1952. After five weeks of frightening interrogation, the two made filmed and taped confessions. The stilted language and sentence structure made it clear the statements were made under extreme stress. "It is very clear that the capitalistic Wall Street warmongers, in their greed, their ruthless greed, have caused this horrible crime of bacteriological warfare in order to get more money for themselves in the hope of spreading the war....I was forced to be a tool of these warmongers, made to drop germ bombs, and do this awful crime against the people of

Korea and the Chinese volunteers....They issued me warm clothing against the cold, gave me excellent food, bedding and a warm place to sleep. I am eternally grateful for their kind treatment. At last, after much patience on the part of the Volunteers, I realized my crime. My own conscience bothered me a great deal, and it is very good to be rid of this burden and to confess and repent. I have realized my terrible crime against the people," the confessions said. Other airmen told after the war of being beaten and tortured, but only a handful "confessed" to dropping germ bombs. In one prison camp, Americans played on the fears of their captors by tying a dead mouse to a handmade parachute with the words U.S. Air Force on the canopy. They tossed it outside their compound, watching with glee when guards gingerly retrieved it with tweezers and stuffed it into a bottle. Still, *Pravda* referred to American generals as "butchers in white gloves, the bloody bigots and traders in death who have unleashed the most inhuman carnage in history, warfare with the assistance of microbes, fleas, lice and spiders."

At the bargaining table, the United Nations had a new negotiator. Adm. Joy stepped down on May 22 into retirement, frustrated that Americans were dying daily on the battlefield for lack of a cease-fire. His

TORTURE

Released prisoners of war told grim stories after being released from Communist captivity. An Associated Press story from "Freedom Village" in August 1953 reported some of them:

FREEDOM VILLAGE, KOREA, Friday, Aug. 7 (AP)—The stories told by soldiers back from Communist captivity turned grim yesterday.

A relative of the chief allied armistice negotiator at Panmunjom said his captors tortured him in a futile attempt to wring military information from him.

The co-pilot of a downed Superfortress said he was tortured for four days.

A U.S. Army corporal said he saw 1,500 of his comrades buried in the brutal winter of 1950-51, dead of starvation, freezing or neglect of wounds.

There was visual evidence too of Communist neglect on the second day of the exchange of prisoners. One South Korean soldier was dead on arrival at Panmunjom. Another South Korean died of tuberculosis as a helicopter took him away from Panmunjom.

Many of the allied prisoners were human wrecks. Some were terribly emaciated. Others could hardly walk. Most were South Koreans.

There were 70 Americans in the second exchange, 42 of them sick or wounded. Most appeared to be in good condition.

There were 250 South Koreans. The others returned were 25 British, 25 Turks, 10 Filipinos, 7 Colombians and 5 Australians. The British appeared in the best physical condition.

Lt. Col. Thomas D. Harrison, Clovis, N.M., a second cousin of Lt. Gen. William K. Harrison, senior allied truce negotiator, told of nine days of starvation and torture.

Harrison lost his left leg when his plane was shot down over North Korea in May of 1951. He said he was taken in September to a building near the North Korean capital of Pyongyang where North Korean civilian police tried to get military information from him.

"For seven days they cut off my food entirely, but at every meal they compelled me to watch others eat," he related.

In November, 10 police entered his room, stripped his clothes from him, wired him to a chair, and pulled his head back.

"They put a towel over my face and poured water on the towel," he said. "This cut off the air and I could not breathe. When I would pass out, they brought me to by stabbing me with [lighted] cigarettes.

"It was so cold the water they poured on the towels ran down me and froze. They didn't get any information."

Lt. Samuel E. Massinberg of Detroit, co-pilot of a Superfort shot down over Pyongyang last Jan. 11, said he was tortured for four days by North Koreans trying to get military information.

He said his frostbitten hands were bound behind him, he was given no food and was beaten. The beatings stopped only when part of his left hand rotted away from gangrene.

Cpl. Russel P. James, Auburn, Wash., said he was on a burial detail in the winter of 1950-51 at a notorious North Korean mining camp known as "Death Valley" and had seen more than 1,500 fellow U.S. prisoners buried.

"Every day there were from 25 to 30 American soldiers who had to be buried. They died of their wounds. We had no medical treatment at all. They froze to death. And they didn't have enough to eat."

Sgt. Robert M. Wilkins of Detroit, on a B-26 shot down last January said he and several others escaped, were recaptured and were tossed into a dungeon.

Later, he said, guards took them to another room "and tied us so that we couldn't move." They were forced to kneel with a stick between their knees, their arms drawn up behind them with a rope tied to the ceiling. A choke rope was tied around their throats. He said a British and an American officer died during the ordeal.

A pattern began to emerge from the soldiers' stories. Foot soldiers captured after the winter of 1950-51 told of somewhat better treatment, but they said food and medical care were inadequate.

On the other hand, airmen in the last two years of the war often were treated with utmost brutality, apparently in reprisal for the endless bombings.

For example, Cpl. Charles F. Hearn of St. Louis, Mo., said treatment in a prison camp was "fairly nice." He was captured April 24, 1951.

Maj. John C. Harlan of Institute, W.Va., said that in the last two or three weeks before the exchange, "it seemed like they emptied their warehouses and did everything possible to make us happy."

Capt. Robert C. Henry, Chicago, a B-26 navigator who also is a minister, said the Reds at first broke up his attempts to conduct religious services. Toward the end, they allowed him to hold services occasionally. He was captured Aug. 10, 1952.

Sgt. Edward Hewlett of Detroit, a Negro, said his captors tried repeatedly to get him to write articles "exposing" racial discrimination in the United States. He said others were approached but "not very many men did."

South Koreans said many prisoners were forced to carry ammunition to the front, and he saw three South Koreans shot to death in September of 1950 when they refused.

President Syngman Rhee is under fire, not only from dissidents in his own government, but from American President Harry Truman who wrote he was shocked that Rhee's police had arrested 12 members of the anti-Rhee Assembly. He holds petitions from citizens asking for a popular election for president.

final statement to the Chinese was: "It has been increasingly clear through the long drawn-out conferences that any hope that your side bring good faith to these meetings was forlorn indeed. From the very start, you have caviled over procedural details; you have manufactured spurious issues and placed them in controversy for bargaining purposes; you have denied the existence of agreements made between us when you found the fulfillment thereof not to your liking; you have made false charges based on crimes invented for your purposes; and you indulged in abuse and invective when all other tactics proved ineffective. Through a constant success of delays, fraudulent arguments and artificial attitudes you have obstructed the attainment of an armistice which easily lay within our grasp had there been equal honesty on both sides of this conference table. Nowhere in the record is there a single action of your side which indicates a real and sincere desire to attain the objective for which these conferences were designed. Instead, you have increasingly presented evidence before the world that you did not enter these negotiations with sincerity and high purpose, but rather that you entered into them to gain time to repair your shattered forces and try to accomplish at the conference table what your armies could not accomplish in the field. It is an enormous misfortune that you are constitutionally incapable of understanding the fair and dignified attitude of the United Nations Command. Apparently you cannot comprehend that strong and proud and free nations can make costly sacrifices for principles because they are strong, can be dignified in the face of abuse and deceit because they are proud, and can speak honestly because they are free and do not fear the truth. Instead you impute to the United Nations Command the same suspicion, greed and deviousness which are your stock in trade. You searched every word for a hidden meaning and every agreement for a hidden trap. After 10 months and 12 days I feel that there is nothing more to negotiate. I now turn over the un-

enviable job of further dealings with you to Maj. Gen. William K. Harrison, who succeeds me as senior delegate of the United Nations Command Delegation. May God be with him." With that, he retired from the service.

Repatriation of prisoners was the one major hurdle left for Harrison, who had been a delegate at the talks for four months. Harrison was a West Pointer from the class of 1917—the same class as Ridgway, Mark Clark and chief of staff Collins. A descendant of a signer of the Declaration of Independence and two U.S. presidents, Harrison spoke Chinese and had grown accustomed to China's tactics at the conference table. He viewed the stalemated talks as a different way of waging war: "fighting it with words and not with guns, just trying to prevent us from getting an armistice which we wanted."

When things deadlocked at the table, American commanders tried to force the issue by stepping up

A leaflet dropped over Korea is a warning from the United Nations Command not to accept stashes of supplies or enemy troops in their homes or run the risk of having their homes destroyed with the resultant threat to civilian life. "Heed This Warning," it says.

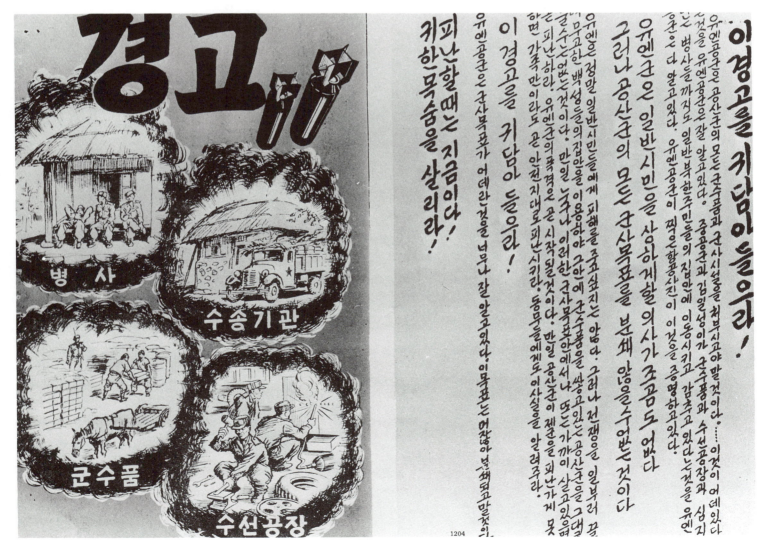

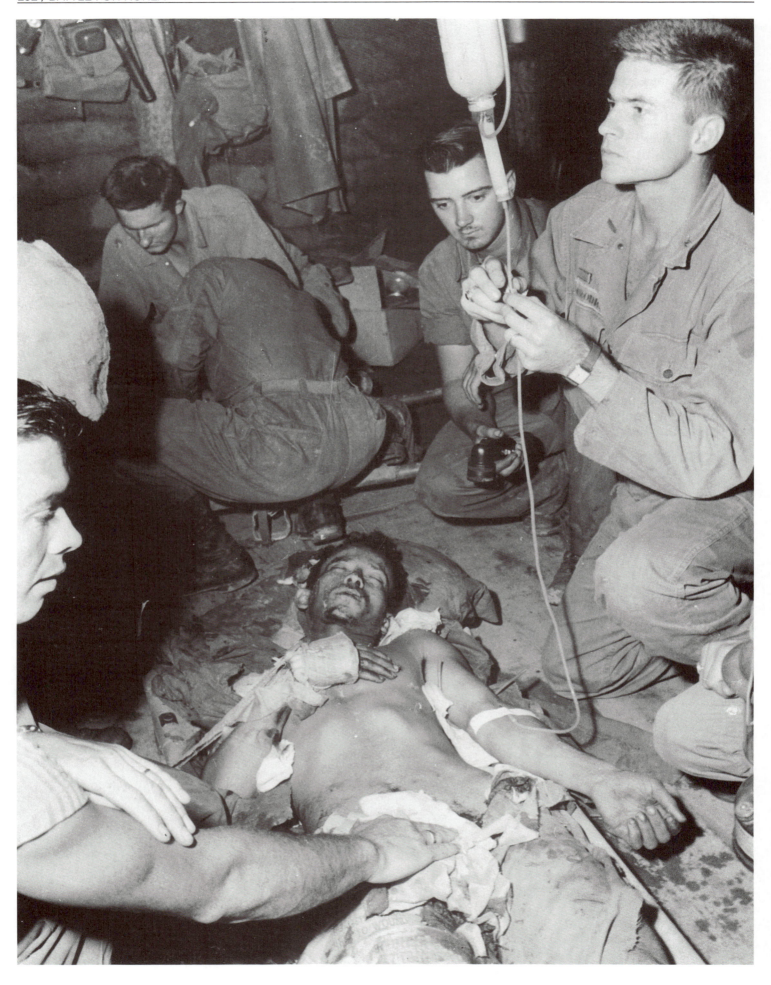

the military pressure—unleashing the Air Force with an intense bombing campaign of North Korea. The tactic resurfaced a generation later when the United States attempted to bomb North Vietnam to the conference table after the Paris peace talks bogged down. In Korea, the targets of the Far East Air Force included 11 hydroelectric plants along the Yalu River. The plants had been considered as targets earlier in the war, but no bombs were dropped because commanders feared it would spread the war beyond Korea. Now, the plants were fair game. "Only through forceful action could the communists be made to agree to an armistice that the United States considered honorable," Gen. Clark said. He wanted to "make the communists realize that the price of peace is not as cheap as they are trying to make it." In three days beginning June 23, land and carrier-based planes flew 1,400 sorties against the hydroelectric stations. The air raids caused a two-week electrical blackout in all of North Korea and affected Manchurian factories which depended on the plants for power. The bombings touched off a worldwide protest because civilians were affected. Even America's allies in London and Paris objected because they weren't consulted beforehand. That summer, three all-out air strikes were launched against Pyongyang. In one raid alone, planes dropped 1,400 tons of bombs and 23,000 gallons of napalm on factories, warehouses, railroad yards, barracks and airfields. The raids flattened what was left of the communist capital and leveled all military targets. Also targeted were 78 smaller cities and an oil refinery just eight miles from the Russian border.

At sea, the American and British navies conducted actions far different from the battles waged over vast oceans in World War II. Their aircraft carriers and dreadnoughts were used to interdict supply lines, support ground forces and flatten land targets. Four U.S. battleships—*Missouri, Iowa, Wisconsin* and *New Jersey*—prowled the coast without much fear of facing enemy ships. Their mammoth 16-inch guns could hurl a one-ton projectile at a target a mile away. The cost of each blast was the equivalent of an American luxury car, so every time the big guns fired, sailors would shout: "One more Cadillac on the way." The shelling made rubble of such places as the oil refinery at Wonsan. The U.S. Navy's harbor blockades were the longest such actions since the Civil War.

On the ground, the armies clashed again near Chorwon and Old Baldy. For 45 days between June 6 and July 21, fighting raged up and down its bare slopes. The U.S. 2nd Division suffered 351 casualties; the Chinese, 1,093.

The trenches were home to draftees and recruits from the city and the farm, most of them on duty for the simple reason their country called. They risked life and limb, and the innocence of their youth could be exhausted in mere seconds of battle under the whistle of shrapnel, the whine of bullets, the blast of a grenade or the moans of a fallen buddy. The warriors in the dugouts quickly learned survival tricks, like using binoculars carefully. Binocular lenses reflected light, and Chinese snipers could pick off the unwary right through the looking glass.

Like the grunts in any army, they were too cold in winter, too hot in summer. They never got enough food and never enough sleep. They ate cold food from tin cans and tried to remember the taste of fresh vegetables and fruit. They lived in the rain and snow, the dust and the mud. On the front, they wore the same clothes for days and weeks on end. Hygiene was a constant concern. Crude toilets were cut out of ammunition boxes and placed on the reverse slope of the hills, hopefully downwind and out of reach of artillery and sniper fire. The only privacy came when they read letters from home, but oftentimes they shared each other's mail. They carried their lives in their shoulder-chafing 60-pound packs—sleeping bag, rations, bullets, communications, rain gear. Sometimes they even hauled their own graves. They were appreciated too little by the home folks and the population for whose freedom they fought. They had no direct knowledge of the nuances of negotiations— like the size of the mahogany table and saving face. Politicians and the top brass never consulted them on the big picture from Washington. They didn't even know much about what was happening on the next hill or other battlegrounds. Most of what they saw of the war was the 50-yard field of fire in front of them. And most of what they cared about was making sure they didn't let their buddies down.

In July, the Marines held a piece of ground the communists wanted. Hill 58 changed hands five times before the Marines were forced off for good. But they captured the neighboring and dominant Hill 122, aptly named Bunker Hill. The Chinese made seven attempts to drive the Marines off Bunker Hill between August 12 and August 25. The outpost changed hands three times, sometimes in periodic heavy rains whipped by Typhoon Karen's 80 mph wind, but it

At a forward aid station in Korea, Lt. Earl Hargroder, medical officer for the 38th Infantry Regiment, gives blood plasma to Pvt. Eulogio Santiago of Puerto Rico, wounded by mortar fire from the hill nicknamed Old Baldy.

ended up in leatherneck hands. Associated Press writer William C. Barnard filed this account of the battle on Aug. 18:

WITH THE U.S. MARINES (AP)—Two Marine sergeants, grimy and red-eyed, came off Bunker Hill after three days and three nights of fighting, full of bitterness of battle and thankful to be alive.

They were two of the many men who staved off seven fanatical Chinese attempts to recapture the scarred and barren hill. It's more a ridge than a hill, sprawling out between the battle line. When you approach it from any direction, you are exposed on both sides.

"I'll tell you how it was," said Sgt. Clarence Wilkins Jr., of Hartford, Conn. "We didn't eat much and we didn't hardly sleep any, and whenever we moved the Goonies could see us do it and they'd let us have it with their big guns. Once they threw 7,000 rounds on us in just a few hours. They came at us in all kinds of attacks. But our boys never griped about anything."

Even the wounded guys didn't gripe, according to Sgt. Howard Ryan of Hempstead, N.Y.

"The first guy I helped carry out was laid wide open under the stomach, but he was grinning and smoking a cigarette. He laughed and said, 'I wear a helmet and flak jacket and they get me below the belt.' He was so cheerful. The rest of us had a hard time keeping him from seeing how sick we felt."

What were the Chinese attacks like?

"You never knew when you were going to get one," said Ryan. "One started when a Goonie ran up a high ridge and fired three shot bursts on a burp gun. That set off the battle and every gun in the world went off. Everybody was waiting. That's the way it always was—everybody waiting."

"Most of the time they attacked at night," Wilkins said. "When we couldn't stand it any longer, we'd doze a few minutes at a time in the daytime, but it was 100 percent watch every night, all night. When

The night sky erupts in light as U.N. and Red fire illuminate the slopes of Old Baldy in a bloody battle for the heights near Chorwon, July 1952

they came up the hill, we'd wait till they got about 30 yards away and open up, firing at their gun flashes and lobbing grenades at them. Afterwards we could hear them rustling and scratching around, getting their dead and wounded out. The wounded would moan but they never hollered."

All night long, each Marine gun would fire sporadic bursts now and then, sweeping a certain sector, Ryan explained. "One night one of our boys didn't see a single Chink, but he kept firing bursts every once in a while. Next morning he was surprised as hell to find 75 dead in front of his gun."

Daytime temperatures reached 100 degrees, which inflicted a rash of sunstroke cases.

"Lots of guys passed out," Wilkins said. "The heat waves came right off the sand and you had your jacket and helmet and all that stuff on you, and you had to be going up and down the hill for ammo.

"When a man would pass out," Wilkins said, "we'd try to get some kind of shade over him. Some were so bad off we had to give them artificial respiration. If they didn't come around, we'd ship 'em back to an aid station. But they'd always be back in a couple of hours."

"You got so hot and tense you couldn't eat," Ryan said. "We had some C rations. Mostly I lived on cocoa."

The men were under constant artillery and mortar fire, which brought its own horrors. They saw a mor-

On the left, men of the 40th Infantry Division test a battery of four bazookas mounted on a homemade rig. Capt. Albert J. Barron is credited with the invention by the Department of Defense.

tar shell land on four stretcher bearers carrying a wounded man, killing all five Americans in one flash. A man who had been relieved of stretcher duty only seconds before survived the explosion. Nothing worked to break the logjam at the talks, however. By the end of September, United Nations negotiators submitted a package proposal involving voluntary repatriation. It was presented as a final offer, but the communists rejected it. Under instructions from Washington, Harrison walked out of the talks. "The UNC delegation will not come here merely to listen to abuse and false propaganda....We are willing to meet with you again at any time that you are ready to accept one of our proposals or to make a constructive proposal of your own, in writing, which could lead to an honorable armistice....I have nothing more to say. Since you have nothing constructive, we stand in recess," Harrison said. After October 8, the main negotiators did not meet again for six months. In Washington, Dean Acheson noted: "We shall not trade in the lives of men. We shall not forcibly deliver human beings into communist hands."

At the same time, a modest ground attack was planned northwest of Chorwon to evict the communists from some hilltop outposts in the Iron Triangle. The area was called the Triangle Hill complex, made up of such terrain features as Pike's Peak, the twin knobs of Jane Russell Hill, Sandy Ridge and Sniper Ridge. Dubbed Operation Showdown, it was approved by Eighth Army commander James Van Fleet and expected to cost 200 casualties over five days of fighting. Instead, the fighting raged for weeks before it petered out on November 18, and the U.S. 7th Division and ROK 2nd Division suffered 9,000 killed or

Dodging the Reds, helicopters are used to move rocket batteries from place to place. They are fired and moved on. The enemy had been directing counter-fire by spotting the firing and tracing rocket trails.

wounded while making minimal gains in territory. The stubborn communists took 23,000 casualties. The Chinese also hit the ROK 9th Division on White Horse Hill on October 6, using their familiar tactic of concentrating troops on a narrow front defended by ROKs. A week later, the Chinese attacked the U.S. 2nd Division on Sniper Ridge. The results reinforced how futile it was to mount direct assaults against fierce resistance, and Showdown was the last U.N. offensive of the war.

White Horse overlooked the main invasion route to Seoul from Chorwon, which made it a prized possession. The crest changed hands 20 times in a five-day October battle, seven times on a single day. Flares lit up the night battles. But at times, it was so dark and fighting was at such close quarters that the South Koreans felt the heads of those around them. If they had longer hair, they were friendlies. If the heads were

It's load, fire and load again for weary artillerymen supporting troops in their assault on Triangle Hill.

Men of the 7th Division and the Korean Service Corps move warily up the slope of bloody Triangle Hill, while to the far left a wounded GI is helped down the hill by a buddy.

close-cropped or shaved, they were Chinese. Hand-to-hand fighting was done with bayonets and rifle butts. Also in October, the Chinese assaulted a spot called The Hook, a mile-long, fish-hooked shaped ridge 10 miles northeast of Panmunjom and about five miles northeast of Bunker Hill. Marines were driven off, then regained it with a counterattack. In November, they turned it over to the British Commonwealth Division.

In a bid to draw the Chinese out of their deep bunkers, the 8th Cavalry Regiment faked an amphibious landing at Kojo on Korea's east coast, 25 miles south of Wonsan. The communists refused to take the bait and stayed snug in their bunkers. Other plans and operations were proposed to get in behind the Chinese and flush them out, but none were ever tried. Ground commanders concluded that the cost in lives of assaulting entrenched defenses was simply not

Infantry of the 7th Division carry a machine gun and supplies to a newly-won position on Triangle Hill.

worth it, even if the Chinese spent soldiers' lives the way the Americans spent ammunition.

With cold weather coming, the infantry braced for the third bone-chilling winter of the Korean campaign. Both sides hibernated in their crude burrows, leaving their relative warmth only for limited patrols while trading artillery and mortar strikes. Scraggly pine trees were sought for another Christmas away from home.

Marine Cpl. James D. Prewitt of the 2nd Battalion, 5th Regiment, described the routine this way: "Days on the MLR (main line of resistance) were slow and sometimes boring. The tedium was broken when someone started shooting at the rats in his bunker. Guaranteed to wake things up and bring some brass up to the line....Nights on outpost duty were long and, as the year waned, became cold. They were always lonely...I would try to tell time by the rotation of the Big Dipper and the North Star—a leftover from my Boy Scout days. There was always the fear of unexplained noises and movements down the draw where the garbage was thrown. Empty C-ration cans were always tossed down into the gullies and ravines leading to the outpost. This trash made the footing very unstable and cut down on the chance of a sneak attack from below. But when the cans clattered in the dark,

A wounded Marine gets a sip of water from buddies after bitter hand-to-hand fighting which dislodged 800 Chinese from Hook Ridge, northwest of Korangpo.

you never knew whether it was the Chinese or just the rats foraging for food....The outposts stank. Flies, rats, garbage, fecal wastes all contributed to the ef-fluvium. The worst job was covering the Chinese bodies that lay on the side of the hill."

10

The Final Battles

When Korea began to look like a bottomless swamp, Far East commander Mark Clark formulated a hard-line, MacArthuresque blueprint for a military solution in late 1952. His plan envisioned amphibious landings, airborne assaults and air and naval attacks on Manchuria. It also recommended dropping the ultimate weapon. "I consider it necessary that plans be made for the use of atomic weapons," Clark messaged the Joint Chiefs of Staff. But Washington said no. A presidential election was being held, and decisions on escalating the war would have to wait until the political fighting was resolved. Harry Truman, whose approval ratings had slipped to around 30 percent, had already decided against seeking re-election. The Democratic nominee to replace him was Illinois Gov. Adlai Stevenson. On the Republican side, Sen. Robert Taft at

President-elect Dwight D. Eisenhower, flanked by Gen. Mark Clark, top commander in the Far East, and James Van Fleet, Eighth Army commander, review troops in Korea.

A Navy fighter-bomber catches on fire landing on the carrier *Essex*. The pilot evacuates and an asbestos-clad firefighter removes 20mm cannon shells. The fire was put out with only slight damage to the plane.

tempted to win the Republican nomination by teaming with Douglas MacArthur, but Dwight Eisenhower won the GOP nod and named Sen. Richard Nixon as his running mate. No one possessed any instant solutions for the Korean mess. But Eisenhower, the supreme Allied commander whose forces conquered the Nazis in Europe, said in an October 24 speech in Detroit that he would "concentrate on the job of ending the Korean War—until the job is honorably done. That job requires a personal trip to Korea. I shall make that trip. Only in that way could I learn how best to serve the American people in the cause of peace. I shall go to Korea." He won the electoral vote in a landslide, the first Republican elected to the White House in 24 years.

President-elect Eisenhower made good on his promise, arriving December 2 in Korea under a tight net of security. He was briefed by his commanders,

visited troops and had a chance to see his son, Maj. John Eisenhower, an officer in the 3rd Division's 15th Regiment. Like his famous father, John had been a battalion commander in the regiment. Ike's top paternal concern was that John not be taken prisoner by the communists. During his trip, Eisenhower also met with Syngman Rhee, but he displayed little enthusiasm for escalated fighting and opted instead for a solution at the bargaining table. Truman called Eisenhower's trip "a piece of demagoguery." In addition to a new administration in Washington, there was a new ground commander in Korea in early 1953. On February 11, James Van Fleet was replaced by Gen. Maxwell Taylor, who had commanded the 101st Airborne Division at Normandy and later commanded U.S. forces in West Berlin. Van Fleet served longer than any commander of Eighth Army in Korea. He had continued Matthew Ridgway's rehabilitation of

Above: Eisenhower lunches with men of his old out-fit, the 15th Regiment of the 3rd Division. Soldiers later made a monument of the crate Ike sat on. With him are Sgt. Jack Hutcherson of Frankford, Missouri, and Cpl. James Murray of Muskogee, Oklahoma.

Right: It's cold and lonely out there. Two GIs walk to their front-line bunker on the central front.

Eighth Army and had pushed the Chinese back above the 38th parallel but he suffered a deep personal loss. His son, James. A. Van Fleet Jr., was killed on a bombing raid in April of 1952. The general also thought the Chinese could have been defeated in the spring of 1951 if there had been a will to press the fighting. "Instead of getting directions for offensive action, we found our activities more and more proscribed as the time went on," Van Fleet said. He also said in a magazine: "I have looked the Chinese Red in the eye and this was my verdict: If ever I should be called back

B-26s are the workhorses of aerial bombardment. One from the Air Force 3rd Bomber Wing unleashes another barrage at a target in North Korea.

to fight him again, I would go with a confident heart. If we retreat from the communists in Asia, we are lost anyway. What are we afraid of?"

Eisenhower's team racheted up the pressure at Panmunjom. In the earliest stages of brinkmanship, the administration hinted that it might sanction an invasion of the Chinese mainland by Chiang Kai-shek's Nationalists, bomb communist sanctuaries outside of Korea and turn parts of the region into an atomic hell. "The prospects of an armistice seemed to improve," Eisenhower wrote later.

Fate took a hand too. On March 5, 1953, Soviet leader Joseph Stalin died and left a void in the communist world. Ten days later, his successor, Georgi Malenkov, made a speech that contained a peace overture. "There is no disputed or unsettled question that could not be settled peacefully on the basis of mutual agreement between the countries concerned," Malenkov said. Washington was still wary of Soviet

trickery, so Eisenhower challenged the Soviets to match words with deeds to bring about "an honorable armistice" in Korea.

Whether by design or coincidence, a breakthrough came March 28 when the Chinese responded favorably to a February 22 proposal by Mark Clark to exchange sick and wounded prisoners. Chou En-lai followed with a conciliatory statement about all POWs, the issue that held up settling the Korean War. "Both parties to the negotiations should undertake to repatriate, immediately after the cessation of hostilities, all those prisoners of war in their custody who insist upon repatriation, and to hand over the remaining POWs to a neutral state so as to ensure a just solution to the question of their repatriation," Chou said.

One of the most recognizable outposts in Korea, and one that symbolized the futility of the last part of the war, was Pork Chop Hill. It was the site of a

The fight for Old Baldy goes on. GIs (upper left) move out from their bunker to take harassment positions against the Chinese who hold the hill.

A wounded Marine is carried to a helicopter bound for a MASH unit from the Vegas Hill sector. The Marines tenaciously hold this outpost in the Bunker Hill area as the Chinese switch from human wave assaults to sneak attacks. Marines counted 298 Chinese dead in three days of fighting.

two-part battle, dramatized later with liberal license in a Hollywood movie. Eighth Army had seized Pork Chop in June of 1952, and the Chinese had tried but failed to evict the Thailand battalion holding it in November. The Chinese made another bid to claim Pork Chop and neighboring Old Baldy in March of 1953. About 8,000 Chinese artillery rounds fell on Pork Chop at the beginning of the month. The infantry assaults came on March 23, and the Chinese seized Old Baldy when the Colombian battalion, in the middle of changing positions, was caught off guard. Plans

to counterattack were canceled by Maxwell Taylor because Old Baldy was not deemed essential to the defensive front. Taylor figured these were face-saving propaganda maneuvers by the communists, and he believed the cost in American lives to retake Old Baldy would exceed its military significance. But Old Baldy overlooked Pork Chop, and from the high ground, the Chinese could fire mortars and artillery with great effectiveness.

Another Chinese bid to capture Pork Chop came on April 16, with 96 soldiers from two platoons of the

More wounded Marines are rushed to the makeshift helicopter landing area on Vegas Hill for transport to the rear. A machine gunner (right) protects the area.

Legless Chinese POW begins first lap of trip home, bound for the repatriation area at Panmunjom.

7th Division's 31st Regiment dug in. The Chinese attacked with two companies and gained some footholds before artillery stopped the advance. After regrouping, the Chinese stormed forward again and held most of the hill except for the crest by 2 a.m. Two hours later, an American counterattack linked up with defenders on the high ground, but not all of the lost positions were recaptured.

Throughout the day on April 17th, 55 determined 7th Division soldiers clung to their perches. A decision

Left: Medics and MPs check out POWs in a medical stockade in Pusan. Many of them are suffering from tuberculosis.

was made to hold Pork Chop at all costs to deny the communists a chance to claim victory at Panmunjom. It was said at the height of the battle, 11 stars worth of U.S. generals were at regimental headquarters. At 9 p.m., two companies of the 17th Infantry joined the battle as both sides threw in reinforcements. The battle raged through the night and next day before the Chinese conceded tactical defeat by the night of April 18. They withdrew from Pork Chop while the Americans rebuilt defenses. Nine U.S. artillery battalions fired 77,349 rounds in the two-day battle. Eventually, five battalions of U.S. soldiers defended the hill, which was under relentless mortar and artillery fire from Old Baldy. Unfortunately, a final, sadder chapter

A U.N. soldier, exchanged by the communists, is strapped to a ski-equipped helicopter for the first leg home, April 20, 1953.

had yet to be written about Pork Chop.

Talks resumed on Sunday afternoon, April 26. And the first exchange of sick and wounded POWs—Operation Little Switch—were carried out between April 20 and May 3. At the Freedom Village in Munsan, 15 miles south of Panmunjom, the communists released 149 Americans, 60 other United Nations troops and 471 South Koreans. A total of 6,670 North Koreans and Chinese were released to the north.

To keep the pressure on at the peace talks, another punishing air assault on North Korea was approved.

Since military and industrial targets had already been flattened, the new objective was to use food as a weapon by destroying the North Korean rice crop. The Air Force targeted a series of earthen irrigation dams 20 miles from Pyongyang in the Toksan and Casan areas, which protected grids of rice paddies.

Right: 3rd Division GIs check over the massed bodies of dead Chinese killed when a Chinese division tried for three straight nights to dislodge the Americans from Outpost Harry. The Americans say the Chinese lost 3,500 killed and wounded.

For two weeks beginning on May 13, bombs fell on the dams. Subsequent flooding damaged 3,200 acres of rice paddies and took out six miles of railroad lines, five railway bridges and two miles of road. North Korea responded by lowering the water levels behind the dikes. Far East Air Force commander O.P. Weyland called the operation "perhaps the most spectacular of the war."

But as the war had dragged on, the Chinese had narrowed the gap in air superiority, although they never closed it. Soviet-made MiG-15s operated from the northwest corner of Korea at a base in An-tung, and trains of 90 or more of the stubby jets swooped down MiG alley to threaten U.N. forces. The MiGs were faster, more maneuverable and had a better rate of climb than America's top plane, the F-86 Sabre, but they were unstable and prone to stall at low speeds. But if their machines were outperformed, American pilots were more experienced and talented, even if they were unable to pursue MiG-15s into Chinese air space. In air-to-air combat, 792 MiG-15s were shot out of the sky in dogfights while 78 Sabres were lost. The principal task of the Far East Air Force remained interdicting supply lines and supporting ground troops. The Chinese worked ceaselessly at patching up transportation systems so they could get bullets and food to their troops.

On the ground, the Chinese struck back on May 25 with powerful offensives along the battlefront. The U.S. 25th Division had to withdraw from the outposts east of Panmunjom, but the main blow was aimed at a soft point in the central sector called the Kumsong Bulge. Kumsong was defended by South Korean troops, and in the concentrated assault, all 21 key ROK positions were under simultaneous attack. The Chinese pushed the ROKs back six miles, eliminating the bulge in the main line of resistance.

Somehow, the negotiators agreed on the details on a prisoner exchange and an armistice in early June. After 18 months of bitter wrangling, procrastination and mistrust, the two sides signed a repatriation document. But like everything else in Korea, nothing came easy.

The final stumbling block to peace was America's ally, Syngman Rhee, who still insisted on driving the communists from the peninsula and unifying Korea under one flag. Rhee told Eisenhower that an armistice that allowed China to remain in Korea would be "a death-sentence of Korea without protest." And

Left: The cleanup after the battle for Outpost Harry continues as another body is added to the graves where the Chinese dead are interred.

when peace seemed at hand, Rhee told Clark on June 8: "I will never accept the armistice terms as they stand. The Republic of Korea will fight on, even if it means a suicide, and I will lead them." He threatened to detach his army from United Nations control and lead them north. Rhee, who had already declared martial law in South Korea, did his best to sabotage the armistice by scuttling the POW issue. Shortly after midnight on June 18, Rhee ordered South Korean guards to cut gaping holes in the barbed wire to turn loose every prisoner who didn't want to be repatriated. In those dark hours, 27,000 of the 33,600 North Koreans in camps at the southern end of the peninsula shed their prison clothes and melted into the population. Fewer than 1,000 were recaptured. The plan had been secretly coordinated at the top level of government, and Rhee stated: "According to the Geneva Convention, and also to the principle of human rights, the anti-communist Korean prisoners should have been released long before this. Most of the United Nations authorities with whom I have spoken about our desire to release these prisoners are with us in sympathy and principle. But due to the international complications, we have been holding these people too long. The reason why I did this, without full consultation with the United Nations Command and other authorities concerned, is too obvious to explain." Far East commander Mark Clark and U.N. negotiator William Harrison acted quickly to contain the damage, apologizing in writing to the Chinese and blaming Rhee for acting alone. The Chinese grudgingly accepted the apology, then asked pointedly if Rhee was under control and if he would fight on even if there was an armistice. "We were now in a place where we could really not vouch that we could keep our end of any bargain we might make with our opponents," Eisenhower wrote. A special envoy dispatched from Washington brought Rhee to heel, but not without a price. Rhee was promised a long-term mutual defense treaty, support for a 20-division army and an immediate $200 million in economic aid. As a last resort, under a contingency called Operation Everready, the United States considered toppling Rhee with a more reasonable leader.

If Rhee wasn't listening to the West, he got a strong message from the Chinese on the battlefield. In early July, 15 artillery-backed divisions charged out of their bunkers and stormed ROK positions near Kumsong. A total of 150,000 troops attacked a 20-mile front in the biggest Chinese offensive since the spring of 1951. The ROKs sloshed backward in sheets of summer monsoon rains, forcing Maxwell Taylor to commit the U.S. 2nd and 3rd Divisions to check the withdrawal.

In addition, the 187th Airborne Regiment was rushed from reserve in Japan to the battle front. The paratroopers were called the Rakkasans, a Japanese word for "falling down umbrella." Their commander was Brig. Gen. William Westmoreland, who went on to become a four-star general and commander of ground forces in Vietnam. The new line formed at the Kumsong River, miles from where the ROKs had stood weeks before. "There is no doubt in my mind that one of the principal reasons—if not the reason—for the communist offensive was to give the ROKs a bloody nose; to show them and the world that *puk chin*—go north—was easier said than done," General Clark noted.

During the peak of the fighting, Rhee caved in on July 9. Although he wouldn't sign an armistice, Rhee said "we shall not obstruct it, so long as no measures or actions taken under the armistice are detrimental to our national survival." The peace delegates resumed talks the next day, with Rhee in tow and some minor procedural issues to be resolved.

The Chinese, desperately seeking a battlefield decision so they could claim a psychological victory, also attacked Pork Chop Hill on July 6. It was a murderous version of king of the mountain. The Chinese attacked and gained positions on part of the crest. Unsuccessful counterattacks failed to dislodge them over the next three days. On July 10, U.S. commanders made a moral decision, concluding that the cost of holding Pork Chop was not worth the price in American blood especially since it would soon be part of the demilitarized zone. Soldiers were withdrawn in armored personnel carriers that normally brought food and ammunition to the front, and the Chinese weren't sure at first if the Americans weren't being reinforced. Many GIs had fought and died to hold this bloody height, only to be ordered off a clump of rock and dirt that became part of no man's land. GIs left behind a snarl of booby traps and greeted the new Chinese tenants with an artillery shower when Pork Chop fell.

By July 14, six Chinese divisions pressed against the Kumsong bulge and virtually destroyed the ROK Capital Division and much of the ROK 3rd Division. The eastern front, which had the northernmost positions, was also under attack. Soldiers were dying for mere yards of territory. The communists had 66,000 casualties in July. In the last four months of the war, total U.N. casualties were 64,703—most of them ROKs resisting the Chinese offensive at Kumsong. During the same period, for day after day and night after night, U.N. artillery fired seven million rounds over no man's land. Weapons such as the 24-tube T-66 rocket launcher were capable of firing 96 rounds of 4.5-inch rockets every five minutes.

Finally, at 10 a.m. on Monday, July 27, William Harrison and Nam Il—without saying a word to each other—signed their names to a document that silenced the guns 12 hours later. Each man wrote his signature 18 times—nine on the blue-bound United Nations copy and nine on the maroon-bound communist volume. The wordless 12-minute ceremony, played out against the thump of artillery guns in the nearby hills, came after 18 million words were spoken at 575 meetings over two frustrating years.

Far East commander Mark Clark signed both documents at the Munsan apple orchard. "I cannot find it in me to exult in this hour. Rather, it is time for prayer, that we may succeed in our difficult endeavor to turn this armistice to the advantage of mankind. If we extract hope from this occasion, it must be diluted with recognition that our salvation requires unrelaxing vigilance and effort," Clark said under the glare of television lights. Clark later noted that he "had gained the unenviable distinction of being the first United States Army commander in history to sign an armistice without victory."

Chinese commander Peng Teh-huai signed in Kaesong. "Because we have done this once, it means that we will do it again and again in the future. This is a happy day for our people. Through three years of fighting together the Volunteers had forged a comradeship in blood with the North Korean people and their army—a friendship which further deepened and strengthened our internationalist feelings," Peng thought.

The final hours were war by the clock, much the way it had been when armies in Europe awaited the 11th hour of the 11th day of the 11th month for the 1918 armistice of World War I. The last bomb from a B-26 fell 30 minutes before the cease-fire; during the war, the Air Force, Navy and Marines had dropped 588,000 tons of bombs and over 32,000 tons of napalm. Artillery thundered until 10 p.m. Arthur Trudeau, commanding general of U.S. 7th Division, pulled the lanyard on his batteries' last round of the war and kept the shell case as a memento. "I was happy it was over. It was apparent that all we were going to do was sit there and hold positions. There wasn't going to be any victory. All we could do was go on losing more lives," Trudeau said. The din of the final bombardments was replaced with the singing of the Ma-

Right: Just one battle alone produces this mountain of empty artillery and mortar casings. This waste heap is the refuse from Outpost Harry's fighting.

Left: A night attack by 15 low-flying communist aircraft started fires in the port of Inchon. A bomb hit a fuel dump.

Above: ROK troops move to mount a counterattack and take back positions on Lookout Mountain, east of the Pukhan River, which they had yielded only four days before.

A truck rescues a jeep in the churning waters of a flooded creek near Kumsong, where GIs supported the 2nd ROK Corps as it recaptured lost ground.

Two Chinese POWs bound for a collection center are guarded by MPs and offered water.

rine Corps hymn, closing insults, the tinkling of rice wine bottles and a silence that was almost as deafening as the pandemonium of war. The Korean War wheezed to an ambiguous conclusion—three years, one month and two days after it started. The 155-mile long line, which runs like a jagged scar across Korea's midsection, was not too far different from the 38th parallel and substantially the same line as when truce talks started in July of 1951. The DMZ predated the Berlin Wall, the enduring symbol of the Cold War, by

eight years and survived long after it crumbled. It has even outlived the collapse of the Soviet Union.

It took some time for the end to sink in for troops asked to fight a war with limits, over ideology rather than territorial gains. Marine Cpl. Robert Hall spoke for many when he recalled: "The cease-fire was announced for 10 o'clock that night. There had been artillery fire all evening from both sides—not a barrage, just banging away. We were all up for it. The artillery gradually tapered off as the hour ap-

Gen. Mark Clark tells the Reds he is willing to sign a truce whatever South Korean President Syngman Rhee's attitude toward a proposed armistice. After delivering his answer, he boarded a plane for Japan after a stop in Seoul.

U.N. Supreme Commander in the Far East, U.S. Gen. Mark Clark, signs armistice documents at his base in Munsan. They had been signed already by both sides at Panmunjom. July 1953.

proached. Flares were shot up by both sides. Then it became very quiet as even the morons who wanted to be the one who fired the last shot of the war quit cranking off. A few showed flashlights. I turned in about midnight. It had grown very still. At earliest light the troops came up out of the ground to look. At first we stood in the trenches. Then some climbed up to the forward edges, then to the tops of the bunkers, for a better look. It was unheard of—standing in the open in daylight. An incredible feeling. I think the infantrymen all across the peninsula, on both sides of the line must have been awed by it. Just the simple,

natural act of standing erect in the sunshine. Then to look, and eventually walk through the land ahead of the trenches, a thing that would have meant sure death 24 hours before. That's when we began to realize that it was really over."

Under the armistice, both sides withdrew 2,000 meters from their forward lines to create a demilitarized zone. But that meant many topographical features that had cost such a dear price in blood were simply abandoned to become part of a no man's land.

At noon on July 28 in Pyongyang, Kim Il Sung claimed victory with his accustomed bluster. "Dear

Fellow Countrymen, brothers, sisters, officers and men of the heroic Chinese People's Volunteers, dear comrades. Although the American imperialists mobilized not only their land, air and naval forces armed with most modern techniques, together with those of their allies, they were defeated with very great losses in men and materiel...Korea belongs to the Korean people. It shall continue to belong to the Korean people." Saluted as the Ever-Victorious Captain of the Korean People in the Great Patriotic Struggle, Kim kept Orwellian control of his portion of Korea for decades to come. His nation, his economy and his people had been devastated.

President Eisenhower, in a national broadcast, told Americans: "There is, in this moment of sober satisfaction, one thought that must discipline our emo-

Far right: Taking the war apart, three mortarmen of the 1st Marines dismantle their weapon before a backdrop of unfired shells and shell casings. Firing stopped at 10 p.m., July 27, 1953.

Below: That's done. Gen. William K. Harrison (seated left) and North Korean Gen. Nam II (seated right) both look up as the signing is completed. With Gen. Harrison, the chief U.N. delegate, is Cmdr. J. E. Shew, U.S.N., at left and Col. J.C. Murray, U.S.M.C., right.

Above: The actual armistice agreements detailing the terms of the truce in which all fighting stops and troops withdraw to agreed-on positions.

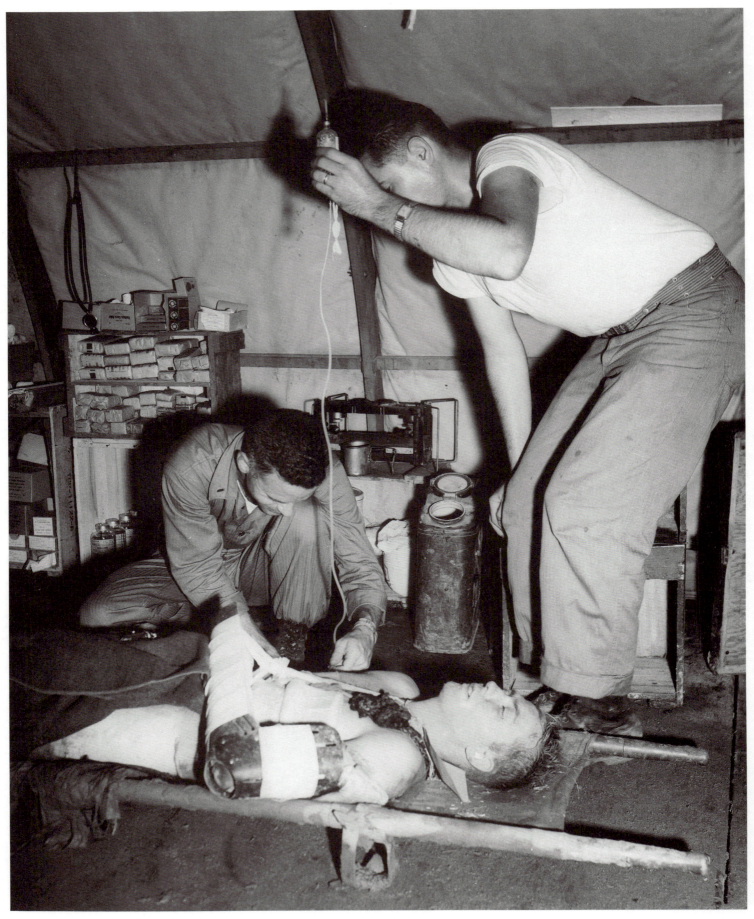

A little short of luck, this Marine was wounded only a few hours before the armistice signing. Navy doctor Lt. William Ridgway of San Francisco works on his wounds and corpsman Stanley Baker of Los Angeles administers albumen and plasma.

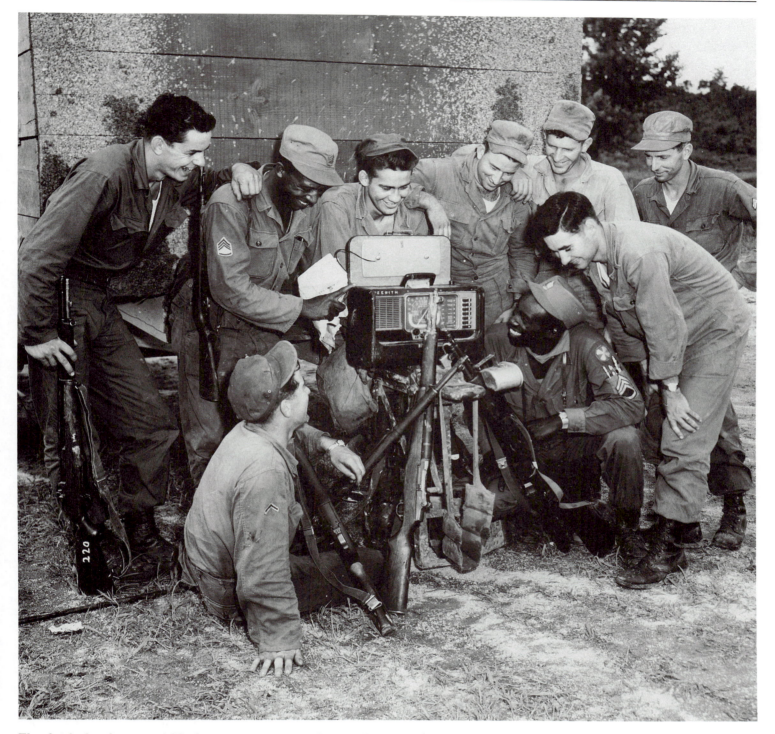

The fat lady sings and Marines at a command post listen to the armistice ceremonies on a hastily set up radio.

tions and steady our resolutions. It is this: we have won an armistice on a single battleground, not peace in the world." The enduring legacy of Korea was that the American military would never be unprepared again.

Paik Sun Yup, South Korea's top combat officer, had seen his country nearly overrun, exalted at the liberation of his hometown of Pyongyang, nearly experienced the unification of his country during the drive to the Yalu, had his hopes dashed after the Chinese intervention, helped rally his army back

across the 38th parallel and negotiated with communists who had tried to kill him on the battlefield. "We gained no victory, true enough, but we staved off a defeat that the infamy of surprise attack had nearly made a sure thing, and we established the cold war policy of containment by bringing the enemy's predatory aggression up short," Paik wrote.

The war ultimately involved 22 countries and left Korea a ravaged, smoking ruin that stank of death. More than 4 million men, women and children were killed, wounded or otherwise incapacitated in the

The bodies of political prisoners suffocated by the communists outside Hamhung are identified by weeping relatives. They were forced into caves which were then sealed.

war—including 2 million civilians in North and South Korea. Harry Truman's police action left 54,246 Americans dead, including 33,629 in combat and 20,617 killed from accidents or illness. There were also 103,284 Americans wounded. In the final two years, after truce talks began, the United States suffered 63,200 casualties, including 12,300 killed on the battlefield. America spent $67 billion on the war, not to mention the billions it took to rebuild South Korea. According to the Pentagon, the total number of United Nations forces killed, wounded or missing was 996,937. South Korea listed 46,812 killed, 66,436 missing and 159,727 wounded while other non-American casualties reached 17,260. The total communists killed, wounded or missing was 1.4 million. North

Left: Thirty-four victims of the Hill 303 massacre are mute evidence of the atrocities committed.

Korea had 214,899 killed, 101,680 missing and 303,685 wounded. Chinese losses were 401,401 killed, 21,211 missing and 486,995 wounded.

The prisoner exchange, called Operation Big Switch, commenced on August 5 and lasted a month. The communists going north—70,183 North Koreans and 5,640 Chinese—stripped off their American clothing, tossed away their boots and shoes, and sang songs to cross the border. The 12,773 United Nations prisoners, including 3,597 Americans, coming south were greeted by a "Welcome Home" arch at Panmunjom and a gaggle of doctors, psychiatrists and interrogators. The exchange was completed on September 6, although 369 Americans are still listed as prisoners of war. One of the last across was Col. Walker Mahurin, who shot down 21 German planes in World War II but had confessed to war crimes three days earlier, well after the truce took hold. "We all think

NORTH KOREAN PRISONERS

The following story, written in 1953 by Associated Press war correspondent John Randolph, goes inside a Communist interview tent for an incisive description of the meetings with North Korean prisoners who rejected communism and resisted repatriation.

INDIAN VILLAGE, KOREA (AP)—The tall, slender Communist lieutenant stood up yesterday, placed his fingers on a small table, and leaned toward the struggling North Korean prisoner.

"Tung-moo," the North Korean officer began, "Comrade..."

The word was like a whip across the prisoner's face.

"Tung-moo," he screamed and hurled himself against the lean, brown arms of his Indian guards.

"Tung-moo, you filthy son of a dog, you dirty communist trainer, you and your Russian Chinese barbarians. Don't 'comrade' me you dirty Chinese lover. I spit on your father and mother."

He spat straight at the officer only five feet away. It missed his face but soiled the crisp olive green uniform with its gleaming belt and gold and scarlet shoulder boards.

The officer stood quietly erect as the prisoner writhed and stomped and kicked to break away from his guards and rush his interrogator.

The Indian neutral chairman in the tent, a Capt. Garaya, looked inquiringly at the Red officer. The Communist shrugged in resignation and started to sit down.

But before Garaya could wave the raging prisoner out of the south door of the tent—where anti-Communists go—the latter hurled himself forward with a supreme effort. He kicked viciously at the little table and sent it hurtling into the Communist's lap.

Then the Indians, patience exhausted, lifted him off the floor and carried him bodily out of the tent. The interview had lasted nearly 40 seconds.

The next prisoner was led in, struggling and sullen, and Garaya read the required preliminaries.

The Red lieutenant stood up, placed his fingers on the table, and leaned forward.

"Tung-moo...." he began, "Comrade...."

The prisoner remained silent but struggling.

"Tung-moo," the Communist repeated. "As a representative of the government of the Republic I can guarantee your personal safety on my own word. You are safe now, and free if you go home now."

"I don't want to be repatriated—I want to stay in South Korea!" the prisoner said.

The North Korean officer did not ever seem to hear him.

"You must think how great the grief of your father and mother will be if they cannot see you," he went on.

The prisoner looked appealingly at the chairman Garaya and pleaded, "Let me go—I don't want to be repatriated."

But he did not show the implacable hatred of the first man.

So began a strange duel that lasted for 123 minutes more.

The duelists, apart from their common language, were distinct contrasts.

The Communist political officer, resplendent in his colorful uniform and black leather Russian boots, showed steady nerves.

The stocky prisoner, wearing olive drab American Army woolens

we are traitors to our country. Some of us confessed and some of us didn't. Those who didn't ought to get the Medal of Honor," Mahurin said. "They were bringing the confessions and making us copy them and sign them. And of course, in their society, those confessions are going to jibe with each other because by that time they had all kinds of information so they could make them interrelate. The nature of the confessions are so ridiculous that a child would not believe if he had any intelligence whatsoever." There were disturbing charges of American POWs collaborating with their captors, but only a few were convicted of misconduct. However, one of the legacies of the Korea War was a new code of conduct for the armed services, which was drafted by a 10-man Advisory Committee on Prisoners of War and signed by President Eisenhower on August 17, 1955.

Prisoners who did not wish to be repatriated were turned over to a neutral nations commission. On January 20, 1954, 21,805 former fighters for communism elected not to return. The parade to the south lasted 15 hours, 43 minutes. A total of 23 Americans and one Briton—Royal Marine Andrew Condon, captured with Task Force Drysdale south of the Chosin Reservoir—defected to communism.

A post-armistice conference called to address the political leftovers in Korea didn't happen until April of 1954 in Geneva. Little was accomplished about Korea. The conference's most notable decision was a partition along a man-made line in Vietnam, which was divided between a communist north and a pro-West south along the 17th parallel.

One of the winners of the Korean War was Japan, or more specifically, its economy. Prior to the war, the Japanese had huge trade deficits; industrial production was just a fraction of pre-World War II levels. But

and muddy boots, clenched his hands tightly and tried to wrench out of the grasp of the Indian guards.

The Red officer talked almost without interruption for an hour and a half, delivering each word with full force.

The prisoner appeared like a bird hypnotized by a snake, wanting but unable to get away. More clever men might have argued. The prisoner just put his head down like a balky mule and let the words roll over him.

"You must come home," pleaded the officer, alternately an orator tense with emotion and then an elder brother, kindly and confidential. "You must think of your father and mother—we are building a new Korea...."

"Let me out of here," the prisoner shouted each time the officer paused for breath.

At 9:58 a.m.—"I don't want to be repatriated!"

At 10:04 a.m.—"I refuse to return!"

At 10:13 a.m.—He whimpered and squirmed.

At 10:15—"I want to go back to my compound!"

At 10:20—"I don't want to go back!"

At 10:21 the Communist broke the rules and threatened, "You must come back—you know that the Peoples Republic will occupy the southern half of Korea...."

Garaya barked the wildly raving Communist to a stop.

"Tell him," he told his interpreter, "that he will not use this threatening language."

At 10:30, more than an hour after the interview began, the weary prisoner turned pleadingly to Garaya:

"I have listened to the explanation and I have said I want to go out that door to South Korea. Can I go now?"

Garaya answered that he must listen until the Reds were finished. The prisoner moaned and slumped back in the guards' arms.

"You must come home," the Red officer said.

"After all, what is there for you in South Korea? All you can hope to be is a shoeshine boy and pick your food out of garbage cans like a dog."

A South Korean observer leaped to his feet and started to scream in Korean at the Communist. Garaya banged the table for order.

At 10:50, Garaya called for a five-minute recess.

Outside the tent, the South Korean observers pointed out that already the prisoner had asked 14 times to stay with the allied side.

An Indian officer said the long interview "shows they're doing some thinking."

When the interview resumed, the incredible Communist officer took up his emotional task with no trace of a hoarse voice.

At 10:57, the prisoner shrieked, "I want to go out."

"Isn't there any time limit?"

Garaya shook his head in the negative.

The prisoner sat down wearily and his head hung low.

Finally, at 11:13, he surged to his feet.

"I refuse to go," he said.

"I have listened to the explanations. Now I want to go out of that door."

He pointed to the one leading back to the allied side.

"Have you finished?" Garaya asked the Red officer.

The orator reluctantly nodded.

The dazed prisoner was allowed to go.

Another prisoner was brought in, screaming, "You sons of dogs."

The Red officer leaned toward him.

"Tung-moo."

during the Korean War, Japan was a staging area and training ground for U.S. troops. The Japanese supplied boots, uniforms and other gear. Ultimately, it became a technological superpower, producing weapons parts, tires, cement and asphalt for roads and steel for railroads and ship repair. The first big postwar jobs for Nissan, Toyota and Isuzu were producing and repairing trucks for Korea, long before their first cars were exported to the United States. At the time of the Korean cease-fire, America and its allies signed a "greater sanctions" agreement to come to Korea's aid if the Chinese violated the terms of the armistice. A million men in arms from North and South Korea still peer warily at each other along the uneasy truce line. Of course, the United States never left South Korea. About 40,000 troops, including one Eighth Army combat division, are on permanent station as a trip wire south of the DMZ—a two and a half mile wide complex of barbed wire, watchtowers with searchlights and loudspeakers. The 1.5 million Americans who served in the Korean War returned home without parades or fanfare, which gave rise to the name Forgotten War. There were no return celebrations, but no campus protests or draft-card burnings. Troops weren't dispatched to Korea with patriotic ditties by Irving Berlin, but there were no anti-war songs either.

"When the war was over, people went back to their jobs and didn't talk about it. When your country asks you to do something, you do it," said Richard Adams, who fought with the U.S. 25th Division.

"We were the silent veterans of the forgotten war. It was like a rock thrown into a pond and there wasn't a ripple," said Frank Kerr, a combat photographer with the Marines at the Chosin Reservoir. "But those who died ennobled that time and place."

Plans for a national monument to their sacrifice

proceeded at a glacial pace. Ground was broken in 1992 for a memorial scheduled for a 1995 dedication in Washington, D.C. The organization No Greater Love in conjunction with the Korean War Veterans Association did place a meditation bench near the Tomb of the Unknown Soldier at Arlington National Cemetery on July 27, 1987. Carved into its granite are these words from Pulitzer Prize-winning novelist Herman Wouk: "The beginning of the end of war lies in remembrance."

Epilogue

by Kelly Smith Tunney, Chief of Bureau, AP Seoul

Korea Today

From a southern guardpost high on a ridge, the rugged outline of the Demilitarized Zone stretches out like a great nature preserve, a swath of underbrush, wild animals, birds, berries and untamed grasses which dips along ridges and mountain valleys from sea to sea.

At night, it is clear enough to see the stars. Soldiers in flak vests and helmets move out on patrol along the barbed wire barriers with M-16 automatic rifles at the ready, hunting knives dangling from their belts. Sound jars the silence: the explosion of a mine, perhaps tripped by a rabbit, a round of fire (a weapon dropped?). Blasts of propaganda from loudspeakers on the northern side echo in the distance.

Four decades after the armistice which ended the Korean War, this two-and-a-half-mile-wide band of no-man's land dividing the peninsula has changed little, a sobering testament to continued tension in the last

Above: All neat and tidy. GIs watch for North Korean troop activity from a security trench that winds its way through hills of the Demilitarized Zone.

Near Kimwa, a guard points to a concrete antitank barrier, part of the DMZ. The DMZ impedes free travel for Koreans who live on both sides.

Americans in an M-56 tank on guard at the DMZ.

theater of the Cold War. More than 1.5 million armed troops are deployed on either side, making it the most heavily fortified demarcation in the world.

Thirty miles to the south is South Korea's capital city, a world where tip-tiled roofs, alleyways and an-

cient stone walls mix with giant apartment complexes, gleaming skyscrapers, luxury hotels, Disneyland-like amusement parks, discos and young people in designer jeans and sneakers. Nothing prepares most visitors for the noise, the hurry, the frenzied

Thirty five years later, the South Koreans host the 1988 Olympics. This is Seoul's Olympic Park with the Athletes' Village in the background and the Fencing Gymnasium in the foreground.

megalopolis which is today's Seoul.

At night, millions of lights and blinking neon signs flash across the broad plain of the Han River which dissects Seoul and disappear behind hillsides and granite mountain peaks as far as the eye can see.

By day, sidewalks are crowded with businessmen, shoppers and secretaries in Western dress, gray-robed Buddhist monks, students with bookbags and old people wearing traditional long Hanbok dresses or silk balloon pants colored in bright pastels.

"It's a Phoenix risen from the ashes," says Ben Nighthorse Campbell, who returned as a Congressman in 1990 for his first visit since 1952. "I marvel at how such total devastation could re-emerge into such prosperity. No one, I mean no one, would believe it who was here in the war. It's like coming back to a different country, a different place."

The sprawling capital and surrounding satellite cities are home to 18 million people, making it the fourth largest metropolitan area in the world. All of them seem to drive. All of them are in a hurry.

Horns blare, tires screech, cars at rush hour seem to ricochet off each other with abandon. Trucks and buses swerving in and out of traffic often clip one another, severing wing mirrors and radio aerials.

Construction workers with jack-hammers and bulldozers build and rebuild city blocks at all hours of the day and night, tearing up pavement laid only months before. Gigantic cranes dangle atop skyscrapers not yet completed. Subways whiz 3.7 million passengers a day underground.

A drive across Seoul can take two hours or more, depending on the gridlock in roadways teaming with Korean-made cars. Parking is often impossible and traffic moves so slowly the Transportation Ministry warns congestion is costing the nation at least $34 billion a year in lost productivity. Outside the city all night, any night, the nation's major freeways and highways are ablaze with headlights as thousands of

Right: Men of the 2nd Division patrol along a fence marking the southern edge of the DMZ.

Busy, productive South Koreans produce more cars than they can sell. The Daewoo Motor Co. at Inchon had to lay off its night shift to cut production by 40 percent. They were turning out 1,200 subcompacts a day where armies once marched.

tractor-trailers, buses, vans and pickup trucks criss-cross the country taking products to market.

South Korea has been one of the fastest-growing economies in the world. The nation's per capita income increased 79-fold, from $82 in 1961 to $6,750 in 1992. The average income in Seoul was nearly $15,000. People of all ages wanted to share in the new prosperity, to join in the economic miracle. The scramble was on.

"Work!" says Kim Woo-choong, founder of the Daewoo Group, one of the country's largest conglomerates with 70 overseas offices and 90,000 employees in construction, shipbuilding, carmaking and electronics. "Nothing comes free in this life, and nothing is accidental."

"My generation didn't eat well and couldn't dress well, but look at the Korea we've built," he tells young people. "Days are too short for me. I wish they were 30 or 40 hours long. I sometimes shave and wash with a towel in the car on the way to work. I even occasionally have breakfast in the car."

Once a month—its only concession to Cold War tensions—the sprawling capital comes to a standstill as shrieking sirens and loudspeakers warn citizens to seek cover in air-raid shelters. Cars pull to the side of the road and for 15 minutes the only movement is by green army jeeps on patrols checking to see if citizens complied.

At Seoul's Hongik University, no one pays attention to the air raid drill. Hundreds of students sitting in cubicles only as wide as their shoulders pore over books in the library. Mozart tapes play in the music

And the fields where mortars once barked and men died now produce bumper crops of rice which this peasant woman is planting.

room where more students study, feet propped up on chairs, empty coffee cups piled on a desk.

These are the new Koreans, the Yuppie generation. A staggering 23 million Koreans, more than half the population, are under age 30.

Few of these students have been to the Demilitarized Zone which is off-limits to ordinary Koreans. Family tales of the Korean War seem to them like ancient history. The 20-somethings are more concerned with finding jobs in the highly-competitive Korean market. Good paying jobs. White collar jobs. They're not interested in the dirty, dangerous or low-paying jobs their parents may have held.

Ma Eun-ji, sits in the student union at Hongik, a leather bookbag in her lap, and pulls a stylish short-cropped black and white jacket down around her waist. She plans to be a teacher.

Eun-ji's uncle was a North Korean prisoner during the Korean War.

"The North Koreans tried to persuade him to fight for them," she says. "When he refused, he was tortured, made to stand for days in shoulder high water and fed only a few noodles. He lost most of his eyesight."

"Our elders want us to remember the war, but young people don't relate to it," she says.

These children of the '90s have been born into rising prosperity. As a group they are not unlike college students in the West. They have leisure time, money to spend, and an explosion of new products on which to spend it.

Seoul, a city which traded hands three times in the war, now sits in the sun. Yoido Plaza is a magnet for thousands.

President Bush and three retired generals view a model of the Korean War Memorial. The generals are, left to right, Richard Stilwell and Andrew Goodpaster of the Army and Marine Gen. Raymond Davis.

THE KOREAN WAR MEMORIAL: AN APT MONUMENT

It took America nearly twice as long to agree on a memorial to its Korean War veterans as it did to wage the war itself—a fact acknowledged by President Bush when he broke ground for the memorial on June 14, 1992. "When tyranny threatened, you were quick to answer your country's call. Sadly, your country wasn't quite as quick to answer your call for recognition of that sacrifice. And today we say, the length of time it has taken for this day to arrive only adds to the depth of our gratitude."

About 5,000 people, hundreds of them veterans of Korea, had gathered in sweltering heat on the Mall in Washington, D.C., for the ceremony. It had been six years since President Reagan signed legislation that authorized a memorial and created the Korean War Memorial Advisory Board. To many veterans of "The Forgotten War," the day seemed long overdue.

In 1988, a site for the monument was chosen on the Mall, across the Reflecting Pool from the Vietnam Veterans Memorial, and the following year a national design competition was conducted. The winning entry, selected from more than 500 submissions by a jury of 12 Korean War veterans, was designed by four architects at Pennsylvania State University. Under the terms of the competition, they received $20,000 and their design became government property.

The design unveiled by President Bush at the White House on Flag Day, 1989, featured a pedestrian corridor defined on either side by a column of 38 sculpted infantry soldiers moving toward a flag. Next, the task of creating a construction design for the memorial was assigned to the Washington architectural firm of Cooper-Lecky, which also had worked on the Vietnam War Memorial. But, the compe-

tition winners regarded their entry as a design, and the advisory board considered it a concept to be fleshed out and adapted. Whatever their own feelings about the aesthetic merits of the winning design, the advisory board and the architects concluded that they had to make substantial changes to reflect the wishes of a slew of reviewing agencies, any of which could veto the whole project.

Although the Cooper-Lecky and the Penn State designers worked together for a while, relations broke down in 1990 and the former filed suit to impose their original design. But Robert Hansen, executive director of the memorial project, said the two designs were basically similar: "In each case, a column of troops is trudging uphill toward a flag; the visitor is led toward a quiet, commemorative area; and a wall of images tells the story of the war."

The Cooper-Lecky design was more realistic and representational; it retained the column of soldiers, but clustered them more closely together and showed some in a battle-ready stance. The design also attempted to comply with requests from reviewing agencies that the landscaping make it an integral part of the Mall.

The plan had to be reviewed by, among others, the Commission of Fine Arts, the National Capital Planning Commission, the National Capital Memorial Commission, the Army Corps of Engineers, the American Battle Monuments Commission and the National Park Service. "We got 50 pages of conflicting comments by the reviewing authorities," recalled Kent Cooper of Cooper-Lecky.

By issuing contradictory criticisms the various agencies often neutralized each other and made "everybody involved look a bit

silly," observed the *Washington Post*. The Cooper-Lecky proposal was modified and scaled down several times—the number of soldiers was reduced from 38 to 16 —before it finally was approved.

The design called for sculptures of slightly larger-than-life soldiers advancing toward an American flag, a reflecting pool and a grove of linden trees. It also featured a low granite wall along one edge of the triangular field, etched with images of those who supported the troops in combat.

Not everyone was satisfied. Joan Abrahamson, the only member of the Commission of Fine Arts to vote against it, said the design "looks like a football game in the rain." The memorial, she complained, " remains unresolved. There is far too much going on for any one memorial; it remains a jumble of elements."

But by spring 1993, $16.4 million had been raised—all through private contributions; an appellate court had ruled against the design competition winners; and the memorial was to be dedicated in July 1995.

As University of Maryland architecture professor Roger K. Lewis noted, the fight over Korea and the fight over the memorial had many similarities: numerous compromises, an ambiguous conclusion and some lingering animosity. Hansen, the project's executive director, had a more optimistic interpretation. With the fall of communism, he argued, the memorial's meaning had changed: "It was supposed to commemorate 'The Forgotten War.' But looking back, we can see the value of having held the line in Korea. Now, this is a monument to the forgotten victory."

At long last, America decides to honor the men who fought in Korea. The war ended in 1953. The site was dedicated in 1989. Warren Ames of Maine, New York, holding an Army Ranger flag, and Andy Gordon of Washington, D.C., are part of the ceremonies.

Born two decades after the end of the Korean War, they are the children of parents who were themselves children during the war. Their elders worry that they don't appreciate their roots and that 5,000 years of Korean culture may dissolve in a vat of fast-food, consumption and disco music. Some, like Eun-ji, earn $400 a month tutoring English in their spare time. So many drive cars that for the first time the nation's universities have parking problems.

The flight of the new generations to the cities—to Seoul, Pusan, Inchon, Taegu—has drained the countryside as the nation moves from an agricultural to an industrial economy. South Korea once was almost totally a nation of fisherman and farmers; there are now less than 6 million, or 13 percent, of South Korea's 44 million people living in rural communities. Only 1 percent are fishermen.

Workers left in the rice paddies are often middle-aged women whose husbands have sought second jobs to bring in more income and whose children have left home.

In Tangjin on the west coast, the open marketplace bustles with small children flinging Frisbees and riding tricycles. Vendors driving motorcycles and pickup trucks hawk dried cuttlefish, and strawberries, bananas, tomatoes and chama, a Korean melon. The rhythms of rural life are less changed than in the cities, but increasing affluence shows. New paved roads, brick schools, a traffic light. Small stores sell Spam, Kleenex and canned juices, symbols of Western affluence in the 1950s and 1960s, as well as a wide array of Korean goods.

Above: Magic Island, part of the world's indoor park. Sights such as these are a great contrast to the stark life in North Korea.

Left: Pedestrians walk through the internationally known Myongdong shopping district in downtown Seoul.

In 1961, North Korea and the Soviet Union signed a mutual defense pact. Nikita Khrushchev said farewell to North Korean Communist Party leader Kim Il Sung and left for Moscow after the signing.

Homes once covered in thatch now sparkle with tops of orange and blue tiles. Television aerials sprout from rooftops. Cars and motorcycles vie for space with the family chickens or farm equipment.

Outsiders sometimes lament that in the haste to rebuild, construction was done with an eye to efficiency rather than beauty as in older days. Many communities are defined by unlovely office blocks, warehouses and one- and two-story buildings covered with a sooty haze from the yontan, the powdered coal briquettes used for warmth in winter.

The prosperity of the homeland even has brought a reverse brain drain. More than 20,000 Koreans who have been living overseas return home each year, many of them with doctorates in engineering, science, law and medicine.

Factionalism is rife in politics and political parties have merged and divided so often that the names blur. Compromise is considered weakness. Protest against authority has been a way of life, not only among students, but among all sectors of society.

In South Korea, the years following the armistice were turbulent as authoritarian leaders grappled to marshal the nation's energies to build a new Korea. Vivid memories of Communist atrocities from the Korean War helped create military-backed governments that supported rigid anti-communist indoctrination and legislation. Dissent was linked to communism.

During the 1970s and 1980s, opposition political leaders were sentenced to house arrest, kicked out of parliament or jailed for criticizing the authoritarian government.

In 1980, in the bloodiest military crackdown in modern Korean history, soldiers fired on civilians in the southern city of Kwangju to put down pro-democracy protests. At least 200 people were killed and some 2,000 wounded in 10 days of fighting which

Two North Korean soldiers keep a watchful eye on U.N. troops in Panmunjom.

An old man throws a casting net in an attempt to catch carps in the Han River, the same river through which many battles were fought forty years previously.

Right: A South Korean guard (right) and a North Korean guard (left) smile for the camera from either side of the DMZ.

Above: American MPs and North Korean guards at their posts.

Right: A North Korean checkpoint at the edge of the truce zone in the DMZ.

Army Pvt. Martin Cook from Cape Girardeau, Missouri, surveys the military demarcation line that separates North and South Korea from a vantage point on the U.N. Command side.

divided the country and left a lasting scar on a generation of political leaders demanding reform.

Dissidents and radical students accused the United States of condoning the bloodshed in Kwangju, saying that they could have stopped it and did not. Washington denied the charges, but anti-Americanism spread.

Radical students yelling "Yankee go home" staged violent anti-government, anti-U.S. protests demanding the withdrawal of thousands of American troops deployed to deter Communist aggression. U.S. facilities were firebombed and American flags burned. Militants blamed the United States for the partition of the peninsula and claimed Washington was keeping the Koreas apart purposely to maintain control of the South as a puppet colony.

In 1987, violent street protests by hundreds of thousands of students and ordinary citizens forced the government to accept direct presidential elections for the first time since 1971.

Democratization took another leap forward when Kim Young-sam, a dissident and opposition leader for 30 years, became president in early 1993—the first civilian to hold the office in 32 years. Kim worked to distance himself from past military-backed regimes. He freed many political prisoners, appointed outsiders and women to his cabinet, purged senior generals and launched an aggressive reform drive to fight corruption.

*   *   *

North Korea exists in bold contrast, politically and economically, to South Korea. Its Communist leaders tell both its people and the outside world only what they want them to know. Visitors to the North see only what its leaders want them to see.

The dearth of hard information about the world's most closed and regimented society is immense, confounding both South Korea and its allies and intensifying tensions.

What is clear, however, is that like the South, North Korea has transformed its war-shattered economy, rebuilt its capital city of Pyongyang and has succeeded in maintaining an industrial-military complex capable of producing sophisticated arms. Billions of dollars are spent by the rival Koreas each year on weaponry.

The dynamic of inter-Korean rivalry is seen as one of the driving forces between the attempts of both nations to excel. Yet unlike the two Germanys, the two Koreas have kept their people apart. There is no mail, communication or travel among citizens of the two sides. The only telephone link is between the Red Cross offices of either side.

In North Korea, there are no commercial billboards, no vendors, no private stores of any kind: everything is owned and run by the government. The few cars are mostly Japanese or Russian and the per capita income is less than $1,000. In the early 1990s, there were frequent reports of severe food shortages with food limited to two small meals a day. Unconfirmed reports said some people were scrounging hillsides for edible food and even eating grass.

Visitors said they were fed well, but their official hosts gobbled up leftovers. Roofs on houses in the countryside were sometimes covered with vines and ripening squash or gourds, but fruit, meat and farm animals were scarce. Corn was ground to the size of rice and the husks eaten.

Pigs near the border with China reportedly were grown in underground caves behind locked doors to protect them from both the frigid winter and theft.

A television program called "Science Common Sense" told viewers they should cinch their belt before eating because not to do so increased the risk of cancer and liver disease, visitors said.

A 1992 AP report from North Korea's main industrial port of Chongjin said it had the air of a ghost town. Soldiers armed with machine guns and bayonets guarded piles of coal. Anti-aircraft guns protruded from bunkers guarding the city.

Politically, there has been no choice for North Koreans. North Korea has had one ideology and one leader since 1948—premier Kim Il Sung who was born in 1912. Kim, called the "Great Leader," has been the object of a slavish personality cult that made him almost a god in an atheistic culture. Dissent of any sort was crushed. Human rights groups claim tens of thousands of people were sent to concentration camps. The worship of Kim was so strong it allowed him to violate basic Communist doctrine to establish a dynasty, designating his son, Kim Jong Il, to succeed him as leader of North Korea's 22 million people.

Despite the hostility and suspicion between the two Koreas and the energy invested in building separate and competitive societies, leaders in both Koreas predict unification by the end of the century. Their ideas on how to go about it, however, are far apart.

In 1988, South Korea was host to the Summer Olympic Games, an event which became a watershed in its foreign policy initiatives. Using the Games as a vehicle, the staunchly anti-communist Seoul government pursued diplomatic and trade relations with the nations of the communist bloc that were backers of its northern rival.

The future of Korea. The parents and grandparents of these children will entrust to them a land they rebuilt from the ashes of war.

By 1992, four years later, it had formed ties with virtually all of North Korea's allies, including the former Soviet Union and China, in hopes of bringing pressure on the North to open its closed society.

In 1991, both Koreas joined the United Nations, temporarily calling a truce to years of competition over which was the legitimate leader of the Korean people.

A few months later, the two prime ministers signed historic agreements calling for peace and reconciliation and setting a broad framework for implementation of political and economic exchanges which could lead to unification.

South Korea's prime minister, meeting his northern counterpart for the first time in 1990, said the two must work together to "thaw the thick ice of distrust."

"I am so glad that you have taken the challenge of blazing an unbeaten trail through the thicket to come," South Korean Prime Minister Kang Young-hoon told his northern counterpart, Yon Hyon Muk.

"National unification cannot be achieved by forcing ideology and thoughts on others," Yon replied. Koreans at the gathering saw it as a turning point in inter-Korean dialogue.

One of the ironies of division is that it's good for the tourist business. Foreigners and dignitaries the world over come to Korea and make the day trip to the Demilitarized Zone to see the village of Panmunjom which sits astride the military demarcation line.

They want to try to understand the depth of feeling over the war that ripped a nation asunder and so enraged and divorced a people that 10 million Koreans have yet to learn if their family members are alive or dead.

Panmunjom is an island of neutrality named after a nondescript village destroyed in the war and is actually a cluster of buildings intended as meeting sites. Its practical purpose is to enable the two sides to keep contact, but most of the time it is a strangely quiet enclave where men in uniform stare at each other through binoculars.

The centerpiece is four narrow 1950s prefabs which make up "conference row." A painted white and concrete strip about six inches wide runs through the middle of the buildings to mark the border.

Ordinary Koreans are not allowed to visit Panmunjom, which requires a drive into the Demilitarized Zone itself. The terminus on Route 1 for South Koreans is at Imjingak, three miles south.

On Sundays and holidays, the big parking area at Imjingak is crowded with tourist buses and cars. Children in picnic areas clamor over howitzer canons, tanks and an S-86 Sabre jet fighter left as memorials.

There are several stone monuments and a characterless building with a small museum, a gift shop and a restaurant where visitors can refresh themselves with rice, pickled kimchi cabbage and coffee.

Around the parking area are rusty chainlink fences topped with barbed and concertina wire, the first and smallest of several barriers marking the beginning of the military security area which leads toward the border.

At some point, every Korean walks to the northern edge of the parking lot, the closest one can go toward North Korea, and looks through the fence toward the distant mountains beyond the river. Even in winter snows and pouring rain, there is someone watching. Some weep.

Some put bamboo mats on the ground and build small altars with incense and fruit and bow to northern relatives they have never seen and ancestors whose graves they can never visit.

You can stand at the fence and see into the Imjin River valley where legions of men fought for three years to preserve their freedom. Cranes often rest on the sandbars in the river on the flight north. At the end of the parking lot is Freedom Bridge, named because it was the route that prisoners of war used when they were returned home. One span of the bridge was destroyed and its pilings punctured with artillery holes can be seen rotting in the river.

From time to time armed soldiers at the bridge allow a tour bus of foreigners to go through, or a distinguished visitor changes cars. The crowd gawks and there is much speculation about what's ahead. For most Koreans, the parking lot is the effective end of the country.

"My parents took us to Imjingak several times," says Park Kyung-hee. "My father's parents were from North Korea and grandfather came South before the war. My parents wanted to show us the North and we went as far as we could get.

"We see the tourist buses go north, but they are not for ordinary people. I want to see with my own eyes what North Korean soldiers look like. I want to see how they talk, how they act. I want to see what it's really like.

"My parents wanted us to know the past in order for us not to make the same mistake, and to know that our country has suffered and my generation mustn't take things for granted," she says.

Someday, she says, maybe she can go beyond the parking lot.

Korean War Veterans' Memorial

Begun in the shadow of World War II, waged in a faraway land, and concluded not with the enemy's surrender but with a negotiated armistice, the Korean War gave most Americans little to remember and much to forget. But for the 1.5 million U.S. men and women who served there and the families and friends of those who did not return, the Korean War could never be The Forgotten War.

The end of the Cold War has brought renewed interest in the conflict that helped determine its course and has generated a new appreciation for the contributions of those who left home and homeland to aid in the struggle against aggression.

The Korean War Veterans Memorial honors the men and women who served in Korea, for their struggles and sacrifices under trying circumstances in service to their country and the cause of freedom.

Visitors approaching the memorial come first to the triangular "field of service." Here 19 stainless steel statues, the creation of World War II veteran Frank Gaylord, depict a squad on patrol and evoke the experience of American ground troops in Korea.

Strips of granite and scrubby juniper bushes suggest the rugged Korean terrain, while windblown ponchos recall the harsh weather also endured. This symbolic patrol brings together members of the Air Force, Army, Marines, and Navy, and portrays servicemen from a variety of ethnic backgrounds.

A granite curb on the north side of the statues lists the 22 countries of the United Nations that sent troops or gave medical support in defense of South Korea. On the south side stands a wall of California Academy black granite, intermingling in its polished surface the reflections of the statues with the etched images of more than 2,400 unnamed service men and women. These images reveal the determination of the U.S. forces and the countless ways in which Americans answered the call to duty.

Louis Nelson Associates, using period photographs, composed the mural; a computer-generated stencil then guided the sandblasting that carved in stone this tribute to all who served. The adjacent "pool of remembrance," encircled by a grove of linden trees, provides a setting for quiet reflection.

Numbers of those killed, wounded, missing in action, and prisoners of war are etched into the curb. Opposite this counting of the war's toll the granite wall bears a message inlaid in silver: *Freedom is Not Free.*

The memorial is staffed from 8 a.m. to midnight every day except December 25 by park rangers who are available to answer questions and present interpretive themes. A bookstore in the nearby Lincoln Memorial sells informational items relating to both the memorial and the Korean War. The Korean War Veterans Memorial is part of the National Park System, one of more than 360 parks representing our nation's natural and cultural heritage . Address inquiries to: Superintendent, National Capital Parks-Central, 900 Ohio Drive SW, Washington, DC 20242.

Bibliography

Dean Acheson. *Present at the Creation*. New York: W.W. Norton & Company. 1969.

Bevin Alexander. *Korea: The First War We Lost*. Hippocrene Books, Inc.

Roy E. Appleman. *South to the Natkong, North to the Yalu*. Washington: USA. 1961.

Clay Blair. *The Forgotten War*. Times Books. 1987.

Omar N. Bradley and Clay Blair. *A General's Life, An Autobiography*. New York: Simon & Schuster. 1983.

J. Lawton Collins. *War in Peacetime: The History and Lessons of Korea*. Boston: Houghton Mifflin. 1969.

David Douglas Duncan. *This Is War!* New York: Harper & Brothers. 1951.

D.M. Giangreco. *War in Korea 1950-1953*. Ringier America, Inc. 1990.

Joseph C. Goulden. *Korea: The Untold Story of the War*. Times Books. 1982.

Charles Heller and William A. Stofft. *America's First Battles*. University Press of Kansas. 1986.

Walter G. Hermes. *Truce Tent and Fighting Front, United States Army in the Korean War*. Office of the Chief of Military History. Washington: U.S. Government Printing Office. 1966.

Donald Knox. *The Korean War. Uncertain Victory*. Harcourt, Brace, Jovanovich. 1988.

Douglas MacArthur. *Reminiscences*. New York: McGraw-Hill Book Company. 1964.

Paik Sun Yup. *From Pusan To Panmunjom*. New York: Brassey's (U.S.) Inc., 1992.

Matthew B. Ridgway. *The Korean War*. Garden City, NJ: Doubleday. 1967.

Russell Spurr. *Enter the Dragon*. New York: New Market Press. 1988.

John Toland. *In Mortal Combat: Korea, 1950-1953*. New York: William Morrow and Company, Inc. 1991.

Harry S. Truman. *Memoirs, Volume 2, Years of Trial and Hope*. Garden City, NY: Doubleday and Co. 1956.

Melvin B. Vorhees. *Korean Tales*. London: Secker & Warburg. 1953.

Index